Living in the LambLight

Living in the LambLight

CHRISTIANITY AND CONTEMPORARY
CHALLENGES TO THE GOSPEL

Edited by

Hans Boersma

REGENT COLLEGE PUBLISHING
Vancouver

Published 2001 by Regent College Publishing,
an imprint of the Regent College Bookstore,
5800 University Boulevard, Vancouver, B.C. Canada V6T 2E4
www.regentpublishing.com

National Library of Canada Cataloguing in Publication Data

Main entry under title:

Living in the lamblight

 Papers from the lecture series, Lamblight lectures, held at Trinity Western University,
1998-2000.
 Includes bibliographical references and index.
 ISBN 1-55361-030-X (Canada)
 ISBN 1-57383-177-8 (United States)
 1. Christianity and culture. 2. Christian ethics. I. Boersma, Hans, 1961- II. Series:
Lamblight lectures.
BV4510.3.L58 2001   261   C2001-910968-7

Contents

Part III
Relating to Our World...127

Contributors

Hans Boersma (ThD, State University of Utrecht) is Assistant Professor of Religious and Worldview Studies for the Geneva Society at Trinity Western University, Langley, B.C., Canada.

John Cooper (PhD, University of Toronto) is Professor of Philosophical Theology at Calvin Seminary, Grand Rapids, Mich., U.S.A.

Marva J. Dawn (PhD, University of Notre Dame) is theologian, author and educator with Christians Equipped for Ministry in Vancouver, Wash., U.S.A., and Adjunct Professor of Spiritual Theology at Regent College, Vancouver, B.C., Canada.

Michael W. Goheen (PhD, State University of Utrecht) is Associate Professor of Religion and Theology at Redeemer University College in Ancaster, Ont., Canada.

Christopher D. Marshall (PhD, University of London) is Reader in New Testament at the Bible College of New Zealand in Auckland, New Zealand.

Arnold E. Sikkema (PhD, University of British Columbia) is Assistant Professor of Physics at Dordt College, Sioux Center, Iowa, U.S.A.

John G. Stackhouse, Jr. (PhD, University of Chicago) is the Sangwoo Youtong Chee Professor of Theology and Culture at Regent College, Vancouver, B.C., Canada.

Rikki E. Watts (PhD, University of Cambridge) is Associate Professor of New Testament at Regent College, Vancouver, B.C., Canada.

John R. Wood (PhD, University of California) is Associate Professor of Biology and Environmental Studies at The King's University College in Edmonton, Alta., Canada.

Acknowledgements

This volume is the outcome of the collaboration of a number of people and institutions, several of whom I wish to mention by name. The essays of this book have been presented between 1998 and 2000 under the auspices of the Geneva Society at Trinity Western University in Langley, B.C. I first of all wish to thank, therefore, the members of the board of the Geneva Society, which is responsible for the LambLight Lectures. I am thankful for their personal as well as organizational and academic support. Trinity Western University has been most encouraging in facilitating this lecture series, and I want to express my appreciation for the wonderful spirit of cooperation between the Geneva Society and TWU.

I am grateful to Trinity students and faculty, as well as to people in the broader community, for the warm reception that they have given to these LambLight Lectures. The response has far surpassed our expectations. Dr. Chris Marshall's lecture was co-sponsored by the M2/W2 Association, a prison outreach ministry located in Abbotsford, B.C. I want to thank its director, Wayne Northey, for his cooperation in the organization of this lecture. A big thank-you also to Christina Battermann, Ken More, Suzanne Staryk and Bob Taylor for their technical and administrative assistance with the lecture series.

The LambLight Lectures have been made possible through the generous financial assistance of the Oikodome Foundation, as well as of a number of other personal and corporate donors. It is good to see that these lectures carry the tangible support of the Church community, within which theological reflection needs to take shape. Further, I wish to acknowledge that the publication of this volume has been partially made possible by a grant from the Social Sciences and Humanities Research Council of Canada.

As editor of this book, it has been a pleasure to work with the various contributors. I want to thank each of the authors publicly for their stimulating lectures, as well as for their cooperation in the editing process. My teaching assistant, Matthew ("Zeke") Zacharias, has been unfailingly helpful in reading through the entire manuscript, as well as in drawing up the list of abbreviations and in crafting the index to the book. Thanks, Zeke! My wife, Linda Boersma, as well as the secretary of the Religious Studies department, Suzanne Staryk, have gone through the laborious process of typing transcriptions of some of the lectures. Rob Clements of Regent College Publishing has also been most helpful in ensuring that these essays now see the light of day.

Hans Boersma
Trinity Western University
April, 2001

Abbreviations

ABD	Anchor Bible Dictionary
BibJudStud	Biblical and Judaic Studies
BAR	Biblical Archeology Review
CTJ	Calvin Theological Journal
CER	Canadian Evangelical Review
CBQ	Catholic Biblical Quarterly
ChCour	Christian Courier
CSR	Christian Scholar's Review
ChrCent	The Christian Century
ChCrisis	Christianity & Crisis
CT	Christianity Today
CH	Church History
ConBio	Conservation Biology
Conc	Concilium
CGRev	Conrad Grebel Review
Eth	Ethics
EvQ	Evangelical Quarterly
Int	Interpretation
JANES	Journal of Ancient Near Eastern Studies
JNES	Journal of Near Eastern Studies
JCS	Journal of Cuneiform Studies
JES	Journal of Ecumenical Studies
JETS	Journal of the Evangelical Theological Society
JR	Journal of Religion
JTS	Journal of Theological Studies
LTJ	Lutheran Theological Journal
MedVal	Media and Values
Mtheo	Modern Theology

NIGTC	New International Greek Testament Commentary
NPCJ	*New Perspectives on Criminal Justice*
NYRB	*New York Review of Books*
NYRBSup	*New York Review of Books Supplement*
Or	*Orientalia*
ProtJI	*Proteus: A Journal of Ideas*
REd	*Religious Education*
Sc	*Science*
SA	*Scientific American*
SJT	*Scottish Journal of Theology*
SBOr	*Studia Biblicus et Orientalis*
SCE	*Studies in Christian Ethics*
SOTT	*Studies in Old Testament Theology*
Th	*Theology*
TM	*Time Magazine*
Trans	*Transformation*
TJ	*Trinity Journal*
VE	*Vox Evangelica*
VT	*Vetus Testamentum*
ZAW	*Zeitschrift für die Alttestamentliche Wissenschaft*

Introduction

The Relevance of Theology and Worldview in a Postmodern Context[1]

Hans Boersma

The current volume is the outcome of three years of LambLight Lectures. In advertising these lectures, the Geneva Society has announced them as being "popular, relevant, and informative." I will leave it to the readers to judge the popular and informative nature of the chapters that comprise this volume. By way of introduction, however, I want to make some comments regarding the claim that these lectures are somehow relevant. All of the chapters in this volume are somehow "worldview" related. A worldview is a framework or set of fundamental beliefs through which we view the world and our calling and future in it,"[2] then the chapters that follow in some way reflect on some of the notions that make up these "fundamental beliefs."[3]

[1] I want to thank Craig Allert, Doug Harink, Richard Middleton and Brian Walsh for their comments on this introductory chapter.

[2] James H. Olthuis, "On Worldviews," in *Stained Glass: Worldviews and Social Science*, ed. Paul A. Marshall, Sander Griffioen, and Richard J. Mouw (Lanham: University Press of America, 1989), p. 32.

[3] These fundamental beliefs are often seen as the answers to a number of "worldview questions." Probably most well known are the questions of Brian J. Walsh and J. Richard Middleton: (1) Who am I? (2) Where am I? (3) What's wrong? (4) What is the remedy? (*The Transforming Vision: Shaping a Christian World View* [Downers Grove: InterVarsity, 1984], p. 35). For a different set of questions, see James W. Sire, *The*

As a theologian teaching worldview studies I am aware that both theology and worldview are concepts whose contents and significance is not undisputed. Both the discipline of theology and the notion of a worldview are under critique. In this introductory chapter I wish to look at the place of theology and worldview in the hope of clarifying both their relationship and the relevance of theology. It is my argument that theology does not need to be *made* relevant, but that it addresses the basic questions of human existence, people's fundamental beliefs and as such immediately *is* relevant. This implies that I see no difference between theology and worldview studies. Theology could be described as the articulation of one's worldview—something that often functions at a subconscious level.

Theology and Enlightenment

Theology, of course, has long been unpopular, and its rightful place has long been marginalized.[4] The Enlightenment project, along with the ascendancy of its twin myths of progress and human autonomy, had little use for the caste of theological clergy. Eighteenth-century Deists, says Arnold Sikkema in chapter 5 of this volume, thought that God's only task was to "design the watch and wind it up." The result was that a "mechanical worldview with God as the watchmaker became firmly embedded in nature." Such a mechanical worldview hardly looked up to the clergy to hold forth on the central mysteries of the faith. John Toland (1670-1722), in his Deistic attempt to extricate all mystery from the Christian faith, decried in 1696 the clergy's attempt not only to make the plainest, but the most trifling things in the Word *mysterious*, that we might constantly depend upon them for the Explication."[5] For Toland, theology displayed clear tendencies to degenerate into an illicit quest for power. Julien de La Mettrie (1709-51), writing half a century later, took the argument to its logical next step: not only had theology been abused by power-hungry clergymen, theology as such had lost its claim to relevance: "[S]ince the existence of [a supreme being] does not prove that one form of worship is more necessary than any other, it is a theoretic

---

Universe Next Door: A Basic Worldview Catalog, 3d. ed. (Downers Grove: InterVarsity, 1997), pp. 17-18.

[4] See Rodney Clapp, "The Ivory Tower Comes to the Windy City: In Defense of Theology," in *Border Crossings: Christian Trespasses on Popular Culture and Public Affairs* (Brazos-Baker, 2000), pp. 53-62.

[5] John Toland, "Christianity Not Mysterious," in *Deism: An Anthology*, ed. Peter Gay (Princeton: Van Nostrand, 1968), p. 55.

truth with very little practical value."[6] Voltaire's well-known watchword, *"Ecrasez l'infâme"* ("Crush the infamous thing") characterizes the Enlightenment desire to rid itself of the superstition and irrelevance of theology and to break the ecclesiastical power structures of medieval Europe. The Enlightenment was a sustained attempt to undermine the relevance of theology in the construction of a sustainable worldview. Theology's claim to be the queen of the sciences (*scientia reginarum*) was deconstructed and unveiled as an arbitrary revolutionary and violent grab for power.

A rigidly enforced democratization of disciplines has since held sway in the academy. Across university campuses, theology has been replaced with the more generic term "religious studies." This change implies a two-fold shift:

(1) First, theology is no longer seen as shaping the heart of the academy. As "religious studies" it is simply one of the many academic subjects that is studied from an objective and detached observer point-of-view. The term implicitly relies on the ability of the autonomous self to obtain a "god's eye view" of all reality, including religious reality. Theology, renamed "religious studies," has been placed in a box that we call "theory," along with other "theories" or areas of academic study, such as psychology, mathematics, etc.[7]

(2) Second, theology has to a large degree lost its close ties with the church. In the Middle Ages, theology was done in and by the church. The church, indeed, formed the heart of society. The Enlightenment has (at best) privatized and marginalized the church. The church (and its theology) no longer addresses public issues. The church has retreated from the realm of public facts into the domain of private values.[8] The public, objective facts of religious studies are now studied in the secular halls of learning, while seminaries (sometimes still with denominational ties) commit themselves to the so-called

---

[6] Julien de La Mettrie, "Man a Machine," in *Les Philosophers: The Philosophers of the Enlightenment and Modern Democracy*, ed. Norman L. Torrey (New York: Capricorn, 1960), p. 176.

[7] Cf. the critique on the distinction between theory and practice in Albert M. Wolters, *Ideas Have Legs* (Toronto: Institute for Christian Studies, 1987); and in Rodney Clapp, *A Peculiar People* (Downers Grove: InterVarsity, 1996), pp. 137-39, 184-86.

[8] Lesslie Newbigin rightly laments this Enlightenment division between fact and value (*The Gospel in a Pluralist Society* [Grand Rapids: Eerdmans; Geneva: WCC, 1989], pp. 14-26).

"practical" skills needed for future pastors and pastoral workers who need to work with people's private issues and values.[9]

It is widely recognized that the eighteenth-century's bold attempt to replace faith with reason has not resulted in the much anticipated paradise of freedom, equality and fraternity. As we see modernity merging into late or postmodernity, the Enlightenment claims of objective knowledge, of an overarching perspective (a "metanarrative"), and of scientific progress no longer ring true. As Michael Goheen puts it in the first chapter of this volume, "Our time witnesses a breakdown in the confidence in these big stories of progress. Many no longer believe them because they have not delivered on their promises." I will not present a detailed critique of the present cultural shift toward late modernity. Goheen's chapter serves this purpose admirably well. I do, however, want to ask the question: what is happening to theology now that the Enlightenment dualism between fact and value seems to have lost much of its currency?

It seems to me that there are a number of different options, and that there is by no means unanimity among Christians on how to practise theology for a generation that has lost faith in progress and human autonomy as the twin pillars of modern mythology. One option would be that of *rational entrenchment*: a re-assertion of the royal status of theology and a return to the abstract and scholastic methodologies of an earlier age. This is not to deny that there are issues where Christians need to speak out on their convictions. As John Cooper makes clear in his chapter on inclusive language for God (chapter 6), there are issues and situations where Christians need to hold on to certain positions that may be quite out of vogue amidst their surrounding culture. At times, however, rational entrenchment is confused with such biblical and theological faithfulness. In some circles, scholastic systematic theological handbooks have never really lost their exalted status. From within a more or less abstract, scholastic paradigm, the loss of the Enlightenment dualism between fact and value is here simply taken as a confirmation of the reasonableness of holding on to the traditional scholastic theologies that have fostered denominational distinctives in the past.[10] Such quests

---

[9] Cf. Richard A. Muller's criticism of the "how-to" approach of DMin degrees and of people's "failure to see the crucial interrelationship of the task of ministry and the work of theology" (*The Study of Theology: From Biblical Interpretation to Contemporary Formulation* [Grand Rapids: Zondervan, 1991], p. vii).

[10] The development of Protestant scholasticism in the late sixteenth century was due to the sophistication of the Reformation debates and of the growing confessionalism

for security in the logical grounding of abstract systems of thought seem misguided, however. They hardly amount to an appropriate response to the uncertainties of a post-Enlightenment society. Ironically, such confessional scholasticism draws on the very over-emphasis of reason that gave rise to the Enlightenment project in the first place. In his provocatively entitled essay, "Why Christians Should Abandon Certainty," John Stackhouse rightly decries such claims to dogmatic certainty: it "renders ecumenism an unlikely project, as alliances fracture time after time as one group judges the other insufficiently pure."

Rational entrenchment is only one of the options open to theology in our post-Enlightenment world. A second response would be what Marva Dawn, in the third chapter, refers to as the *subversion of pride*. It is tempting to give up on the notion of a metanarrative altogether, so that we fail to see any longer a common thread in the biblical narrative. As it seems more and more difficult to tell the history of salvation as a coherent story, we may be tempted to read it as a wildly chequered collage, as a patchwork of which the pieces seem randomly stitched together. The result may well be that it becomes more and more difficult for the church to be bold in its theological assertions. In fact, it seems fair to say that in many churches issues of style (liturgy) are hotly debated, while questions of contents (theology) are routinely shrugged off as irrelevant.[11] Shouldn't the question at least be asked, however, if there is perhaps a connection between contents and style? Is there not also in the church truth to the statement that the medium is the message?[12] Dawn points out that despite the apparent humility of this position ("I don't claim to have a better story than you do") there is an element of pride in the rootlessness and the loss of metanarrative of postmodernism: "It is prideful to presume that merely our own epoch is enough, that our theology and music need not submit to the whole Church."

---

and institutionalism in the church. See Alister E. McGrath, *A Life of John Calvin: A Study in the Shaping of Western Culture* (Oxford: Blackwell, 1990), pp. 202-11; Ian McPhee, "Conserver or Transformer of Calvin's Theology? A Study of the Origins and Development of Theodore Beza's Thought, 1550-1570" (Ph.D. diss., University of Cambridge, 1979), pp. xvi-xvii.

[11] Cf. the intriguing article by Michael S. Hamilton, "The Triumph of the Praise Songs: How guitars beat out the organ in the worship wars," *CT*, 12 July, 1999, 28-35.

[12] Cf. Marshall McLuhan, *Understanding the Media: The Extensions of Man*, new ed. (Cambridge: MIT Press, 1960).

Worldview and Neo-Calvinism

Worldview studies appear to have less of a struggle for survival than theology—at least in Christian colleges and universities. The notion of a "worldview" has figured prominently in the neo-Calvinist tradition associated with the Dutch theologian and politician, Abraham Kuyper (1837-1920). In his 1898 Stone Lectures delivered at Princeton University, Kuyper set forth the notion of a neo-Calvinist "worldview" that would have implications for all areas of life. Over against Enlightenment modernism, Kuyper made a case for a Calvinist "life system" that "must start from that point in our consciousness in which our life is still undivided and lies comprehended in its unity,—not in the spreading vines but in the root from which the vines spring."[13] Kuyper associated this undivided point of unity with the moment of God's sovereign act of regeneration in the individual.[14] Within the Dutch neo-Calvinist tradition following Kuyper, the heart is often seen as the place where one's worldview operates on a "supra-temporal" level, as the root of human existence. In our supra-temporal heart we grasp the basic motifs of the Christian life—or, perhaps better, the power of the Holy Spirit takes the human heart in its grip.

According to the Dutch neo-Calvinist tradition, therefore, one's worldview precedes any theoretical exposition of the various disciplines within the academy. As Peter Heslam puts it, Kuyper "seized on the concept of worldview in the specific 'pre-philosophical' (or 'pre-scientific') sense of *Weltanschauung*, casting his entire thought-world within its conceptual framework."[15] The Spirit touches the heart not by means of formulas or theological statements. As one of many academic disciplines, theology needs to be clearly distinguished from a Christian worldview. The latter, the biblical theme of creation, fall and redemption—which has a radical unity of meaning—forms the pre-

---

[13] Abraham Kuyper, *Lectures on Calvinism* (Grand Rapids: Eerdmans, 1931), p. 20.

[14] Kuyper's notion of a Calvinist worldview logically downplayed the importance of the community of faith and emphasized individual predestination: "The 'Deo Soli Gloria' was not the starting-point but the result, and predestination was inexorably maintained [in Calvinism], not for the sake of separating man from man, nor in the interest of personal pride, but in order to guarantee from eternity to eternity, to our inner self, a direct and immediate communion with the Living God. The opposition against Rome aimed therefore with the Calvinist first of all at the dismissal of a Church which placed itself between the soul and God" (*Lectures*, p. 21).

[15] Peter S. Heslam, *Creating a Christian Worldview: Abraham Kuyper's Lectures on Calvinism* (Grand Rapids: Eerdmans; Carlisle: Paternoster, 1998), pp. 95-96.

theoretical basis for all academic endeavour. This theme "is the religious presupposition of any theoretical thought," argues the neo-Calvinist philosopher, Herman Dooyeweerd.[16]

The neo-Calvinist or Reformational tradition has consistently emphasized this pre-theoretical character of one's worldview. One sees this emphasis, for instance, in the well-known volume of Brian J. Walsh and J. Richard Middleton, *The Transforming Vision*, in many ways a wonderful text, that has shaped an entire generation of college and university students. Walsh and Middleton argue that "knowledge" in the biblical sense is often different from theoretical knowledge. The former has to do with one's worldview and is pre-theoretical, while the latter has to do with the academic disciplines and is therefore theoretical in character: "World views ... are not theoretical in nature; they are pre-theoretical answers to ultimate questions."[17]

The term "worldview" has lately undergone some important scrutiny, from among neo-Calvinist scholars themselves. First, it is being recognized today that worldviews are not simply lenses that we take from Scripture in order make sense of the world around us. As James Olthuis puts it, worldviews are not only "visions *of* faith *for* life," but they are at the same time "vision *of* life *for* faith." People's worldviews are formed "in dialogue with a particular people's historical experience and categorical frameworks."[18] In other words, our faith does not simply and unilaterally prescribe the way we deal with reality. Our faith is not immune from its surroundings. Instead, people's general cultural situation and their personal circumstances shape their faith and influence the way they subconsciously experience and make sense of the world around them. What is more, the "view" element of "worldview" has been criticized because of the cognitive or theoretical element that it would introduce. Nicholas Wolterstorff, in particular, is concerned that

---

[16] Herman Dooyeweerd, *In the Twilight of Western Thought: Studies in the Pretended Autonomy of Philosophical Thought* (Nutley, N.J.: Craig, 1980), p. 125.

[17] Walsh and Middleton, *Transforming Vision*, p. 171. Albert M. Wolters argues similarly that "philosophy and theology, as academic disciplines, are scientific and theoretical, whereas a worldview is not. A worldview is a matter of the shared everyday experience of humankind, an inescapable component of all human knowing, and as such it is non-scientific, or rather ... *prescientific*, in nature (*Creation Regained: Biblical Basics for a Reformational Worldview* [Grand Rapids: Eerdmans, 1985], pp. 8-9).

[18] James H. Olthuis, "On Worldviews," in *Stained Glass: Worldviews and Social Science*, ed. Paul A. Marshall, Sander Griffioen, and Richard J. Mouw (Lanham: University Press of America, 1989), p. 32.

an emphasis on "worldviews" in education "puts too much emphasis on a 'view,' that is, on what we have called cognition."[19] Wolterstorff believes we need to shift toward an emphasis on discipleship and a Christian way of life. Discussions on worldviews have too much of a tendency to remain theoretical and abstract.

The interim balance so far seems to be that both "theology" and "worldview" are in flux. Is it possible to do theology without falling back into timeless truths abstracted from the biblical account? Should we return theology to the church, and should theology take back its supportive function toward the other disciplines? If so, what would this do to the idea of "worldview studies," firmly entrenched as they are in Christian educational institutions? Also, if we abandon the "worldview" notion (as perhaps being too "viewish"), do we not run the danger of losing all reflection on Christian presuppositions for the various academic disciplines? Is our postmodern confusion such that we are perhaps in danger of losing both theology (due to Enlightenment criticism) and worldview studies (due to internal critique among neo-Calvinists)? Is it still possible, in the face of this criticism, to be faithful to the call to search out and give shape to our basic faith commitments?

Theology as *ancilla scientiarum*

In what follows I want to put forward some ideas for discussion, in the hope that they may prove helpful in dealing with the relationship between theology and worldview (studies) in a post-Enlightenment age. Is it possible somehow to overcome the dichotomy between fact and value, the separation between religious studies and worldview studies? I do not believe that there is a simple or straight-forward answer to these difficulties. Exposing the dichotomy — as I have done in this chapter — is something which will hopefully contribute to further reflection on the issues before us. At the same time, I submit that the following items may be helpful in developing a theology for a post-Enlightenment age:

1. *Narrative theology.* Ever since the "biblical theology" movement of the 1950s, the acts of God in history have been in the centre of theological reflection. This has resulted in an emphasis on the importance of

---

[19] Nicholas P. Wolterstorff, *Educating for Responsible Action* (Grand Rapids: Christian Schools Internationa; Eerdmans, 1980), pp. 13-14; cf. Harry Fernhout, "Christian Schooling: Telling a World View Story," in *The Crumbling Walls of Certainty: Towards a Christian Critique of Postmodernity and Education*, ed. Ian Lambert and Suzanne Mitchell (Sydney: Centre for the Study of Australian Christianity, 1997), pp. 75-98.

salvation history and biblical narrative, nearly across the theological spectrum. There are remarkable parallels between the neo-Calvinist "creation-fall-redemption" paradigm and, for example, N.T. Wright's notion of a biblical drama, in which we today take the stage to perform the last, unfinished act.[20]

2. *Centrality of the church.* The emphasis on the biblical story often goes hand in hand with a renewed emphasis on community and on the church. The introspective and individualist concerns of the modern period have lost a much of their appeal today. The church needs to re-emerge from the shell of its "Babylonian captivity" and re-assume its central place. It is the church, after all, that claims to offer hope to the world and that wants to be a light to the nations. Robert Webber rightly emphasizes in his *Ancient-Future Faith* that "the challenge of the church in the postmodern world is to recover community within the local church and the community of the entire church throughout history."[21] Such renewed emphasis on the importance of the community of the church is among the more hopeful signs of theological life within the evangelical tradition.

3. *God's communal character.* Also, if we take the continuing biblical story seriously as the revelation of God's character—most clearly and definitively revealed in the human face of Jesus—this requires a renewed reflection on the character and being of God. Renewed theological exploration of the Trinity has resulted in the three-ness of God receiving more explicit attention, which appears to have significant implications for human relationships.[22] The relational character of God is also at stake in the current debates surrounding open theism. These discussions are an indication that many evangelical theologians feel the need to have their understanding of God shaped by salvation-historical rather than Greek notions.[23]

---

[20] N.T. Wright, "How Can the Bible Be Authoritative?" *VE* 21 (1991): 7-32; N.T. Wright, *The New Testament and the People of God,* Christian Origins and the Question of God, vol. 1 (Minneapolis: Fortress, 1992), pp. 139-42.

[21] Robert E. Webber, *Ancient-Future Faith: Rethinking Evangelicalism for a Postmodern World* (Grand Rapids: Baker, 1999), p. 80.

[22] Jürgen Moltmann, *The Trinity and the Kingdom: The Doctrine of God,* trans. Margaret Kohl (Minneapolis: Fortress, 1993).

[23] See Clark Pinnock, et al., *The Openness of God: A Biblical Challenge to the Traditional Understanding of God* (Downers Grove: InterVarsity, 1994); Gregory A. Boyd, *God of the Possible: A Biblical Introduction to the Open View of God* (Grand Rapids: Baker, 2000).

4. *Embodiment of theology.* Our ability to spell out the contents of a Christian worldview in some theoretical format should not be seen as an excuse for a return to an intellectualism that values faith over works or mind over body. I affirm, therefore, Wolterstorff's underlying concern for the importance of discipleship. William Dyrness has recently expressed a similar concern by saying that we need not just the biblical *story*, but that we also need the categories of *space* and *sight*. It is by means of space and sight that we encounter the world around us. For Dyrness, the notion of "story" is not enough: "We can hear the story and sing it for ourselves. But how do we embody this story? How does it influence a whole culture? Better yet, how do we dance and sing it together?"[24] In our embodied existence here on earth, we are made dance partners with the Triune God.[25] This means, for example, that theological notions of justice and atonement have implications for the way in which justice and forgiveness function in our relationships and in the judicial system. As Chris Marshall puts it so well in chapter 9: "God's justice cannot be vindicated ultimately by retribution, but only by reconciling forgiveness and healing, for only thus are things made right." Theology needs embodiment, also in the judicial system.

5. *Theology as service.* Rikk Watts argues in chapter 7 that human beings are images of God and live in the created order as his temple. This implies an enormous responsibility toward the world in which we live. As Watts puts it, "There are a lot of Christians unfortunately, who would look after their lounge rooms better than they look after God's palace temple." My plea to restore theology to a more central place may instill certain fears of oppression and domination: we have seen how in the Middle Ages theology exercised its regal function as queen of the sciences, and we are perhaps afraid of its oppressive and violent tendencies. This fear is not without warrant. It is important, therefore, to emphasize theology's role as that of a servant, both toward the other disciplines and toward the created order and our contemporary society. John Wood rightly concludes, therefore, that love of nature ("biophilia") and the gospel must necessarily go hand in hand (chapter 8). The metaphor of *ancilla* (handmaid) may be more

---

[24] William A. Dyrness, *The Earth Is God's: A Theology of American Culture* (Maryknoll: Orbis, 1997), p. 11.
[25] See my essay in chapter 4, "The Feet of God: In Stomping Boots or Dancing Shoes? The Trinity as Answer to Violence."

adequate to describe the role of theology than that of the medieval notion of *regina* (queen).[26]

Theology as worldview studies

This brings me to one last step, which I believe is necessary to escape the Enlightenment dualism between fact and value, and the corresponding separation in Christian colleges and universities between "religious studies" and "worldview studies." Doug Harink, in a recent essay in *Christian Scholar's Review*, laments the fact that "theology in many Christian liberal arts colleges finds itself being pushed aside and replaced by 'Christian worldview' studies."[27] It seems to me that Harink hits the nail on the head. In order to safeguard students' Christian convictions and Christian perspectives on the various disciplines, Christian colleges and universities have bought into the neo-Calvinist notion of "worldview." At the same time, in order to uphold the objective, public truths of the study of religion, they have tended to introduce "religious studies" departments.

One of the positive insights of Reformational worldview studies is the notion that our worldviews often function at a subconscious level. Our basic motives are often obscure to ourselves. In other words, our worldviews tend to influence us in ways of which we are often only dimly aware. There is a real sense, therefore, in which our worldviews often operate on a non-theoretical (that is to say, non-academic) level. So I do not share the fear that the "worldview" notion is too cognitive in character. To be sure, we need to watch out that we do not intellectualize the faith. One could argue, however, that the notion of a worldview has a built-in resistance to intellectualism: worldviews—at least according to the neo-Calvinist tradition—usually function not at a cognitive, but at a pre-theoretical level. We therefore do not need to give up on the idea of a worldview.

---

[26] The popular notion of "servant leadership" may be helpful to describe the task of theology. At the same time, as any course in leadership will highlight, practising "servant leadership" is far more difficult than explaining it.

[27] Douglas Harink, "Taking the University to Church: The Role of Theology in the Christian University Curriculum," *CSR* 28 (1999): 390.

We do need to ask ourselves, however, what we do when we take the next step and explore these pre-theoretical commitments in our worldview *studies*. It seems to me that when we do this—whether by means of a creation-fall-redemption paradigm or in any other way—we will soon find ourselves engaged in some serious theological enquiry. As many courses in worldview studies make clear, a great deal can be said or theorized with regard to our worldviews—even if we often do not realize their impact on our daily activities. The story of salvation (or, in neo-Calvinist terms, the creation-fall-redemption paradigm) is a story that can only be told by means of words and sentences. "Worldview studies"—the *study* of worldviews—implies as much. It seems unavoidable, therefore, that we end up with the question: are we perhaps unwittingly theologizing when we study people's world-views?[28] If the answer to this question is affirmative, perhaps it is time we have another look at the despised medieval queen of the sciences and restore her to a position in which she is at least interacting once again with her cultured despisers—the other disciplines.

I believe that it is time to return theology to a more central position in the university—at least in the Christian university. Theological exploration and teaching will always deal with the basic questions in life. As a result, such exploration cannot but shape people's world-view—their fundamental beliefs through which they interpret the world and their calling and future in this world. The so-called "worldview questions"—the questions we struggle with as we make sense of the world in which we live—can only be properly phrased and addressed if we see theology as relevant for the other disciplines and to our postmodern world: "You stir man to take pleasure in praising you,

---

[28] It could even be that the theologizing of our "worldview studies" is inherently unstable in the sense that it has too much of an anthropological bias. The standard worldview questions (Who are we? Where are we? What's wrong? What's the solution?) are typically Western in their emphasis on the human situation and their focus on the human predicament.

because you have made us for yourself, and our heart is restless until it rests in you."[29]

---

[29] Saint Augustine, *Confessions*, trans. Henry Chadwick (Oxford: Oxford University Press, 1998), p. 3.

Part I

Relating to Our Culture

Chapter 1

Charting a Faithful Course amidst Postmodern Winds

Michael W. Goheen

How should the believing community relate to our postmodern culture? Paul gives us clear direction on the relationship of the church to her culture when he says that we are not to be conformed to the world but to be transformed by the renewing of our minds (Rom 12:1-2). From time to time God uses dramatic changes in history to shake his people out of conformity with the world. The church has lived in the context of the modern worldview that has shaped Western culture for centuries. I agree with Lesslie Newbigin when he says that this long association between the church and Western modernity has led to a situation where the Western church is an "advanced case of syncretism."[1] We have been far too much conformed to this world, to the modern worldview that has shaped our culture for so long. To use a marine analogy: the church has been sailing along with the winds of modernity far too peacefully. Today those winds are shifting; new winds are blowing—winds we might call postmodern. We are living in the midst of dramatic changes often described as the movement from a modern to a postmodern world. Two well-known observers of our situation have described it this way. Diogenes Allen of Princeton observes: "A massive intellectual revolution is taking place that is perhaps as great as that which marked off the modern world from

---

[1] Lesslie Newbigin, *The Other Side of 1984: Questions for the Churches* (Geneva: World Council of Churches), p. 23.

the Middle Ages."[2] Alexander Solzhenitsyn says: "If the world has not approached its end, it has reached a major watershed in history, equal in importance to the turn from the Middle Ages to the Renaissance."[3] I believe that God uses dramatic changes in history to shake his people out of conformity with the world. Thus the postmodern challenge presents us with an opportunity to examine the direction we have been going and perhaps to make some drastic adjustments.

When winds shift and cause us to see our conformity with the world, our job is not to push over the tiller and sail before these new winds of change. We are not simply to exchange modern winds for postmodern winds. We would then be "infants, tossed back and forth by the waves, and blown here and there by every wind of teaching" that moves our culture (Eph 4:14). Our task is to look again at our chart and compass, to hear afresh our sailing orders, and to ask how we can use these new winds and new tides to carry out the directions that have been given to us by Christ, our captain. Our new situation gives us an opportunity to place once more our lives under the searching light of the Word of God.

If we are to heed the Word of God and chart a faithful path amidst postmodern winds, our first task is to examine and understand these winds. Let me quote from a speech given by Lesslie Newbigin in 1962. It is the question he poses at the beginning of this quotation that can help us in our examination and understanding of postmodernity. In the year 1962 missions was facing enormous and revolutionary changes. Newbigin was involved as a world leader in the missionary task of the church. The changes of that time threatened the whole enterprise. Colonialism was rapidly breaking up; the newly independent nations were quickly being taken up into the movement toward globalization. The sixties were the "decade of the secular" as unbridled optimism intoxicated western man.[4] All of this threatened the missionary enterprise as it had been known and practised for over 150 years. It was

---

[2] Diogenes Allen, *Christian Belief in a Postmodern World* (Louisville: Westminster/John Knox, 1989), p. 2.

[3] Aleksandr Solzhenitsyn, "A World Split Apart," in *Solzhenitsyn at Harvard: The Address, Twelve Early Responses, and Six Later Reflections*, ed. Ronald Berman (Washington: Ethics and Public Policy Center, 1980), p. 20.

[4] Throughout this chapter, I am using masculine pronouns and the word "man" in their generic, inclusive sense, since modernity used to define humanity in masculine terms.

this dramatic, changing, and revolutionary time that provides the context for the following words:

> The real question is: *What is God doing in these tremendous events of our time?* How are we to understand them and interpret them to others, so that we and they may play our part in them as co-workers with God? Nostalgia for the past and fear for the future are equally out of place for the Christian. He is required, in the situation in which God places him, to understand the signs of the times in the light of the reality of God's present and coming kingdom, and to give his witness faithfully about the purpose of God for all men.[5]

The parallel between the dramatic changes facing Newbigin and the dramatic changes we face makes his words intensely relevant for us today. We see many in North America with nostalgia for the past. Postmodernity with its relativism and pluralism presents a threat; the desire is to hold on to the good old days when our country seemed to be more compatible with the Christian faith. There is a genuine fear for where the future might take us. While there may be some legitimacy in this concern, I believe Newbigin is correct when he says that this should not be the primary response of the believing community. Our task is to understand and interpret the current context through the lens of Scripture so we can play our part as God's covenant partners. The vital question that must be pressed is: "*What is God doing in these tremendous events of our time?*"

To ask what God is doing in these events means that we must attempt to understand our times in the light of God's kingdom and faithfully bear witness to God's purpose for his creation. These are the questions I pose in this chapter: what is God doing in these times? How are we to understand these events of our day in the light of God's kingdom? How can we witness in postmodern times to the purpose of God for his creation? It will only be when we understand what God is doing in these times that we can chart a faithful course amidst postmodern winds.

Postmodernity Is Incredulity toward Metanarratives

Jean Francois Lyotard has given the most well-known definition of postmodernity: "Simplifying to the extreme I define postmodern as

---

[5] Lesslie Newbigin, "Rapid Social Change and Evangelism" (unpublished paper, 1962), 3.

incredulity toward metanarratives."[6] Now this definition might make one think that postmodernity is simply an academic issue and unrelated to the average person. Yet it points to something that all of us know, feel, and sense at a deep level. The modern worldview has been shaping Western culture for centuries. That worldview is characterized by a deep confidence and faith that autonomous rational man can progress toward a better world by science, technology, and the rational organization of society—including politics, economics, and education. Progress would bring about a world where people were happy, materially prosperous, free from disease, oppression, ignorance, poverty, suffering, primitiveness—a world of truth, justice, peace, harmony, and prosperity. In other words, science would counter the effects of sin and usher in the kingdom of man. Science is at the heart of this worldview, which is often referred to as the "modern scientific worldview." Science as applied to the non-human creation in technology and to human society in rational economics, politics, and social order would lead to this utopia of freedom. The modern worldview, then, is the confident belief in a story of progress—progress toward a better world that man himself is progressively improving and perfecting through his own efforts.

Modernity has been filled with stories of progress. The two most common in the twentieth century have been the liberal, capitalistic, democratic story characteristic of North America and Western Europe and the collectivist, communist story of Eastern Europe and the Soviet Union. It is these kinds of big stories of progress that Lyotard is referring to when he speaks of "metanarratives."

Postmodernity is "incredulity toward metanarratives." Our time witnesses a breakdown in the confidence in these big stories of progress. Many no longer believe them because they have not delivered on their promises. A growing gap between rich and poor, the threat of a nuclear holocaust and escalating militarization, the degradation of the environment that threatens our future, growing economic problems (including chronic unemployment), burgeoning social and psychological maladies, and bureaucratic bungling, inefficiency, and corruption of our "rational" institutions all contribute to disillusionment with stories of progress to a better world. Our contemporaries do not believe them anymore.

---

[6] Jean-François Lyotard, *The Postmodern Condition: A Report on Knowledge* (Minneapolis: University of Minnesota Press, 1984), p. xxiv.

How do we interpret this radical change in the light of God's Word? How do we understand what God is doing in these events of our day? The first thing that must be observed is that these modern stories of progress are heretical counterfeits of the biblical story. What has happened in the modern West is that the modern worldview took over a biblical understanding of the linear movement in history toward a better world—the kingdom of God. From the time of Augustine, this biblical story—shaped by neo-Platonism—of the movement of history toward the kingdom of God—a world of peace, truth, justice, freedom—was stamped on the consciousness of European people. Other worldviews untouched by the gospel are essentially cyclical and have no conception of history moving toward a goal. It is only when the Bible permeates a culture that hopes of a better world are awakened. The radical secularization of modernity preserved the biblical notion of the movement of history toward a goal but placed humanity at the centre in the place of God. No longer would the sovereign work of God by his Spirit and gospel move history forward to a world of freedom, truth, peace and justice, but rather the human activity of science, technology and social planning would do this.

Thus at the heart of the modern worldview is idolatry. An idol is an aspect of creation in which we place ultimate commitment and trust—our faith. We have trusted science, technology, social planning, economic growth, and political bureaucracy to lead us to the secular kingdom of man. The language of Philip Handler, a former president of the USA National Academy of Science, in an essay entitled "In Praise of Science," betrays an idolatrous faith in science. In spite of obvious challenges to his faith that he is facing in the latter part of the twentieth century he maintains his deep commitment:

> Our current malaise stems from a few bad experiences—from time-delay in meeting the high hopes and expectations raised in the minds of those who appreciate the great power of science, the force of technology. Those expectations have taken on a new light as science has also revealed the true condition of man on earth.... *I retain my faith* that the science that has revealed the most awesome and profound beauties we have yet beheld is also the principal tool that our civilization has developed to mitigate the condition of man.[7]

---

[7] Philip Handler, "In Praise of Science," *NYRBSup*, 27 September, 1979, 15 (emphasis added).

Walsh and Middleton use an evocative image to portray this idolatry. They adopt the image of Daniel 2—an idol with a head of gold, chest and arms of silver, belly and legs of iron. They compare the belly and legs of iron to scientism—an idolatrous faith in science. They speak of the chest and arms of silver as technicism—our idolatrous faith in technology. Finally, the head of gold is economism—our idolatrous faith in economic growth as the goal of human life.[8] Together they form the idol of Western culture. But these idols have not delivered on their promises. They have not delivered prosperity—poverty is growing. They have not delivered freedom—we are more controlled by media, education, big business, and government than at any other time in history. They have not delivered truth—we face a proliferating pluralism that betrays a lack of agreement on truth. They have not delivered justice and peace—oppression, war, and violence abound. These idols have not delivered the goods, and people are abandoning their misplaced faith.

The Bible is ruthless in its castigation of idols and their inability to deliver: "Of what value is an idol, since a man has carved it? Or an image that teaches lies? For he who makes it trusts in his own creation; he makes idols that cannot speak" (Hab 2:18). "[T]heir idols are silver and gold, made by the hands of men. They have mouths, but cannot speak, eyes, but they cannot see; they have ears, but they cannot hear, noses, but they cannot smell; they have hands, but cannot feel, feet, but they cannot walk; nor can they utter a sound with their throats. Those who make them will be like them, and so will all who trust in them" (Ps 115:4-8).

Perhaps another way of putting the same thing in New Testament terms and in light of the coming of the kingdom is to see that modernity is based on false messiahs. The hope of the Scriptures is that the kingdom will be ushered in by the Messiah—one anointed by God to accomplish this work. Jesus announces that he is the Messiah. He calls people to follow him and to be heralds of this good news. This announcement of the gospel awakens an interest in a future world where all the effects of sin will be overcome. It proclaims Jesus Christ as the One who will accomplish this work. However, modernity has placed its faith in false messiahs—science and technology—to usher in the kingdom of man. It is instructive to note that in many Third World countries it is the children of Christians or those who have received their education in missionary schools that quickly embrace either Marxism or capitalism as the way to

---

[8] Brian J. Walsh and J. Richard Middleton, *The Transforming Vision: Shaping a Christian World View* (Downers Grove: InterVarsity, 1984), pp. 132-39.

improve their country. They are filled with a future vision of the kingdom of God from Scripture. Ultimate issues are raised: who or what will usher in this world of truth, justice, peace, and freedom? When the gospel does not bring this about in their timing they seek more expedient ways to bring about this world. They turn to false messiahs. The gospel raises ultimate issues: who or what can be trusted to usher in a world in which sin and its effects have been eliminated?

This is what we should expect if we are interpreting things from the standpoint of Scripture. In Mark 13 Jesus gives us a glimpse of some of the dynamics of world history that will come about as a result of his messianic mission. He predicts that the preaching of the gospel will give rise to numerous false messiahs that will offer the kingdom of God without death and resurrection. But Scripture leads us to expect the failure of false messiahs the same way we are led to expect the impotence of idols. These false messiahs are unable to usher in the kingdom. The only way our sinful world can be healed is by death as God's judgment on sin and by resurrection to new life.

What is God doing in the momentous events of our time? We might answer in a word: "judgment." We need to interpret our times in terms of the collapse of idols and the failure of false messiahs as a result of God's judgment. Science, technology, economic and political systems, education are all good parts of the creation but cannot rise to the place of creator or messiah. Instead of ushering in the secular kingdom of man, they have shaped a world of oppression that postmodern interpreters have rightly excoriated and denounced. Western man has misplaced his faith and "you shall suffer the penalty ... and bear the consequences of your sinful idolatry" (Ezek 23:49). Jeremiah proclaims:

> O LORD, my strength and my fortress, my refuge in time of distress, to you the nations will come from the ends of the earth and say, "Our fathers possessed nothing but false gods, worthless idols that did them no good. Do men make their own gods? Yes, but they are not gods! Therefore I will teach them—this time I will teach them my power and might. Then they will know that my name is the LORD. (Jer 16:19-21)

Postmodernity Displays a Non-Rational Anthropology

Let me press my analysis of postmodernity further by examining a second theme of postmodernity—non-rational anthropology. All cultural stories or worldviews are rooted in a certain understanding of the human person. What understanding of the human being undergirds the modern story? The modern story is deeply rooted in the human person as autonomous and rational.

The word autonomous comes from two Greek words meaning "self" (αυτο) and "law" (νομος). This means that human beings are their own source of meaning and authority. They define what happiness is; what it means to be human; what the meaning and purpose of life is. There is a rejection here of the divine and ecclesiastical authority of the medieval period. It is no longer the church or the biblical story that defines human life. People no longer acknowledge the authority of church or Bible. Human beings are at the centre of the world displacing God as the maker of history. This autonomous humanism was eloquently articulated by Pico della Mirandola in the fifteenth century at the birth of modernity, in his *Oration on the Dignity of Man*. In this text from 1486 God is speaking to man:

> The nature of other creatures, which has been determined, is confined within the bounds prescribed by us. You, who are confined by no limits, shall determine for yourself your own nature, in accordance with your own free will, in whose hand I have placed you. I have set you at the center of the world, so that from there you may more easily survey whatever is in the world. We have made you neither heavenly nor earthly, neither mortal nor immortal, so that, more freely and more honourably the moulder and maker of yourself, you may fashion yourself in whatever form you shall prefer.

What distinguished man in his dignity and equipped him to define his own purpose, to be his own authority, and to shape history his way, was primarily his rationality. The human ability to reason distinguished man from nature. We will not dig into the historical roots of this anthropology; however, what would clearly emerge is the powerful culturally formative influence of Hellenistic culture, and especially the influence of Plato and Aristotle. So the view of man lying at the base of the modern worldview is the human person as free to determine his own course and purpose and equipped with reason to do so.

When some aspect of human functioning is absolutized and raised above all others, it leads to a depreciation of the other aspects of human functioning. The Bible views human beings as primarily religious creatures; that is, created as God's image, human beings are made first of all to live the whole of their bodily and creational lives in response to and in covenant partnership with God. There are many aspects to human functioning. We are bodily creatures, emotional creatures, rational creatures, linguistic creatures, social creatures, imaginative and creative creatures, ethical creatures, faith creatures, and so on. When one aspect is idolized all the other aspects of human life are depreciated. Indeed, this is what has happened in modernity. With the exaltation of reason the body, feelings, imagination, and more have been suppressed and depreciated. However, because God's creation is a cosmos—a harmonious interrelated unity—and because God will not let his creation go, when something is suppressed it forces its way back. Al Wolters compares it to a spring: when you try to push down a tightly coiled spring, you can only do it for so long. Finally, it will recoil and spring back.

The postmodern situation is characterized by a non-rational anthropology. That is, the non-rational aspects and functions of human beings have come to central stage in our time. The primary postmodern analysts that have detailed this are Gilles Deleuze and Felix Guattari. They see the dethroning of reason and the rise of feeling and desire as the key to understanding the postmodern condition. According to Deleuze and Guattari, intuition functions as the source of knowledge, an intuition shaped by feelings, desires, and passion. The ominous implications of this view of humanity have been observed by Roger Lundin when he comments that "there is no goal for the actions of the self save the fulfillment of its desires."[9]

We see signs of the correctness of this insight all around us. The body that was diminished and depreciated during modernity has now become the object of veneration in a growing body cult seen in the rise of health clubs as well as in the explosion of pornography. Emotions that were minimized have become the primary authority for the average person. "I feel that" settles it for most people. The primacy of emotions can also be seen in our new styles of worship geared primarily to an emotional experience and in the proliferation comedy and horror flicks which titillate our emotions of gaiety or terror. Walk through your local video store and note the number of times you find "desire" and "passion" in the title. Freud, Jung and the whole discipline of psychology have undermined rationality by demonstrating that we are all driven by subconscious drives. While the imagination and creative or aesthetic function of humanity was undermined in modernity it has a new lease on life in our postmodern times. What is most unexpected is the stress

---

[9] Roger Lundin, *The Culture of Interpretation: Christian Faith and the Postmodern World* (Grand Rapids: Eerdmans, 1993), p. 75.

put on the imagination by philosophers of science. The scientific method is not simply an exercise of methodological reason. The imagination plays a central role in the determination of theories. The doctrinaire secularism of modernity denied any kind of reality that could not be explained by cause and effect relationships. However, the religious, spiritual, mystical—call it what you will—aspect of human beings has come back with a vengeance. Psychics, Eastern religions, native spirituality, occult, age old religions and cults are evidence of this new interest. We could continue multiplying examples.God has made human beings as richly diverse creatures with a variety of functions and abilities. When these are not unified in service and knowledge of God, one of those functions will be absolutized to give direction to human life. In the case of modernity it was human rationality. This resulted in a society based on science, technology, and the rational organization of society. However, no function of humanity can bear this weight. Other aspects suppressed and diminished rise up in rebellion and demand to be noticed. Today we see a new, often idolatrous, appreciation of the body, emotions, desire, passions, subconsciousness, imagination, intuition, creativity, and religious aspects of human beings. As Calvin has pointed out, the heart of humanity is a fabricator of idols. As it turns its back on the illusion of modernity, postmodern humanity is not about to turn to the living God in Christ. Another aspect or other aspects of human functioning will replace reason as the central idol or idols. It seems that where we have driven out the demon of rationalism and seven other demons stand ready to take its place. I wonder if the final condition is not worse than the first (Matt 12:43-45).

And so we ask again: what is God doing in these tremendous events of our times? For those with eyes to see—eyes equipped with the spectacles of Scripture—God is announcing in the events of our time that autonomous man cannot achieve his own salvation. Human reason does not have the capacity to bring about redemption or bring the abundant life. Human beings are made to live in communion and covenant partnership with God. Human beings are religious creatures who will always serve some Ultimate. If they do not serve God and follow Christ they will serve another—an idol of their own making. In the end, what defines humanity is faith and obedience, not rational activity. Indeed, all rational activity will be shaped by some faith.

Postmodern Knowledge Is Social Construction

I turn now to a third and final element of postmodernity—the notion of knowledge as social construction. The modern worldview took form as stories of progress. Those stories of progress were built on a confident humanism that invested man with the authority to shape history and a rationalism that equipped man with the ability to accomplish his goals. The primary way that autonomous man could build a better world was through science. Science played a central role in the modern worldview—so central that many speak of the "modern scientific worldview." The scientific method was the means by which human rationality could realize its goals. The scientific method would give human beings an objective understanding of the world that could then be applied to the non-human world in technology and to human society in a rational organization of society. Science would be the instrument to control the non-human creation and to shape human society.

The confidence that modern humanity put in science can perhaps be captured best in the couplet of Alexander Pope during the Enlightenment—a time when modernity fully matured. Pope wrote the famous lines: "Nature and nature's laws lay hid in night. God said, 'Let Newton be' and all was light." Newton, of course, was the one that fashioned the scientific method. It is that scientific method that is the light of the world and provides the truth that is needed to build the kingdom of man.

On this view, science gives us knowledge that is objective. Our minds can mirror the world faithfully. The knowing subject can gain a neutral and dispassionate standpoint outside the relativities of culture, history, or language, from which he or she can represent the world as it really is. This neutrality comes from the proper use of the scientific method. One can rise above all historical contingency by the use of this method. This objective and neutral knowledge gives modern man what he needs to shape the world with technology and social planning.

In postmodern thought this neutrality and objectivity is seen as an illusion. Reason is not a neutral instrument that can represent the world truly without any subjective context. Advances in anthropology, sociology, history, and linguistics have underscored the relativity of human knowledge. Knowledge is a social construction. Our rationality is shaped by a host of social factors (tradition, community, language, culture, history, faith) and personal factors (feelings, imagination, subconscious, gender, class, race). There is no universal truth for anybody, according to the postmodernist. Many postmodern authors deal with this theme from a variety of angles—Michael Foucault, Jacques Derrida; but perhaps the first name that should be mentioned here is Thomas Kuhn. In his book, *The Structure of Scientific Revolutions*, Kuhn attacked the central shrine of the modern worldview—the objectivity of science. He argued that scientific work is not neutral, dispassionate, and objective but rather is shaped by prevailing worldviews or paradigms. As the intellectual historian Richard Tarnas notes: "The prevalence of the Kuhnian concept of 'paradigms' in current discourse is highly characteristic of postmodern thought, reflecting a critical awareness of the mind's fundamentally interpretive nature."[10]

A stark example of this shift can be seen by looking at the famous political philosopher, John Rawls. In 1971 he wrote a book entitled *A Theory of Justice*. There he sought to establish a universal claim for justice. He attempted to develop a theory of justice that could be established on a rational basis. This rational basis would make the theory universal—standing above all cultural particularity. The power of the postmodern critique can be seen in that nine years later (in *Kantian Constructivism in Moral Theory*, 1980) Rawls said that his theory could only be rationally defensible within this particular culture. It was a product of the reasoning of the West. Whether it was applicable to other situations must be left to other cultures to decide. Justice is not universal and objective; it is social construction.[11]

The well-known and much-used joke of the three umpires is a good illustration of the postmodern condition. They are having a beer after the game, and the first says, "There are balls and strikes and I call them as they are." (This is the modern realist.) The second says, "There are balls and strikes and I call 'em as I see 'em." (This is the critical realist.) The third says, "They ain't nothing until I call them." The first umpire is naive, we now see. The second umpire recognizes an objective reality but also recognizes that his subjective perspective shapes that reality. The third umpire believes that reality is as he constitutes it. The fact that the debate today centres around the last two is indicative of the postmodern shift.

---

[10] Richard Tarnas, *The Passion of the Western Mind: Understanding the Ideas that Have Shaped Our World View* (New York: Ballantine, 1991), p. 397.
[11] Philip Sampson, "The Rise of Postmodernity," in *Faith and Modernity*, ed. Philip Sampson, Vinay Samuel, and Chris Sugden (Oxford: Regnum, 1994), pp. 37-38.

Since there are so many subjective factors that shape our knowledge, there is not one truth about the world, about politics, about economics, about ethics. We are left with a bewildering pluralism, a cacophony of voices, all proclaiming their desires with no umpire to adjudicate. The certainty of scientific knowledge characteristic of modernity has given way to a profound uncertainty that despairs of any universal truth.

This profound uncertainty demonstrates the failure of an attempt to undergird ethics with a rational foundation. Modernity took over norms and standards from the Christian worldview of the medieval period. Our cultural commitment to freedom, justice, righteousness, compassion, and so on come from the biblical story. However, in the modern period autonomous rational man sought to establish a rational and scientific foundation for each of these ideals. Today's ethical relativism and debilitating pluralism signifies the failure of modern humanity to undergird ethics by human scientific rationality. The whole modern period can be seen as providing negative proof for the fact that the fear of the Lord is the beginning of wisdom and that the scientific method cannot replace Christ as the light of the world.

And so we conclude this section again with the question: what is God doing in the events of our time? Our deep cultural crisis comes from a misplaced faith. Too much was expected of methodological rationality or scientific reason. Science, indeed, has been a tremendous gift of God. Our world is a better world because of science. So our tongues should not vilify what our lives embody. The problem is not science but scientism. We have assigned a redemptive role to science especially by assuming that science has the ability to determine norms for politics, society, economics, education, and so on. Pope proclaimed that the scientific method was the light of the world. Jesus has proclaimed that he is the light of the world. What do we see God doing in the events of our time? He is announcing that science has failed as the light of the world. Science as a human creaturely endeavour needs a more ultimate light; philosophy and history of science has shown this. What will that more ultimate light be? Scripture has proclaimed that it is Jesus Christ. Postmodern humanity must either embrace that light, reject that light and find another, or reject that light and despair of ever finding one. Our times have brought ultimate issues to the fore. It must be the believer who sees this in the light of the gospel and bear witness faithfully to the purpose of God for all men.

The Conclusion of the Matter: I am the LORD

The modern worldview is characterized by stories of progress toward a better world. These stories take over the biblical view of history and rewrite them in humanist discourse. Progress is dependent on free and rational man who builds a world of freedom, justice, and truth with science and technology. However, the wheels have come off this confidence. Postmodern humanity no longer believes this story. Every part of that worldview is under attack today, including the rational anthropology and the view of objective scientific truth that undergird this confidence. Disillusionment is the order of the day. Listen to the words of the famous psychologist, Carl Jung:

> I believe I am not exaggerating when I say that modern man has suffered an almost fatal shock, psychologically speaking, and as a result has fallen into profound uncertainty.... I realize only too well that I am losing my faith in the possibility of a rational organization of the world, the old dream of the millennium, in which peace and harmony should rule, has grown pale.[12]

When we ask what God is doing in the momentous events of our time, the answer we give is the answer of Isaiah: "I am the LORD; that is my name! I will not give my glory to another or my praise to idols" (Isa 42:8). Or, in the words of Paul: "They exchanged the truth of God for a lie, and worshiped and served created things rather than the Creator—who is forever praised. Amen. Because of this God gave them over ..." (Rom 1:24-26).

Lest we become triumphalist or self-righteous in our joy at the fall of idols and the failure of false messiahs, I end by adding two things. First, the Christian church has been deeply compromised by the idols of modernity. The postmodern shift ought to lead the Christian church to new reflection and a deep repentance. We are called to give a faithful witness of the purpose of God for the world and all its people. That witness is the witness of one beggar telling other beggars where bread is to be found. It is as humble beggars who have too often chased the crumbs of modernity that we must give witness to Christ as the bread of the world. Second, faithful living in a postmodern world will involve a sympathetic entering into the pain and confusion of our contemporaries. Hopeful and joyful living by a Christian community that believes that

---

[12] Carl Gustav Jung, *Modern Man in Search of Soul* (New York: Harcourt and Brace, 1933), pp. 231, 234-35.

God is sovereign in history will bear eloquent witness to a disillusioned and confused world. However, it is not a joy or hope that raises us above our cultural condition but a joyful confidence in the Lord of history in the midst of dismay and bewilderment. May God grant us that joy and hope that comes from faith in Christ and discernment in the light of his Word.

Chapter 2

Why Christians Should Abandon Certainty

John G. Stackhouse, Jr.

S ome things ought to be seen as black and white, as the choice between extremes. The Christian religion teaches that we are "dead in trespasses and sins" before we become "alive to God." "You must," Jesus declared as an absolute requirement, "be born again." Either we are doomed in a "kingdom of darkness" or we have been transferred by God's grace into "the kingdom of his beloved Son."

We believe that there is only one God. We believe that God is Father, Son and Holy Spirit, and not anything or anyone else. We believe many things, that is, in an "either/or" way, and the gospel requires us to do so.

What I suggest in this chapter is how we are to believe these truths that Christians hold to be absolutely, even "extremely," true. And the first suggestion I offer is that we understand our believing as lying between two extremes: dogmatism and despair.

The dogmatist is "often wrong, but never in doubt." He believes what he believes with the total confidence that he is right and could not possibly be wrong. It is this form of believing, what I am calling "certainty" in this essay, that is not only unattractive to many of our neighbours, but also untrue to the Bible's teaching about the nature of human belief.[1]

---

[1] See Clark H. Pinnock, "The Conservatives," in *Tracking the Maze: Finding Our Way through Modern Theology from an Evangelical Perspective* (San Francisco: Harper & Row, 1990), pp. 33-53.

Such dogmatism, that is, compromises our evangelism in that we turn off and turn away people who are fed up with know-it-alls. Dogmatism compromises our apologetics as we refuse to actually argue with people in an authentic give-and-take, but instead simply assert our point of view and accuse those who refuse to be persuaded of the obvious truth of our position either of stupidity ("I guess you just can't see the truth of what I'm saying") or of sinfulness ("You perversely refuse to see the truth of what I'm saying"). And such dogmatism compromises our ability to engage in the common life of our society, engagement that necessarily involves compromise, ambiguity, and shifting alliances with those who do not share all of our ultimate values.[2]

Within the church, dogmatism renders rigid our sense of discipleship: there is only one way to be a Christian, and this is it; no allowance for personal or communal differences; no recognition that perhaps God has shared his Spirit with Presbyterians and Mennonites and Roman Catholics and Pentecostals. Such dogmatism makes Christian education a matter of mere indoctrination in which questioning and creativity are feared and correctness prized above all. Dogmatism renders ecumenism an unlikely project, as alliances fracture time after time as one group judges the other insufficiently pure. And dogmatism, finally, renders our worship dangerously narrow: our "God" becomes too small, too much restrained by our ideas and preferences, too much a projection of ourselves and not the sovereign, mysterious, transcendent God of the Bible whose ways are far above our ways and whose thoughts are far above our thoughts.

Dogmatism seems safe. Dogmatism seems flattering to oneself and — of course! — to God. But it instead renders both self and God, both the Christian church and the Christian religion, brittle, constrictive, and harsh.

Yet if dogmatism grasps the truth too tightly, despair lets it go entirely. Many of our compatriots, and some within the Church itself, find it both fashionable and freeing to ask questions without embracing answers. To be sure, some persistent questioners currently walk paths of genuine inquiry. Some of them understandably are reacting against repressive authorities. These must be met with loving care.

---

[2] On this last point especially, see Donald C. Posterski, *True to You: Living Our Faith in Our Multi-Minded World* (Winfield, B.C.: Wood Lake, 1995); and Glenn Tinder, *The Political Meaning of Christianity: An Interpretation* (Baton Rouge, La.: Louisiana State University Press, 1989).

Many others, however, simply do not want to submit to any truth. Their "incredulity toward metanarratives," in the phrase of postmodernist Jean-François Lyotard, is political in a deep sense. They do not want to acknowledge, much less submit, to anyone's "Grand Story," to anyone's master scheme of things. A posture of continuous questioning, then, provides such people with the short-term enjoyment of a form of liberty. But their liberty is, finally, the liberty of flotsam, the liberty of the dustmote, the liberty of the ungrounded, untethered, and unconnected thing. This liberty is, at last, only a freedom to die, as an untethered astronaut is free from his spacecraft only to eventually succumb to his own fatal limitations.[3]

If dogmatism seems safe, despair is sad. And it devastates any attempt at Christian mission to the neighbour, any attempt at Christian fellowship based on common commitment to "one Lord, one faith, and one baptism," and any transformative worship. If the dogmatist's "God" is too small, the despairer's "God" is too vague. Authentic Christian commitment, therefore, must lie between these two extremes.

Biblical Anthropology Meets Contemporary Epistemology

Christians should affirm what we affirm because we believe God's revelation points that way. It turns out that what the Bible affirms about human believing correlates nicely with some assertions in contemporary epistemology (that is, philosophy of knowledge).[4]

First, our perception of the world, and our reflection upon it, is finite. We see what we see, hear what we hear, sense what we sense, and then think what we think with all of the limitations of the particular human being: in my case, being male, white, Anglophone, middle-aged, married, a graduate of particular schools with particular courses of

---

[3] This point has been raised many times. For two very different versions, see Terry Eagleton, *The Illusions of Postmodernism* (Oxford: Blackwell, 1996); and Gene Edward Veith, *Postmodern Times: A Christian Guide to Contemporary Thought and Culture* (Wheaton: Crossway, 1994). The most appreciative, yet also critical, evangelical response to postmodernism is J. Richard Middleton and Brian J. Walsh, *Truth Is Stranger than It Used to Be: Biblical Faith in a Postmodern Age* (Downers Grove: InterVarsity, 1995).

[4] The contemporary epistemologists to whom I am most indebted are Alvin Plantinga and Nicholas Wolterstorff. See Nicholas Wolterstorff, *Reason within the Bounds of Religion*, 2d. ed. (Grand Rapids, Mich.: Eerdmans, 1984 [1976]); Alvin Plantinga and Nicholas Wolterstorff, eds., *Faith and Rationality: Reason and Belief in God* (Notre Dame, Ind.: University of Notre Dame Press, 1983); and Alvin Plantinga, *Warranted Christian Belief* (New York: Oxford University Press, 2000).

study, located at the turn of the twenty-first century in the city of Vancouver, and so on. Such a radical finitude of both perception and reflection can lead to wildly wrong conclusions about things. I have badly misjudged traffic patterns, the temperature of coffee, the handwriting on a student essay, the intentions of colleagues, and a million more things because of my lack of knowledge.

Human believing, furthermore, is deeply interested—especially as Marx used the term. That means that we come to a situation with certain allegiances, preferences, and agendas—we are never disinterested. Such biases are not always bad things, to be sure. It sometimes helps that I care enough about a situation to continue to investigate it even when the initial findings are not promising or even contradictory. It sometimes helps that I badly want to believe a person who seems at first to be mistaken or even dissembling. But sometimes my interests interfere with my recognizing that the data are not coming out "right," or that someone has motives I do not want to suspect. My interests may even interfere with my looking in the right direction for the truth.

Indeed, the third important qualifier of human believing is that it is fallen. I tend to see what I want to see, hear what I want to hear, and believe what conveniences me to believe. Philosophers refer to this phenomenon as "the noetic effects of sin." Such a clinical phrase, however, doesn't come close to evoking the terrible reality we face every day as our spiritual and psychological darkness and distortion interferes with our recognizing the way things really are.

So in our knowing we are inescapably particular, located, and non-certain. We think we know this or that, but we know what we think we know only in part, in a biased way, and in a way subject to moral distortion. Furthermore, we cannot get out of our own heads to see how well we do know things from some objective point of view. Science fiction is full of stories that describe someone being actually in one situation (say, lying in an isolation chamber) but perceiving his situation quite differently (say, as a busy street or even another planet) because of other people manipulating his mind through drugs, computers, or other means. This fanciful imagining only dramatizes the everyday reality that we cannot escape our highly qualified epistemic predicament.

Some have suggested that we can escape in time, however, through the work of the so-called hermeneutical spiral. One version of this spiral sees us beginning with our preconceptions, whatever they are and however we acquired them, and then examining some new data—a book, say, or a set of geological specimens, or the view from a tower we've never climbed before. Our preconceptions dispose us to experience this new data in particular ways and not other ways. Yet the data themselves "push back," as it were, on these preconceptions, validating some and perhaps questioning others. As we move back and forth between preconceptions and data, we move along (so the happy version of the hermeneutical spiral goes) toward more and more harmony between the parts (the data) and the whole (our governing worldview as operative in our preconceptions), refining our knowledge toward greater and greater accuracy and comprehension.

— Or not. For the sober truth seems to be that both individuals and communities can ride a hermeneutical spiral away from reality and toward error. Racist individuals and societies have become more and more convinced, not less and less, of the virtues of discrimination and even slavery. Germany, the nation that set the pace for so much of Western culture by the end of the nineteenth century, helped foment two world wars, and the rise of Nazism. No, it seems that even the hermeneutical spiral, promising as it is for a model of how human thinking ought to work, cannot fully rescue us from our epistemological troubles, and can even exacerbate them as we become more and more convinced of what is in fact an error or a lie.

So who can deliver us from this slough of despond?

Faith: Between Dogmatism and Despair

Christians rightly praise God for their deliverance from evil. One of the evils from which God seeks to deliver us today, then, is our epistemological confusion. He delivers us, however, according to the same principle by which he delivers us from other problems as well: by faith. It is commonplace in modern times to put faith over against knowledge, as if the former is mere wishful thinking and the latter hard fact. Instead, however, according to both Christian tradition and contemporary currents in epistemology, all of our intellectual commitments — whether we call them "faith" or "knowledge" — ride on a sea of non-certainty. As the eminent scientist and theologian John Polkinghorne concludes, it's all faith. Human thought is nothing other than our best guesses on the basis of what we trust are helpful avenues to knowledge. We can never be entirely sure that what we think we know matches up precisely with the way things are. We can only trust what we think has worked in the past, or what seems promising to work in the future, and make our best guesses.[5]

Thus it is all faith, in the sense of faith as a commitment to act in the light of what one believes one knows to be true with the recognition that one might be wrong—and will act anyway. One might be unsure about the roadworthiness of this borrowed car, but one can't go anywhere without getting in and driving. One might be unsure about the reliability of this treasured friend, but one can't get married without getting entirely married, giving one's whole self to the joint enterprise of matrimony. One can't even perform a scientific experiment without a belief in the regularity of the cosmos and scientific laws, the reliability one's memory of scientific formulae, the competence of one's assistants, and so on. Faith is something we exercise all the time, and necessarily so.

This isn't, moreover, an entirely bleak situation. For sense experience seems normally pretty reliable in making contact with the external world. Reason has proven to be limited, of course, but still eminently useful—a terrible master, but a fine servant, as many have observed. And so for other ways in which we seek to access and make sense of things: memory, testimony, authority, spiritual experience, history, philosophy, and so on.

Furthermore, to say that none of our media of investigating or reflecting upon the world can provide certainty is not to conclude that all are of equal value. Some beliefs seem much more powerfully warranted than others. There are people who trust their lives to the deliverances of ESP or numerology, but most of us think the preponderance of evidence leads away from such reliances and toward confidence in other media of knowledge instead. In the face, then, of both New Age oddities and of postmodernist despair, Christians can still affirm reason, experience, tradition and Scripture as gifts of God to be used well in making sense of things and making the most of them in God's service.

Christians, that is, should not claim certainty, affirming that what they know is true and they could not possibly be wrong about it. Instead, Christians must be people of confidence (note the Latin word for "faith" in the midst of that word, *fides*). Christians trust the good means God has given us to make sense of the world. Furthermore, Christians rejoice in assurance, the gift of the Holy Spirit in our hearts that testifies that we

---

[5] John Polkinghorne, *The Faith of a Physicist: Reflections of a Bottom-Up Thinker* (Minneapolis: Fortress, 1996 [1994]); and idem, *Belief in God in an Age of Science* (New Haven: Yale University Press, 1998).

belong to God in Christ. Again, there is no way for us to get outside ourselves and test to see whether this experience of spiritual encouragement is actually caused by the Holy Spirit or not. But it both feels like it is and it coheres with what else we think we know about God, ourselves, and so on—so it is rational for us to trust that experience as such unless we have some sufficiently powerful reason to doubt it. Finally, on the basis of Christian confidence and assurance, we embrace commitment, the actual living out of life in the light of these beliefs and experiences. We live as if we know Christianity is true, because as far as we know, Christianity is true. And it is both well-warranted and marvelously good news!

Such a posture of happy trust in God and in the great things of the gospel is true to the apostolic pattern. The early church did not say, "We have considered all of the religious and philosophical options in the world, weighed them up with complete knowledge and disinterested analysis, and thus find Christianity to emerge as the world's best religion." Instead, they said things such as we find at the start of John's great letter: "That which was from the beginning, which we have heard, which we have seen with our eyes, which we have looked at and our hands have touched—this we procalim concerning the Word of life. The life appeared; we have seen it and testify to it, and we proclaim to you the eternal life, which was with the Father and has appeared to us. We proclaim to you that we have seen and heard…" (1 John 1:1-3).

We do not have to claim more than we rightly can ("We know it all" or "We couldn't possibly be wrong") to join the missionary work of the Church through the ages in saying, "What we have seen and heard about the word of life, this is what we have to offer you. We're as convinced of the truth of this word as much as we are convinced of anything else, so we have no choice but to joyfully share it with you."

Epistemic Duty and Christian Vocation
Let us then consider the place of Christian thinking in the larger issue of the Christian vocation. What does God want to accomplish through our thinking in the light of his great purposes for the world and his calling of the Church to work with him toward those ends?

To begin, consider two axioms of the Christian vocation: (1) The primary calling (vocation) of earthly human life is to grow in love with God and to fulfill God's will; (2) God loves us and so we can trust him to provide all that we need in order to grow in love with God and to fulfill his will.

It seems to me that from these basic affirmations flow crucial episte-mological implications. In particular, because (1) and (2) are so basic to Christian life, Christians can therefore expect that if they pursue knowledge responsibly, for the right reasons (love of God and pursuit of the interests of his kingdom), then God will provide what knowledge they need to fulfill their vocations. To put it another way, I am commending the idea of responsible Christian thought rather than correct Christian thought. We are responding to God's calling by doing what is up to us to do while trusting that God will do his part. We engage in Christian thought in just the way we engage in every other activity of the Christian life: in faith that the great God will take our finite and fallen efforts and make out of them, with us, something pleasing to him and beneficial to the world. Our thinking thus shares in the great exaltation of all things human in God's great sharing of his glory with us as his images and, even better, his children.

The reverse side of this confidence, however, is the humbling recognition that we may have nothing more than this state of knowledge. Consider that our primary vocation is not "to know things." Consider further the interesting fact that God seems manifestly content with Christians everywhere not knowing many things, and with us actually believing that we do know this or that when it appears to others or even later to ourselves that we are in error. So confidence in God's providing for us what knowledge we need to fulfill our vocations does not entail confidence that God will render Christian thought infallible. Not at all. It doesn't even mean that Christians will always think more correctly and creatively about things than non-Christians, even with their advantage of beginning with a Christian worldview. The history of human thought as it has unfolded under divine providence shows that Christians have played their part, but not the only part and not always the best part in the human search for knowledge. Instead, this proposal suggests instead that Christians ought to give up the quest for certain knowledge, and instead redirect, and truly subjugate, our epistemological concern to the more basic concern to love God and serve him.

The model presented here says, "We rely on you, God, to show us each day what we need to know in order to love and serve you. We understand that we will often not recognize what in our minds is in fact erroneous or incomplete. Yet we trust you to make of our efforts in thought, as well as our efforts in every other respect, something acceptable to you and useful to others." This model, therefore, is determined to please God above all else—even above the quest for knowledge itself. In this, I believe, the priorities are Christian.

Christian Thought as a Means of Grace

Let us consider, then, an awkward question. If, on the one hand, there is no certainty to be had; and if, on the other hand, God can be relied upon to show us what he wants us to know; then why go to all the trouble of serious thought? Why read challenging books, and industriously seek out more? Why engage in rigorous conversation about difficult subjects? Why go to seminars, attend expensive schools, support Christian education in the church? Why work so hard at Christian thought?

Christian tradition through the years has formulated the category of a "means of grace." This phrase denotes some vehicle, some instrument by which God conveys good things to his people. For most Christians a means of grace has been the Lord's Supper, in which Christ blesses his church as they worship in this way. For all Christians, the Bible has always been a means through which Christ nourishes his people. Preaching, music, prayer—all of these and many more have been recognized by Christians as means of grace. When handled by us in all of our finitude and fallenness, their goodness becomes fragmented and corrupted to some extent. Yet they have shown through the centuries that they are reliable sources of blessing, and we rightly rely on them for guidance.

Could God not give us the results of these means more directly, bypassing them entirely? Perhaps he could. The point is, however, that God has ordained these means of grace. He has sovereignly chosen to work through them. Therefore the appropriate response of the Christian is to receive and use them gladly.

Christian thought, I suggest, can be considered helpfully in this way. Responsible Christian thought gladly uses the resources God has made available to it. And we are responsible to use them gladly and well.

It is not for us to discard them in the name of postmodern doubt, because they do seem to help us negotiate reality: in predicting future events; in sowing and then reaping; in following directions to reach destinations; in giving advice to others that seems genuinely to help them also; and so on. In particular, we must not allow ourselves to become epistemologically paralysed just because we cannot refute a skeptic's clever argument.

It is also not for us to lie down in a lazy, pseudo-spiritual stupor or retreat fearfully from the rigors of serious thought into the dogmatic pronouncements of our traditions or favourite authors. It is not for us to remain immature when God calls us to maturity through these disciplines. It is not for us to disobey God by ignoring or avoiding his means, and especially odious to do so in the name of piety. No, we use what God has given us in faith that he will accomplish his good will in us thereby.[6]

Conclusion

I recognize that this proposal seems a long way from the popular evangelical sentiment that "the Bible says it; I believe it; that settles it." It also has moved away from more sophisticated forms of evangelical Christian thought, rooted as they are in one or another form of modernity's epistemological over-confidence.

To be sure, this proposal shares some of that confidence in that it values reason and experience as genuine means of divinely-given grace. This proposal, however, takes other things more radically into account, including sin in the hearts and minds of us all. It tries to keep first things first. It does not promise certain knowledge, but it does promise God's sufficient provision for the basic calling of every Christian. And I suggest that that is enough.

For on that great day, no one will hope to hear from our Master a commendation such as, "Good for you. You figured it out." Instead, we will yearn to hear the strong, soft music of "Well done, thou good and faithful servant. Enter thou into the joy of thy Lord."

---

[6]So the argument in Mark A. Noll, *The Scandal of the Evangelical Mind* (Grand Rapids: Eerdmans, 1994).

Chapter 3

The Subversion of Genuine Worship

Marva J. Dawn

If we want to consider the subject of worship, it is essential that we hear what the Scriptures say on the topic. Therefore, this chapter will use reflections on some Psalms to deal with aspects of "the subversion of genuine worship." The most important word in that title is the word *of,* since it can be read in two ways. First, what are the forces in our culture that subvert genuine worship? Second, what in our worship will subvert the culture?

We need to contemplate both aspects, because I think—and I believe many others in the Church also think—that worship is in serious trouble in North America. Churches are being buffeted by cultural influences that are formidably strong and are pulling us away from biblical foundations into patterns of behaviour that are not as formative of Christian identity as we might wish. Therefore let us look at what some of these forces are and see what resources we have to counteract them. Especially, let us consider what kind of questions we should be asking about worship, so that we can more faithfully plan worship, lead worship, and participate in worship. Everyone reading this chapter is probably involved in at least one of those three. How could we be enabled to participate in worship and lead worship in ways that are more godly, more biblical and more formative of genuine Christianity?

The psalms teach us many essential truths about worship. One morning while praying Psalms 81-84, I discovered that excerpts from these passages expose many of the idolatries that invade churches. Let us consider seven of these idolatries, so that we may counteract them with seven subversions on the part of worship.

The first subversion is exposed in Psalm 81, which begins with the following words: "For the choir director; on the Gittith. A Psalm of Asaph." As a preface to studying these psalms, let us remember that it is helpful to pay attention to the psalm titles. The titles themselves are often verse 1 or part of verse 1 in the Hebrew Bible and tell us the canonical context of the poem. Psalm 81's particular title tells us that this was a song used in public worship. Such a title is thrilling to me, because it indicates that Jesus no doubt sang this song as he participated in the worship of Temple and synagogue. It is a great delight to sing the psalms with this title because we are knit to all the Christians and Jews, especially Jesus, who have sung this song throughout time and space. We can date the psalm because it was Asaph's (see especially 1 Chronicles 16), and we can surmise, from the structure and content of the psalm, that it was probably used for a festival celebration.

The Subversion of Narcissism

After its title the psalm enjoins, "Sing for joy to God our strength; shout aloud to the God of Jacob! Begin the music, strike the tambourine, play the melodious harp and lyre. Sound the ram's horn at the New Moon, and when the moon is full, on the day of our feast." We can't help but notice in these beginning verses, first of all, the call to use many instruments and a great diversity of them. Second, these verses do not say one whit about one's emotions (except joy, which we shall see below is more than merely emotional). This leads us to contemplate first the idolatry of feelings, which is terribly destructive in subverting Christian worship. The pervasive notion that our self is what is most important and that what we get out of worship is what determines whether the worship service is a good one or not is a total reversal of what genuine worship truly is.

Notice that this psalm begins with the command, "Sing for joy *to* God." The point of worship is to adore God.[1] If worship is for God it doesn't really matter what we feel. But take note how often we hear this kind of complaint in our churches: "I didn't get much out of that worship service" — to which I always want to respond, "How much did you put in?" Or the complainer declares, "I didn't like that worship

---

[1] This is one of the primary points of my book, *Reaching Out without Dumbing Down: A Theology of Worship for this Urgent Time* (Grand Rapids: Eerdmans, 1995).

service." Does that really matter? The point is whether God liked it, since worship is for God. If we determine what is happening in worship by how we feel about it, then we are worshipping ourselves. We are caught up in a terrible paradigm in North America that says that we go to worship to please ourselves. This notion should be exposed for the narcissistic idolatry that it is: worshipping myself instead of worshipping God.

The psalm invites us to praise. Praise has been so mis-defined in our culture that people confuse the word *praise* with "upbeat music." To be sure, upbeat music is sometimes praise, but not always. Sometimes praise is upbeat, but not always. In fact, one of my favourite praise songs is a dirge; in our sorrow, we praise God for being present with us at a funeral. Praise means to attribute to God his character or to recognize God's intervention or to name something about God. Therefore, when I praise God I am noticing what God has revealed about God's self. This means that praise can take all kinds of forms. It can use the harp, the lyre, the trumpet; it can sound melancholy, it can sound upbeat. We need all kinds of praise, or else we do not have a big enough God, nor a large enough vocabulary to know God's presence in all the dispositions and circumstances of life. Our God, the Triune God, is a God who reveals himself in all of our moods and feelings. When I go away from worship, the question is not so much "do I feel better?" as "do I know God better?"

Let me modify this last question a little bit, because by saying "know God better" I do not mean merely cerebral knowledge. Knowing God is a more holistic notion, which we misunderstand if we are too modern Western-minded. The contemporary tendency is to dissect body, mind, soul and spirit into separate parts. Hebrew thinking, in contrast, recognizes that all of this is connected in one undivided self. To know God engages me wholly.

In a culture that over-accentuates feelings, it is essential that believers learn not to build our knowledge of God on them. Otherwise, how do we cope when we are in pain, when we don't feel good about God, when our feelings would convince us that God is absent?

Knowing God requires, as Paul tells us in Romans 12, the renewal of our minds. That is not purely cerebral either, not just mechanical brain work. It is recognizing with wisdom the truths that we know about God, regardless of how we feel. The reason our culture has so much trouble understanding this is that our culture is so data laden it has trouble distinguishing between facts and knowledge, much less knowledge and wisdom. Data isn't strong enough to overcome negative feelings, but wisdom is.

When we gather together with others for worship, the truths of God we celebrate can subvert the idolatry of our selves so that we can discover who our true self really is. Our true self is much larger than the way we happen to feel at the moment. If worship can easily be subverted by the contemporary culture of narcissism, then one gift of genuine worship is that it invites us to know God, to praise God, to sing for Joy, because no matter what is going on in our lives, God is there.

Let's distinguish between happiness and Joy, which I always capitalize to underscore its divine source. Happiness is a feeling contingent upon circumstances; Joy is a truth.[2] Picture the difference this way: in most of life people's emotional state is predicated on their happy or sad feelings, dependent upon whether life is going smoothly or whether life is a mess. As Christians we have another dimension. What matters to Christians is not so much our emotions—whether happy or sad—but the firm foundation underneath those emotions. That foundation is created by the resurrection of Jesus Christ, which has changed everything. Though throughout history the LORD has been a God of deliverance, his most decisive emancipation occurred in the resurrection of Christ. The pattern of rescue which God reveals throughout the metanarrative of our Scriptures culminates in our deliverance from sin, death, and the devil when Christ arose and defeated all the powers. Therefore, we recognize that this God is a source of Joy, regardless of what is happening in this particular moment of life.

We can experience Joy even when we are not happy because of who God is. God will always be the same, and nothing can change the fact that Christ has delivered us from our captivities (including our bondage to feelings!). God's character remains infinitely true, no matter what happens in the circumstances of our lives. Thus when Psalm 81 says, "Sing for joy" it doesn't promise that you will be happy. Nor do the psalms ever say, "Praise the Lord because you are happy." Rather, Psalm 9:1 says, "I will praise you, O LORD, with all my heart," and the biblical word *heart* signifies our will. With our minds we know that God is worthy of being praised, and so with our wills we can rejoice in God all the time regardless of what is happening to us.

---

[2] This is explored much more thoroughly in Marva J. Dawn, *Joy in Our Weakness: A Gift of Hope from the Book of Revelation* (St. Louis: Concordia, 1994).

This suggests a difference between praise and thanks. Thanks is directly related to me: "I *thank* you, God, because you got me here safely tonight." But we could say, "I *praise* you, God," even if the airplane had crashed because he would still be God and still be worthy of praise. There is a self-abnegation in genuine worship. Truly to adore God is mortification, for what really happens in worship is that my self dies. Of course it rises again, too. But if we haven't died, we cannot really rise.

Part of the reason why Christianity is so wimpy in North America is that there is not enough death happening. We haven't died to ourselves enough to really let Christ live through us.[3] Just think how it would change the picture of North America if every person in the pews of our churches so died to themselves that Christ could really live through them all the time, if all of us lived missionally twenty-four hours a day, seven days a week.

This is subversion #1: worship gets subverted when we let our own narcissism influence how we participate in it. Contrarily, our narcissism gets subverted when we genuinely worship, when we praise God, name God for who God is, and claim that God as the one whose calling us "beloved" is true whether we feel it or not.

The Subversion of Choice

Psalm 81:4-5 declares, "this is a decree for Israel, an ordinance of the God of Jacob. He established it as a statue for Joseph when he went out against Egypt, where we heard a language we did not understand." At first glance, these verses seem quite odd. It helps us to understand them if we recall that the previous verse speaks about the new moon. Probably this psalm was used for the tabernacle festival, "the feast of booths," when the Israelite families all built little tents or shelters and lived in them for a week to remember their wanderings in the wilderness. Notice in all of this that to worship is a "statute," an "ordinance," a "testimony," a language we are not used to hearing.

The second subversion of genuine worship happens when we turn it into a matter of choice instead of obedience to God's command. One of the worst things that has happened to the faith formation of our churches' children is that they are allowed to choose whether to go to public worship. I thank God I grew up in a family for which participating in worship was never offered to me as a choice. My father

---

[3] To pursue this subject in more depth, see Marva J. Dawn, *Powers, Weakness, and the Tabernacling of God* (Grand Rapids: Eerdmans, 2001).

was the organist, and we all joined him in corporate worship every Sunday. I am so grateful that the delightful and formative habit of weekly worship was instilled in me in my childhood. For one thing, it saves a lot of time. My husband and I never have to waste time Sunday morning figuring out whether we're going to go or not. We simply go. What a wonderful habit!

Similarly, there is no question about tithing. We never have to ask *if* we are going to tithe. It is just what a family does! (Actually, the question for all of us in North America, where we are so rich compared with the rest of the world, should be how much beyond the tithe we can go. Can we aim for half this year?)

When we have these habits, these practices, these obediences, then we will be able to resist the subversion of choice. We certainly won't harbour the notion that we decided to go to worship out of our own brilliance or benevolence. Instead, we will realize that creatures owe their Creator praise!

Psalm 81:4 reminds us that worship is an obligation. Isn't that a radical idea in North America? Every Christian college I know is doing away with required chapels. Don't think that I'm necessarily opposed to that, but it does illustrate that a command to worship no longer seems intellectually credible. The point is that we have fallen into North America's notion that we can just do whatever *we* want about participating in worship or not. I would like to recover the sense that our God is so wonderfully worthy we can't help but worship. We obey the deepest law of the universe: to have no other gods above this One.

Furthermore, what audacity it is to show up and not recognize that if God wanted to, God could just blast us out of there. Annie Dillard comments that if we really knew what we were about when we gather for worship, the ushers would hand out crash helmets at the door! In his *Theology of the Old Testament* Walter Brueggemann talks about God being "wild." Why have we so tamed and reduced the LORD of the cosmos that we think we are doing God a great honour by showing up on Sunday mornings? How have we lost our awe in being so amazingly blessed that God deigns to let us into his presence? But we have turned God into a cuddly teddy bear or into something small enough to put into our pockets, and we do not realize that this is GOD we are talking about.

This is the God before whom people fell on their faces in the First Testament. This is the God who came down on Mount Sinai and caused such a ruckus that the Israelites said to Moses, "Speak to us yourself and we will listen; but do not have God speak to us, or we will die" (Exod 20:19). Jesus didn't change that, for God is still the same yesterday, today and forever. Jesus has showed us much more about God, has opened the way of access for us to God, but he did not negate what we already knew about God. Sometimes we get so Jesus-centred that we are not Trinitarian. The atonement of Jesus makes no sense if we don't know that God's righteousness is radically perfect and cannot endure our sinfulness. If we had a larger view of God, we would not make the mistake of saying only "God is love" while never saying "God is holy." When asking people about their goal in life, I have never yet heard a teenager say, "My goal is to be holy." Nonetheless, that is what God has declared to us: "You shall be holy, for I, the LORD your God, am holy."

That we have lost this sense of God is obvious if we ask a person on the street, "What does it mean to participate in worship?" We are not likely to hear that it is an enormous privilege, that the person is so grateful to have the opportunity to gather with the saints for worship in a corporate setting.

We can easily see how much we have been subverted by the idolatry of choice. We have turned churches into "vendors of religious services and goods" where people shop for worship, instead of "a body of people sent on a mission."[4] People choose a church by what makes them feel good (notice how the subversions support each other—choice and narcissism), instead of belonging to a community in which God will kill us, and then raise us up into the new life of obedience! Many Christians want to jump to Easter without working through Lent and especially Good Friday. We choose the victory and the resurrection and the blessings without the suffering. We really don't want to take up our cross and follow Jesus. Too often in the churches of North America people act as if the text says, "Take up your teddy bear and follow me," for the only reason to carry a cross is to die to ourselves on it.

It might seem like this section is all bad news, but that is not the case at all. However, we cannot experience the true Joy and freedom of real worship unless we recognize what subverts it and what a great honour it is to obey God's command to worship. We can't really experience the fullness of Joy in God's presence unless we realize how utterly we don't deserve to be there.

---

[4] See George R. Hunsberger, "Sizing Up the Shape of the Church," in *The Church Between Gospel and Culture: The Emerging Mission in North America*, ed. George R. Hunsberger and Craig Van Gelder (Grand Rapids: Eerdmans, 1996), pp. 333-46.

Think of the most noble person in whose presence you have ever been and what a great honour it was. When I was in college I took part in a choir tour around the world. In Thailand, we sang a command performance for the King of Thailand and were treated as VIPs consequently throughout our stay in the country. Be assured, we trembled a bit after the concert, when we stood at the base of the stairs and the king came down in a stately procession to shake our hands. Multiply that privilege by a zillion and then we are just beginning to imagine the unfathomable grace it is that we can gather for corporate worship. What an obligation!

This, then, is subversion #2: worship gets subverted when we think that we participate in it by our own noble choice. Contrarily, our cultural emphasis on choice gets subverted when we genuinely worship and realize what a privilege it is that God condescended to deliver us from ourselves and to set us free to obey his command to worship him.

The Subversion of Meta-Narrative or The Subversion of Pride

In Psalm 81:6, 7, 10 and 16, this is the LORD speaking: "I removed the burden from their shoulders; their hands were set free from the basket." (God is referring to Israel's slavery in Egypt, to what it was like to gather the raw materials and then make bricks for Pharaoh's massive building projects.) "In your distress you called and I rescued you. I answered you out of a thundercloud [Mt. Sinai]; ... I am the LORD your God, who brought you up out of Egypt. Open wide your mouth and I will fill it ... But you would be fed with the finest of wheat; with honey from the rock I would satisfy you." These scattered verses sketch some of the main points of Israel's master story and challenge us to recognize how much our culture and our worship is subverted by the postmodern lack of (or prideful rejection of) a metanarrative.

As postmodern philosophers and our increasingly postmodern society insist (falsely) that every description of universal, overarching truth is a hidden bid for power and that any larger narrative is by nature oppressive, people are more and more being robbed of any grounding story. It is certainly true that many metanarratives have been oppressive. The United States formerly told an appalling myth that Christopher Columbus "discovered" America, that the pioneers were noble as they swept across the country and bravely annihilated the "Indians." We can all fill in gruesome details of that story, which was indeed a very grievous metanarrative to African Americans and to native Americans. It was a horrendous account and bespoke much godlessness, as well as much simplistic misunderstanding.

The result of the postmodern rejection of that metanarrative, however, is that now U.S. citizens have none. There is absolutely nothing in the United States that holds people together. There is essentially no common story, and because there is no communal past or future the United States is splitting in the present into more and more victim groups. There is an escalation of blaming others and a decreasing sense of the common good. This is the nature of our times if we have no unifying larger story.

It is true that many metanarratives have been oppressive, but human beings can't get along very well without them. We intrinsically need some deeper source and sense of identity. We have to have something that gives us roots. Instead, postmodernism has been coupled with the technological milieu's tendency to change focal practices that produced engagement in the larger world into merely the use of devices that produce commodities.[5] This has led to a terrible rootlessness in our culture, with people not having any social (or mental) "web of reality" that equips them with enough inner resilience to be committed. If people haven't any larger story by which to understand their own, what sort of self do they have with which they can be committed? (This was illustrated well by the movie, "Runaway Bride," in which the lead character several times at her own weddings ran away from the grooms and marriage—and at the end of the film confessed that it was because she didn't know who she was.)

Psalm 81:6-16 recounts several aspects of Israel's story and suggests that Israel's worship was powerfully founded in their metanarrative, in the common story which is ours, too. Our metanarrative begins with Abraham and Sarah, with God calling and thereby creating a people for himself. That is very different from any other metanarrative. No other religious story begins with a god choosing and then rescuing a people. This metanarrative is not oppressive like others, because it is the master account of a gracious, merciful, promising, and promise-keeping God. The book of Deuteronomy especially uses the phrase "the LORD thy God" almost 350 times to set out the uniqueness of Israel's story. Moses asks in Deuteronomy 4:34 if

---

[5] See Albert Borgmann, *Technology and the Character of Contemporary Life: A Philosophical Inquiry* (Chicago: University of Chicago Press, 1984), especially pp. 196-209.

any other god has ever gone "to take for himself one nation out of another nation ... like all the things the LORD your God did for you in Egypt before your very eyes."

Many religions have creation myths, but Israel's creation account is dependent upon their knowing that the God who called Abraham and Sarah was also the God who created them. Consequently, Israel's narrative of the beginning of the world is more like a liturgy exulting, "This is how our God created the cosmos." The beginning of our story is phenomenal: we know the creator God personally as well as majestically. Both of these elements are present in the two names used in the two creation accounts. The name *Elohim* is actually the Hebrew plural form, which might suggest that this magnificent God is more than gods, and the name *YHWH* ("I AM") refers to our covenant promising LORD in relationship with us. We know God both ways, and Scripture is filled with the dialectical combination of this transcendence and immanence.

Our metanarrative is highlighted by all the First Testament accounts of what the LORD promised and how he fulfilled those promises. God is always performing what was pledged to Israel, is always there to rescue them. He delivers them out of Egypt; he rescues them through the judges every time outside threats wake them up from their periods of rebellion; and he liberates them from Babylon.

As the apostle Paul directs us in Romans 9-11, Christians cherish the Jews' extraordinary metanarrative because it is our story, too, since we have been grafted into it. Thus, we share in God's promise-filled call to Abraham, "I will bless you, /I will make your name great; /and you will be a blessing" (Gen 12:2). We recognize ourselves as a rescued people, called by the LORD to be his own for the sake of the rest of the world. Then, of course, Jesus is the high point of the whole biblical metanarrative, and the absolute culmination of everything that God promises is found in his resurrection. It is because of the resurrection that we can trust God for all the rest of the promises.

The metanarrative goes on with the story of the early church, and it also has an ending on that last great day when God will do away with all struggle and strife forever. In the meanwhile, we live in these in-between times, waiting for Christ to come again, improvizing our part in the eternal metanarrative, living the story of our daily lives as part of God's whole graced narrative about the cosmos. In a world that is starved for some sort of bearings, isn't this story a great gift we have for the Church's neighbours?

In a world that wants to subvert worship by limiting it to just a few years of the story, we instead want to give as much of the story as we can give each time we gather. There is a subtle rebuke in those words. It seems to me to be extremely dangerous to have only "contemporary" services. Hear me clearly: I love using new music, new worship forms, so-called contemporary songs; but if our worship includes only the contemporary, how do we display the picture of an eternal and cosmic metanarrative? If we act as if we invented Christianity in the last ten years, that is awfully arrogant.

It is equally idolatrous, however, to emphasize only "tradition" without employing anything new, as if God died fifty years ago. That is comparably arrogant. We want in our worship to have a sense of the whole story, and a sense of all God's people throughout space and time.

Therefore, we need what our forebears learned about God; we aren't smart enough to figure out all of theology today. Nor can we stop at what our forebears knew; we must have new theology, and new songs, and new creative expression, because God is alive, and the Spirit is at work. Nor can we just settle for the German tradition, because God is working in Tanzania, and God is working in Korea, and God is working in Brazil. We need music and theology from those places. Instead of limiting ourselves to just one little piece of Church, could not our worship give us the sense that we are part of the whole Church throughout space and time?

Could not our worship subvert at the same time both this cultural rootlessness and the opposite problem of being stuck-in-the-mud? Both are dangerous because we miss out on an "awe-full" lot of God if we confine the eternal LORD to just one epoch. God is too big for that, and we are too small. Earlier, we considered the subversions in our culture of narcissism and of choice. This subversion (or loss of) metanarrative in our culture is also a subversion by pride. It is prideful to presume that merely our own epoch is enough, that our theology and music need not submit to the whole Church. The subversion of worship by pride fails to recognize how the Gospel's glorious good news has encompassed and been expressed by a great company of people throughout space and time.

Many old German churches utilized an architectural practice to illustrate this all-encompassing character of the good news. In their sanctuaries the congregations would make the kneeler for the people at communion in the shape of a half circle. Members understood that the other half of the circle was in heaven (or in the churchyard in the cemetery). During communion there was a sense that all the people of God were present. (This idea was illustrated in the movie, "Tender Mercies," which ended in a scene of the Lord's Supper, where suddenly those who had been killed by racial violence during the course of the movie were present, sitting with their families or next to their former enemies.)

Similarly, once I asked my cancer doctor, who is Greek Orthodox, why their worship services named so many ancient saints. He replied, "Because they are there." Do your worship services give participants the sense that the great saints are present? What can we do in our worship to have a better sense that the whole people of God worship here?

The ancient catholic liturgy includes in Sunday worship the Sanctus: "Holy, holy, holy, LORD God of power and might! Heaven and earth are full of your glory. Hosanna in the highest. Blessed is He who comes in the name of the LORD. Hosanna in the highest." I love singing this because of its cosmic connections. The first part of the text comes from Isaiah 6, where the seraphim are singing it. This became part of Jewish worship, so Jesus probably sang it. The second part of the text is what the children sang on Palm Sunday (quoting Psalm 118:26), so we join with children at Jerusalem and with all the saints welcoming Jesus into our lives when we sing it. When I was teaching in Madagascar and Poland we sang it. Many denominations sing it. Altogether, that is a big choir! To sing the Sanctus on Sunday mornings and to be conscious that people have sung this song since at least 700 years before Christ is to experience the fullness of the "cloud of witnesses" that cheer on our faith!

This, then, is subversion #3: worship gets subverted when our culture's pride and its rejection of metanarrative limit our worship forms to those of just one epoch. Contrarily, our cultural arrogance and antipathy to a master-story get subverted when we genuinely worship using forms from the whole Church throughout space and time and when we remember the fullness of our biblical story and our particular place in it.

The Subversion of Rebellion

The rest of Psalm 81 deals with the next idolatry: "I tested you at the waters of Meribah. Hear, O my people, and I will warn you; if you would but listen to me, O Israel! You shall have no foreign god among you ... But my people would not listen to me; Israel would not submit to me. So I gave them over to their stubborn hearts..." (7c-9a, 11-12a). These words show that worship is often subverted by the human need to "get my own way." We don't want to be mentored by anyone else. We want to do everything by our own selves. This is the idolatry of rebellion, which has been practised throughout time, but especially since the 1960s in new forms. Sometimes I want to say, "Come on, churches, grow up!" because many of the worship wars in churches are the result of sheer rebellion.

Recently I participated in an endowment-sponsored conversation between a number of people who represented a diversity of opinions on worship. One of the speakers was asked to enumerate what those self-described as "contemporary" musicians could learn from the "traditionalists." Among the several items he listed, he stressed that they could have gained deeper theology, better skills for musical leadership and for inviting the people to sing, more quality in music. I couldn't help but ask him point-blank, "Then why did you rebel against the Church? All the experienced musicians could have taught you those things." He responded, "No one has ever asked me that before."

That points out the need for all of us to do some self-reflection: have some of our attitudes about worship arisen out of rebellion against our forbears? Some people comment about worship, "I don't want to do things like my parents did." On the opposite side, why do older people often rebel against change? Both kinds of rebellion are equally destructive. It doesn't ultimately matter which end of the spectrum contention comes from. The real problem in all of it is that we destroy the possibility of being a genuine community, characterized by unity in our diversity.

The result when the subversive power of rebellion, truly a destructive force in North American culture, invades our churches is that we don't display the comprehensive nature of the God we worship. Moreover, we don't know each other or love each other well enough to sing songs we don't particularly like for the sake of the community. (Notice that I'm not referring to songs that are theologically askew or musically incoherent or incongruent, but only to those that might be of styles that aren't our favourites.)

Ken Medema is a wonderful pianist/composer, who can make up a matching song instantly for whatever story he is told. At a recent conference, he suggested that in congregations people could tell the stories of why a certain piece is spiritually strong for them. He gave an example of when it was a German fellow's turn—a guy with long hair, who didn't look like the traditional sort. Consequently, the whole congregation was totally shocked that he chose an old German chorale. They could hardly wait to hear the story; why did this guy pick such a song? He told them how he had grown up in the Church and had rebelled against it, how he got into drugs and alcohol and rebelled against worshipping God. One day he hit the lowest of lows and could barely stagger down the street. Needing to sit down and finding a church door open, he walked in and sat in the back pew. The organist happened to be practising, playing this chorale for which the German fellow knew the words from his childhood. He said to the congregation, "That song brought me back to the Lord. That song rescued me from my despair." Now everyone in the congregation loves that song.

Couldn't we similarly be a community of care first, so that we don't fight over such silly things as musical taste? Couldn't we teach each other to appreciate each other's songs so that all together we have a bigger vision of God? Couldn't we sing songs we don't like because we love our brothers and sisters?

This is just one of many rebellions I could have picked. The point is that we need to resist the subversion of worship by the societal forces of rebellion that say that nothing old can be good or that nothing new can be good. God's presence in our worship calls us away from these rebellions into humility.

Do we have enough humility to listen to a choir anthem that is rather esoteric without blaming the choir for singing a mysterious song? Could we rather acknowledge that our understanding is a wee bit too limited so that we couldn't yet appreciate it but might learn to? Too often, instead our tendency is to grumble, complain, protest, withdraw. On the other hand, musicians sometimes need to sacrifice their own good taste for something a little less exalted, that is more accessible to all the people. The real key to using all sorts of music has five simple steps: educate, educate, educate, educate, educate. We can educate people to appreciate a wider diversity of forms and styles, so that they don't have to rebel against elements of worship.

A long time ago when I was a choir director, the choir was going to sing Bach's beautiful Advent piece, "Wachet Auf" ("Wake, Awake, for Night is Flying"). At various points, the male voices enter with a different melody in the midst of the organ theme. Because the congregation was perhaps not ready to understand it, I explained to them why Bach does what he does in his faithful setting of the text. He creates real tensions: sometimes the organ melody isn't finished when the men break in; sometimes the organ rhythm doesn't seem to go with the choir rhythm. The result is that people experience some jarring when they listen to it. Not being able sometimes to concentrate on hearing both elements at once, the listener might be pulled to the one or to the other. What better way to envision the tension of Advent? Advent envelops us in many tensions of the aeons—of preparing for Christ to come and yearning for the kingdom's culmination, yet knowing that his first coming has brought the new creation already into conflict with the old. Moreover, we recognize that we don't deserve Christ's salvation and are not ready for his coming, but we want to prepare his way and receive the gifts of his coming. I tried to help the congregation hear this clash of the two aeons in Bach's music.

One of the high school students in our congregation usually hated coming to worship, but the day we sang this particular piece, he commented to the youth director, "That was so cool!" He had understood it and had been caught up by Bach's vision.

Many of the rebellions over aspects of worship could be avoided if we educated to prevent the rebellions. We could help older people learn to sing the syncopation of new music instead of needing to resist it. We could help young people appreciate the value for faith of the old songs. Remember that we educate against rebellion because ultimately it is not solely directed against each other; it is rebellion against the God whose primary goal is to unify us. God does not want us to be split over such minor things as taste.

This is subversion #4: worship gets subverted when our cultural rebellion encourages subgroups of the congregation to demand their own worship forms and styles of music. Contrarily, our society's rebellions get subverted when we genuinely worship a God who wants to unite us, who wants to "feed [us] with the finest wheat"—his own presence. Also, our worship itself subverts rebellion when we educate people to look for God's uniting presence in what they usually resist because they don't understand it.

The Subversion of Materialistic Consumerism
This leads to the next subversion, which is closely intertwined with all the rest (as is true with all these subversions). Let us now turn to Psalm

82 in order to subvert our society's materialistic consumerism.
Consumerism manifests itself in numerous ways, such as the huge
proportion of many congregations' budgets which is spent on their own
buildings and furnishings or when Christians want their churches to
follow the church growth principle of homogeneity (which usually
means "upscale"). Do we really want the riff-raff, the "down-and-out-
ers" to show up at our houses of worship on Sunday mornings? Are we
really ready for the tax collectors and sinners to come and eat with us?

A new research study reports the shocking statistic in the U.S. that
only 2-3% of mainline Protestant churches are racially integrated. Eight
percent of conservative Protestant churches could be considered
"mixed" in that at least 20% of the members have a racial or ethnic
heritage different from the largest group, while 20% of Catholic parishes
and 22% of non-Christian communities (Muslims, Jehovah's Witnesses,
etc.) are integrated.[6] We would probably be similarly shocked if we had
statistics of how poorly most churches have accomplished mixing across
social classes.

Psalm 82:1-4 declares, "A Psalm of Asaph. God presides in the
great assembly; he gives judgment among the 'gods': How Long will you
defend the unjust and show partiality to the wicked? Defend the cause of
the weak and fatherless; maintain the rights of the poor and oppressed.
Rescue the weak and needy; deliver them from the hand of the wicked."
That speaks pretty strongly against churches that are "successful" in the
world's terms of wealth and elegance! To really be the Church is to go
down into the slums. To really be the Church is to be radically changed
by God's frequent call to work for peace and justice.

We have made salvation too small. We have subverted salvation
by turning it into our own personal little cozy relationship with Jesus
Christ—which can also easily take on consumerist overtones. Don't get
me wrong: I am not denying the need for such a personal relationship at
all, but salvation in the Bible is much bigger. It includes God's desire to
reconcile the cosmos, God's plan to save the universe.

Salvation is never our own private possession. Rather, it always
calls us beyond ourselves and our own relationship with God to be
ambassadors in the ministry of reconciliation. We have mistranslated 2
Corinthians 5:17 all these years by rendering it, "If anyone is in Christ, he

---

[6] The Congregations Project, based at Rice University under the leadership of
sociologist Michael Emerson, reported these findings in John Dart, "Hues in the
Pews," *ChrCent*, 28 February 28, 2001, 6-8.

is a new creation" (nor is the proper translation, "If anyone is in Christ, she is a new creature"). The original Greek literally says, "If anyone is in Christ, *there is* a new creation." Our whole world is different if we are in Christ! Now we become agents of reconciliation. If our own salvation always calls us to participate in God's saving of the world, then God's work will flow through us to feed the hungry, clothe the naked, welcome the homeless into our own homes, and never turn away from a human being (Isa 58:5-12). So churches, let's get on with it! Many people in the world are starving!

Paul rebukes Christians concerning this in 1 Corinthians 11, where he writes about the need to "discern the body" when we come to communion. This discerning of the body was necessary in Corinth because of a conflict between the congregation's rich and poor members. When we go to the Lord's Supper, are we conscious that 40,000 people each day die of starvation and malnutrition-related diseases? Are we discerning the body? At one church in South Bend, Indiana, when the members go forward to communion, they drop money over the altar rail and use that money to feed the neighbourhood a Sunday noon dinner. Thus their eucharistic practices subvert societal materialism.

In a culture dominated by, and delighted with, the success model, we Christians are called to be different. We are called to be people whose primary concern is the spreading of the gospel. That includes reconciliation, peace building, justice producing. It means that we all participate in caring that the needs of the hungry be met.

This is subversion #5: worship gets subverted when our salvation becomes a gift for our own consumption. Contrarily, our society's consumerism get subverted when the texts of our worship call us back to being God's agents in feeding the hungry and securing justice for the downtrodden. When we genuinely worship the God who judges the earth (Ps 82:8), we will know that our own materialism is judged; when we worship the LORD who became poor for our sakes (2 Cor 8:9), we will be formed into his generosity.

The Subversion of Utilitarianism and Efficiency

Finally, let's turn to Psalm 84 to consider two more idolatries. Psalm 84:1-4 proclaims: "For the director of music. According to *gittith*. Of the Sons of Korah. A psalm. How lovely is your dwelling place, O LORD Almighty! My sould yearns even faints, for the courts of the LORD; my heart and my flesh cry out for the living God. Even the sparrow has found a home, and the swallow a nest for herself, where she may have her young – a place near your altar. O LORD Almighty, my King and my God. Blessed are those who dwell in your house; they are every praising you." The delight of the psalmist in simply praising God subverts our society's utilitarianism.[7] That cultural pressure causes many churches to turn their worship into the primary means for accomplishing the task of appealing to people. I have read the Bible through numerous times, but I have never yet found a verse that says, "Worship the Lord to attract the unbelievers." And yet we confuse that all the time. We make worship utilitarian and turn it into a marketing tool.

When we genuinely worship God, we are wasting our time in the world's terms. We are not trying or needing to accomplish anything. It is similar with worship's larger framework in the Christian's Sabbath Day. What a great day, one whole day a week when we don't have to accomplish anything! We are commanded by God not to work—and we discover that all the tensions about work and our fundamental need in the first place to accomplish it are also work that should be given up.[8] Worship, too, is not intended to achieve anything. Instead, in worship we become "lost in wonder, love and praise." We simply revel in God's presence.

Let me stress also that one of the ways in which worship gets subverted is by private utilitarianism. Corporate worship is not the same as private devotions. I have experienced too many church services in which everyone seemed to be off in his/her own little worship world or in which the worship leader actually invited everybody to enter into a time of (private) intimacy with God. That is not congregational worship! Public worship is intentionally a *corporate* thing, in which we help each other encounter God's presence. If we all simply enter our interior world, we might as well do that at home. Psalm 84:4 emphasizes that blessings are upon "those" (plural) who dwell in God's house and continue together to praise the LORD.

Do we love "wasting" our time together in worship? If I were a pagan, I'm not sure I would bother to be with Christians on Sunday morning. Do they demonstrate a way of life different from the frenzied

---

[7] My second book on worship is called *A Royal "Waste" of Time* (Grand Rapids: Eerdmans, 1999) because it attempts to counteract the subversion of genuine worship that happens when we misconceive its purpose to be the utilitarian function of attracting unbelievers to our churches.

[8] See Marva J. Dawn, *Keeping the Sabbath Wholly: Ceasing, Resting, Embracing, Feasting* (Grand Rapids: Eerdmans, 1989).

utilitarianism of the technological milieu? Does the world notice how we have an entirely different attitude toward time, how we honour a complete Sabbath day, how we never watch our watches during worship (because it doesn't really matter how long the service is since the whole day is God's anyway)? Are our neighbours observing such things about us and about our church communities?

Genuine worship is subversive of our society's utilitarianism because it enfolds us in the absolute delight of simply being there in God's house with the LORD's people. There is absolutely nothing utilitarian about worship, for it won't change one whit how God feels about us.

Correlatively, there is nothing efficient about worship. Prayer and singing hymns are both grossly inefficient. So is growth in the Christian life. In a culture driven by technicization, we are formed to expect that everything has to be efficient. Consequently, many people want instant spirituality. My favourite book title in the whole world is Eugene Peterson's *A Long Obedience in the Same Direction: Discipleship in an Instant Society*.[9] That kind of obedience and discipleship is what truly subversive worship develops in us.

Many Scripture and hymn texts used in worship form us to resist the world's utilitarianism and efficiency. Those are the world's values, but they are not biblical values. To care compassionately for our neighbours will not be efficient. It is not genuine love for our neighbours if it becomes utilitarian — nor is it true love for God if we want something out of it (see Job 1:9-11, 2:4-5). It is a good thing that God does not love us utilitarianly, or God would have given up on us long ago. Because the LORD loves us totally and inefficiently, without expecting it to do him any good, to worship the Triune God will form us to imitate his love.

This, then, is subversion #6: worship gets subverted when we think it has to be useful and to be accomplished quickly. Contrarily, our society's utilitarianism and correlative efficiency get subverted when the texts of our worship call us back to God's wanton, prodigal, totally lavish love. Genuine worship will be a royal "waste" of time and will form us not to measure our compassion by how much we accomplish or how quickly we solve problems.

---

[9] Let me stress that this is also a very good book about the Psalms of Ascent. See Eugene H. Peterson, *A Long Obedience in the Same Direction: Discipleship in an Instant Society* (Downers Grove: InterVarsity, 1980).

The Subversion of Works Righteousness

Psalm 84 concludes by saying, "They go from strength to strength ... Blessed is the man who trusts in you!" (7a and 12b) These lines suggest the last subversion to be highlighted here: works righteousness. Such trust in self and deeds appears when worship leaders think that they are the ones who will manufacture the results. I am super-guilty of this myself, for often I find myself preparing a sermon with the question in mind, "How can I influence the people?" Instead, I should let the Word prune me and call me to confess the sins it exposes. Then I would be free solely to proclaim the Word to the congregation.

I'm sure many preachers and musicians run into the same problem. We try (perhaps even subconsciously) to manipulate the people's response, while instead God has called us simply to be heralds. A herald merely proclaims the good news and is not liable for anyone's reaction to the news. We, as worship leaders and worship participants, are not responsible for our neighbours' responses to the gospel, as if it were our work instead of the Holy Spirit's. We simply make sure that we are faithful in clearly proclaiming biblical truth in all its goodness. As the psalmist reminds us, our strength does not come from our own abilities. Our power and effectiveness come entirely from the Lord of the text. Jesus' parable in Matthew 25:13-30 about the slaves who were entrusted by their master with one, two, or five talents captures the issue well. How will we respond to God's gift of his righteousness?

Worship is not about earning God's favour or influencing the people. Nor are we mistakenly to go and hide in a field that treasure which God has entrusted to us. What a silly thing to do, for we would miss the opportunity to experience God's Joy! And worship is not done for the people by the pastors or worship leaders (as performance), for they only "stand at the threshold" (Ps 84:10b) as servants. What happens in the Christian life is that God pours out his grace in bringing us to believe and then by grace God condescends to allow us to worship him. In response to the LORD's prior mercies, the believers come in genuine worship bringing all their talents,[10] which our Master gave us first. Worshippers come with their money, their time, their selves, their musical abilities, their skills for listening. They come and love letting God's gifts work to praise him. Consequently, the Master says, "Bravo!

---

[10] The Matthew 25 text is actually where the English word *talent* comes from, for the Greek word in the parable is *talenta*.

You had such a good time that I'll give you even more to do. Enter into the Joy of your Master" (cf. Matt 25:21, 23).

This is not to cop out of our responsibilities as worship planners and leaders or as participants. It is simply to recognize that God has given us our gifts in the first place, and we use them by his grace to glorify God. When in worship we sit under texts from his Word, we are formed and transformed more thoroughly to glorify him in public praise and in life.

This is subversion #7: worship gets subverted by our society's dependence on our own human efforts and work. Contrarily, our society's self righteousness and dependence on human strength get subverted when genuine worship teaches us that we obtain our strength from God, that "the LORD bestows favor and honor" (Psalm 84:11b). How blessed are those whose worship forms them to trust in the LORD!

When we let these subversions—narcissism, choice, pride, rebellion, consumerism, utilitarianism and works righteousness—pull us away from true worship, we give up the Joy of the Master. Instead, could our churches' worship subvert those cultural lies and mistaken values? Could our worship be so filled and fill us with Joy—not just a temporary high, but the deep, abiding Joy that penetrates us seven days a week, twenty-four hours a day—that the world will see the presence of the LORD in our midst, beg to participate, and say, "We want a Joy like yours"?

Part II

Relating to Our God

Chapter 4

The Feet of God:

In Stomping Boots or Dancing Shoes? The Trinity as Answer to Violence[1]

Hans Boersma

In 1989, as the Germans were tearing down the wall dividing East and West Berlin, many in the West naively thought that this signalled the beginning of a new world order, an order of peace and harmony, an end to the violence and destruction that had characterized the modern world. The collapse of modernism, symbolized by the fall of the Berlin wall, has not coincided, however, with the establishment of a more peaceful society. The fears of a nuclear holocaust may have (temporarily) subsided with the disintegration of the communist bloc, but violent wars and conflicts have not disappeared. If anything, violent regional conflicts are on the increase as a new tribalism is asserting itself. Rwanda, Somalia, Serajevo, Kuwait, Kashmir, Kosovo, East Timor.... these names

---

[1] I presented this chapter as a lecture on the occasion of my inauguration as the Geneva Chair in Reformational Worldview Studies at Trinity Western University (September 23, 1999). I published an earlier version in CER 18 (1999): 2-18. I want to thank Dr. John Stackhouse, Dr. James B. Torrance, Dr. Miroslav Volf and Dr. Albert M. Wolters for their insightful comments on earlier drafts. I also appreciate the interaction with my paper at the annual meeting of the Canadian Theological Society in Edmonton (May 25, 2000).

tell horror stories of mass murder, squalid refugee camps and ethnic cleansing.

What is more, violence has penetrated into our own back yards—and perhaps our front yards: the school shootings in Denver, Colorado and in Taber, Alberta prevent us from isolating violence in the other. We worry that we may come to experience senseless acts of violence first-hand, that our own friends and children, our own churches and schools, may be next. Violence appears to be closing in on us. "Violence," says Walter Wink, "is the ethos of our times. It is the spirituality of the modern [and, we might add, the postmodern] world. It has been accorded the status of a religion, demanding from its devotees an absolute obedience to death."[2] Indeed, the media inundate us with violence. At times, the bombardment is blatant and unconcealed, in films such as Jonathan Demme's *The Silence of the Lambs* (1991), James Cameron's *Terminator 2: Judgment Day* (1994) and Oliver Stone's *Natural Born Killers* (1995). There is little doubt that these films desensitize our culture to violence.[3] Violence also affects us in more subtle ways, however, by means of sit-coms, soap operas, cartoons and even our news media.[4] The humorous tricks of Tom and Jerry and of Roadrunner may be on an entirely different level than the hard-core violence in *The Silence of the Lambs*, but the underlying "myth of redemptive violence" is the same:

> An indestructible good guy is unalterably opposed to an irreformable and equally indestructible bad guy. Nothing can kill the good guy, though for the first three-quarters of the strip or show he (rarely she)

---

[2] Walter Wink, *Engaging the Powers: Discernment and Resistance in a World of Domination* (Minneapolis: Fortress, 1992), p. 13

[3] A remarkable feature of *Terminator 2* is that in the midst of the numerous violent scenes, John Connor is able to teach the robot that is protecting him not to murder at random. The film ends with the words of John's mother, Sarah: "The unknown future rolls toward us. I face it for the first time with a sense of hope, because if a machine, a terminator, can learn the value of human life, maybe we can too." At the same time, however, these qualifying elements also serve to justify the extreme violence characterizing the film.

[4] Cf. J. Francis Davis's comment: "Media critics often focus on violent entertainment dramas such as cop shows and movies like *Terminator 2*. But graphic reports of crime and terror on the news probably have greater influence in creating our feeling that the world is unsafe. Newsmakers feature shocking, violent stories because they sell newspapers and raise ratings. And our belief that news stories are 'real' and thus could happen to us heightens their impact" ("The Power of Images: Creating the Myths of Our Time," *MedVal* 57 [1992]: 5).

suffers grievously, appearing hopelessly trapped, until somehow the hero breaks free, vanquishes the villain, and restores order until the next installment. Nothing finally destroys the bad guy or prevents his reappearance, whether he is soundly trounced, jailed, drowned, or shot in outer space.[5]

It is not my intention to turn this chapter into a cry of protest against today's media. They are not the ultimate cause of the spiral of violence that sucks down our culture and its values.[6] The violence of our modern media is first of all not a cause but an expression of human violence. Accordingly, we need to analyze the underlying causes of the violence that we witness around us and present a Christian alternative that can put a halt to this destructive cycle.

One of the ways in which Christians react is by praying to God. We ask God to end the senseless violence, to bring relief and harmony, to replace the stomping boots of war with the dancing shoes of peace. But we start second-guessing even the usefulness of prayer. Is it possible to pray in a postmodern world in which all order and meaning seem to have disappeared? Several postmodern writers have argued that the God of the Bible is implicated in the chaos and violence of our world. The biblical picture seems to be one of violence from beginning to end, from Genesis to Revelation. For some inexplicable reason, it is said, God accepts Abel's sacrifice, but rejects Cain's. Doesn't God exclude Cain before he has done anything wrong? Is not God, in a real sense, responsible for the violence that Cain commits? In her book, *The Curse of Cain*, Regina M. Schwartz asks in exasperation, "What kind of God is this who chooses one sacrifice over the other?"[7]

The Geneva Society carries "In the LambLight" as its motto. But is not the Lamb in the book of Revelation at the same time a lion that

---

[5] Wink, *Engaging*, p. 17.
[6] What is more, the media are but one cause of the violence in our world: "Many blame media for the rise in violence, but of course that's not the whole story. It's also clear that overcrowding, pervasive life-long poverty, hunger, joblessness and drug addiction—as well as the ready availability of guns—also contribute to our skyrocketing homicide rate" (Elizabeth Thoman, "Making Connections: Media's Role in Our Culture of Violence" *MedVal* 62 [1993]: 2).
[7] Regina M. Schwartz, *The Curse of Cain: The Violent Legacy of Monotheism* (Chicago: University of Chicago Press, 1997), p. 3. For a carefully balanced critique of Schwartz's book, see Miroslav Volf, "Jehovah on Trial," *CT*, 27 April, 1998, 32-35; "Original Crime, Primal Care," in *God and the Victim: Theological Reflections on Evil, Victimization, Justice, and Forgiveness*, ed. Lisa Barnes Lampman (Grand Rapids: Eerdmans; Washington: Neighbors Who Care, 1999), pp. 17-35.

makes its enemies cringe (Rev 5:6; 6:16-17)? One contemporary author, Gilles Deleuze, denounces the Lamb in the book of Revelation as "the carnivorous lamb, the lamb that bites and then cries, 'Help! What did I ever do to you?'"[8] We cannot ignore postmodern complaints against the God of Cain and Abel (Schwartz) and against the Lamb of Revelation (Deleuze). If, in the face of violence, we are to be able to turn to God, we must have reason to trust that he does not wear the stomping boots of which we are so afraid.

The Modern God of Monotheism

The criticism of Schwartz and Deleuze rings true to many people today. One of the reasons for this is the picture of God with which they have grown up. I am afraid that the picture entering the minds of many people, when they close their eyes to pray for an end to violence, is not too dissimilar from William Blake's picture of *God creating Adam* (1795): a solitary bearded old man, powerfully domineering creation. The god of the brilliant Romantic poet, painter and engraver, William Blake (1757-1827), is unable to help people today.[9] Postmoderns are unable to pray to such a god. Why? The characteristics of the god of Blake's engraving speak for themselves. This god is a violent god. And he is violent for at least two reasons. First, he is male. A leading feminist theologian speaks

---

[8] Gilles Deleuze, "Nietzsche and Saint Paul, Lawrence and John of Patmos," in *Essays Critical and Clinical*, trans. Daniel W. Smith and Michael A. Greco (Minneapolis: University of Minnesota Press, 1997), p. 39. Deleuze builds on the work of D.H. Lawrence, who denounces the violence of the Lamb in Revelation with the words: "John insists on a Lamb 'as it were slain': but we never see it slain, we only see it slaying mankind by the million. Even when it comes on in a victorious bloody shirt at the end, the blood is not its *own* blood: it is the blood of inimical kings" (*Apocalypse*, rev. ed. [London: Heinemann, 1972], pp. 50-51). Miroslav Volf deals both with the Cain and Abel narrative and with the question of violence in Revelation (*Exclusion and Embrace: A Theological Exploration of Identity, Otherness, and Reconciliation* [Nashville: Abingdon, 1996], pp. 92-98, 286-306).

[9] It is true that Blake had his own, eccentric notion of God. To Blake it was a perplexing reality that the creator of the lamb, the symbol of innocence, was also the creator of the tiger, the symbol of repression and violence. In *Songs of Innocence and Experience* (1794), Blake agonized over his question to the tiger: "Did he who made the Lamb make thee?" For Blake, violence is ultimately rooted in the god who created not only the lamb, but also the tiger: "To the idea that only lamblike virtues are holy, the poem opposes a God who is just as violent and fiery as the tiger himself. He is not a God whose attributes are the human form divine, but a God who is fiercely indifferent to man" (E.D. Hirsch, *Innocence and Experience: An Introduction to Blake* [New Haven: Yale University Press, 1964], p. 245).

Illustration 1
William Blake,
"God Creating
Adam" (1795)
© Tate Gallery,
London, UK
Used by
permission of
Art Resource,
New York.

Illustration 2
Andrei Rublev, "The Holy Trinity" (15th century)
Reproduced by permission of Art Resource, New York.

for many when she comments that the terms Father, Son and Spirit have become "literal portrayals of maleness in God." She comments:

> Through art forms which continue to our present day, we see the results: the old man, the young man, and the dove become unspoken depictions teaching us that God is male. The inevitable societal effect makes men the primary representatives of God. Paradoxically, the very means initially used in the biblical context to break down injustice became a means of reinforcing the societal injustice against women. The "walls of partition" broken down by God have been raised again in the very name of God.[10]

The complaint is clear: a male god leads to a male dominated society. Blake's picture of god is no longer considered acceptable in our postmodern world. Blake's god is hardly a god to whom people can turn today in their fear of violence. It is this very picture of god, after all, which is considered responsible for the oppression and violence of our modern, patriarchal world.

Blake's god is violent not only because he is male, but also because he is a solitary god. He is all by himself. He is the god of radical monotheism. And monotheism does not fare well in our postmodern world. Regina Schwartz links violence to monotheism in *The Curse of Cain*. Her book carries the subtitle *The Violent Legacy of Monotheism*. This subtitle captures it all: monotheism leads to violence. Why is this so? Let me lift a few elements out of Schwartz's book. She deals with a number of related problems that she claims are linked to monotheism:

(1) *Identity formation*. In the preface to her book, Schwartz, a Professor of English and Religion at Northwestern University in Chicago, describes how, one day, she was teaching in one of her undergraduate classes about the exodus. She told the class that the story was a deeply inspiring story about liberation from slavery. As Schwartz puts it:

> I added some remarks about class consciousness and liberation theology to make the story more contemporary, and lingered over the fact that this story has now come to have urgent political force in Latin America and South Africa as it had during the U.S. civil rights movement. Then, in the midst of this celebration, the student raised his hand and asked simply, "What about the Canaanites?" Suddenly all the uncomfortable feelings I had been repressing about the Bible for years flooded me. Yes,

---

[10] Marjorie Hewitt Suchocki, "The Unmale God: Reconsidering the Trinity," *QRev* 3 (1983): 43-44.

> what about the Canaanites? And the Amorites, Moabites, Hittites? I
> now began to see some complicity, for over and over the Bible tells the
> story of a people who inherit at someone else's expense.[11]

Schwartz's difficulty is that in the Bible some people inherit at the
expense of others. She argues that the liberation of the Israelites from
Egypt has its inevitable shadow side in the violence committed against
the Canaanites and others. The reason for this violence has to do with the
way in which people forge their identities. Too often, identities are
shaped negatively, in opposition to others, rather than positively, in
harmony with others. This negative way of identity shaping shows up in
the Bible in a number of different ways.[12] Underlying this negative
identity is monotheism, the idea that there is only one God. Schwartz
recalls how in public school she pledged allegiance to the flag and the
republic, "one nation under God." She then comments: "Monotheism is
a myth that grounds particular identity in universal transcendence. And
monotheism is a myth that forges identity antithetically—against the
Other."[13] Monotheism tends to be tied up with particularism: one nation
under one God. What is needed, therefore, is a move away from this
particularism of monotheism to the appreciation of differences, which
comes with polytheism.[14]

(2) *The principle of scarcity.* Scarcity is a second problem that
Schwartz argues is linked to monotheism. In the monotheistic vision of
reality there is not enough to go around: land, love, food, everything is
scarce in a monotheistic worldview. This, according to Schwartz, is the
root of the violence in our world:

> When everything is in short supply, it must all be competed for—land,
> prosperity, power, favor, even identity itself. In many biblical
> narratives, the one God is not imagined as infinitely giving, but as
> strangely withholding. Everyone does not receive divine blessings.

---

[11] Schwartz, *Curse of Cain,* pp. ix-x.

[12] Schwartz deals with "covenant" as a way of inventing identity (chapter 1), with
"land" as a way of owning identity (chapter 2), with "kinship" as natural identity
(chapter 3), with "nations" as a way of dividing identities (chapter 4) and with
"memory" as a way of inscribing identity (chapter 5).

[13] Schwartz, *Curse of Cain,* p. 16. It is not entirely clear to me how Schwartz believes
monotheism is linked with a negative way of forging identities. She qualifies the
connection between the two by maintaining that the relation can be conceived in
different ways (pp. 17, 31) and by arguing that the Bible also offers glimpses of a more
positive vision of monotheism (p. 36).

[14] Schwartz, *Curse of Cain,* p. 36.

> Some are cursed — with dearth and with death — as though there were a
> cosmic shortage of prosperity. And it is here, in this tragic principle of
> scarcity, that I find the biblical legacy to culture so troubling. . . .
> Scarcity is encoded in the Bible as a principle of Oneness (one land, one
> people, one nation) and in monotheistic thinking (one Deity), it
> becomes a demand of exclusive allegiance that threatens with the
> violence of exclusion. When that thinking is translated into secular
> formations about peoples, "one nation under God" becomes less
> comforting than threatening.[15]

Monotheism has a preoccupation with one-ness.[16] This preoccupation shows up in the story about the first murder, the story of Cain and Abel. For some inexplicable reason, God accepts Abel's sacrifice, but rejects Cain's. Why does God not accept the sacrifice of both brothers? It is, says Schwartz, the monotheistic principle of scarcity at work: "This God who excludes some and prefers others, who casts some out, is a monotheistic God — monotheistic not only because he demands allegiance to himself alone but because he confers his favor on one alone."[17] The world in which we live is a world in which exclusion (God's rejection of Cain's sacrifice) leads to murder (Cain murdering Abel), which in turn leads to further exclusion (God banishing Cain). It is a vicious circle. It now becomes clear why Schwartz's book is called *The Curse of Cain*: "[E]ven God, the very source of blessings, does not have enough to go around,"[18] since without any motive this God blesses Abel and curses Cain. The God of monotheism is ruled by a principle outside of himself: the principle of scarcity.

(3) *Memory fixation.* I want to take a look at one last way in which monotheism turns out to be problematic for Schwartz. This third problem has to do with memory fixation. All groups have memories. People tend to share stories about the past that give them a shared identity. The more protective a group becomes about its identity, the more such a group will insist that only one way of reading the stories of the past is possible, the more the memories are being fixed. In Schwartz's words: "The more rigid the group identity, the more rigid its memories."[19] These memories serve political agendas. When those

---

[15] Ibid., p. xi.
[16] Ibid., p. 89.
[17] Ibid., p. 3.
[18] Ibid., p. 82.
[19] Ibid., p. 145.

memories are fixed, when they are frozen, the result is hatred and violence:

> Abraham came to be remembered as father not only of the ancient Hebrews, but also of Christians and Muslims. It could have been one community. Sadly enough, these revisions succumbed to competition for the status of the true children of Abraham, to the scarcity principle. The myth of common humankind – the sons of Adam – splintered all too quickly into the terrors of Cain and Abel and their legacy of ethnic, national, and religious hatred.[20]

Schwartz ends her discussion with the call to open up our memories, to open up the biblical canon to newly invented stories: an "alternative Bible" that replaces monotheism with multiplicity. Schwartz insists that this is the only way to deal with scarcity and with violence. We need a different Bible because we need a different god (or gods). To return to Blake's picture: the violent, male, solitary god of modernity needs to be replaced in our postmodern society by a pantheon of peacefully relating divinities.

Schwartz is by no means alone in her criticism of the god of modernism. There are some important studies on how monotheism functioned in the fourth century, around the time that Emperor Constantine converted to Christianity.[21] The conversion of Constantine meant a radical change in the position of Christians in the Roman Empire. Suddenly Christianity found itself in the position of the official state religion. The Christians, who had been persecuted for hundreds of years, were understandably delighted. The so-called "Constantinian arrangement" looked as a God-sent. One of the results of this newly found freedom of religion was a close link between church and state. Eusebius, one of the great theologians of the time, was entirely enthused about the new arrangement. He saw the *pax Romana* as God's gift. The Roman Empire had been a huge help in the spread of Christianity. Eusebius interpreted the situation under Constantine as the fulfilment of the biblical prophecies of the end time. He saw four elements as

---

[20] Ibid., p. 159.

[21] In the following paragraphs I have benefited especially from the ground-breaking studies of Erik Peterson, "Der Monotheismus als politisches Problem," in *Theologische Traktate* (Munich: Kösel, 1951), pp. 45-147; and George Huntston Williams, "Christology and Church-State Relations in the Fourth Century," *CH* 20.3 (1951): 3-33; 20.4 (1951): 3-26. Cf. also Yves Congar, "Classical Political Monotheism and the Trinity," *Conc* 143 (1981): 31-36.

inextricably tied together: (a) the Roman Empire; (b) peace; (c) monotheism; and (d) monarchy. Clearly divine monarchy and human monarchy seemed to fit hand in glove.[22] Eusebius defended the power of the emperor with an appeal to monotheism. It is difficult to avoid the impression that the emperor's footwear was not that much different from that of the God he worshipped.

Around the same time that Constantine converted to Christianity, the church was struggling with the Trinitarian issue. Was the Son simply *like* the Father, as Arius asserted, or did he have the very same essence as the Father, as Athanasius maintained? Was Arius right in arguing that there was a time when the Son did not exist, or was the Son truly co-eternal with Father? While the Arians wanted to look at Christ as a highly exalted being, they believed he was nonetheless subordinate to the Father. The Father stood at the highest level, entirely alone. Arianism, it has been argued, "is monotheistic Christianity in its purest form."[23] As it turned out, the Council of Nicea (325) decided against Arius in favour of a truly Trinitarian understanding of God.

The remarkable fact is that the followers of Arius tended to be fervent upholders of the authority and power of the emperor, while the Nicene theologians were more careful in how they acknowledged his authority. What were the underlying reasons for this difference in approach? G.H. Williams points to the following factors:

1. The subordination of the Son. Bishop Eusebius, who had Arianizing tendencies, had difficulty accepting that the church was ruled directly by Christ. He "was unable to make a clear distinction between the Church founded by the Incarnate Logos and the Empire—once its ruler had become Christian."[24] Once the position of Christ was devaluated, his authority over the church was curtailed as well.

2. The quasi-divinity of the emperor. Since Christ was merely *like* God, his position was no longer unique. The emperor also held a highly exalted position, so that the two could almost be regarded as being on a level playing field. The result is that the Arians tended to accept more readily than the Nicene party the authority of the emperor also in church affairs. Radical monotheism went hand in hand with the

---

[22] Cf. Jürgen Moltmann, *The Trinity and the Kingdom* (San Francisco: Harper, 1981), pp. 132-34, 195; Jan Milic Lochman, "The Trinity and Human Life," *Th* 78 (1975): 180; Thomas D. Parker, "The Political Meaning of the Doctrine of the Trinity: Some Theses," *JR* 60 (1980): 169.

[23] Moltmann, *Trinity*, p. 133.

[24] Williams, "Christology," 17.

defence of a concentration of power in the person of the emperor.

It is not surprising, therefore, that some of the strongest opposition to monotheism has recently come from liberation theologians who want to stand up for the cause of the poor and the oppressed in the Third World. These liberation theologians typically turn to the issue of monotheism. Out of fear that monotheism automatically leads to political oppression and violence, the word "monotheism" is looked at as an inadequate description of the Christian belief about God. "Strict monotheism," warns Leonardo Boff, "can justify totalitarianism and the concentration of power in one person's hands, in politics and in religion."[25]

So, radical monotheism is under attack: Schwartz opposes the biblical understanding of monotheism; Arianizing tendencies in church history appear to support structures of power in society; and liberation theologians agitate against monotheism out of fear for totalitarianism. And indeed, where a radical form of monotheism pits an aloof, solitary god over against the creatures who worship him, Christians should be on the alert. If monotheism is understood in the way in which Schwartz tends to view it, there is indeed reason for concern about monotheism. If Blake's god is the god of our worship, huge problems do arise. Disturbing questions cannot be avoided about the solitary god of modernity: is it possible for the god of modernity to love the world? Is it possible for such a god to care passionately for the world? Is it possible for such a god to take human form in order to make our suffering his own? I believe it would not be right to respond to Schwartz's critique of monotheism by digging in our heels. The way in which monotheism has functioned in the history of the church, and also in the history of Western culture, may well be in need of some criticism. Perhaps radical monotheism and modernism have formed an unholy alliance for too long. Perhaps we are more influenced by the violent picture of William Blake and by a modern worldview than we like to admit. The demise of modernism may well mean the demise of radical monotheism, and this

---

[25] Leonardo Boff, *Trinity and Society*, trans. Paul Burns (Maryknoll: Orbis, 1988), p. 20. Both Boff and Moltmann criticize what they term "strict monotheism," although it is clear that even the word "monotheism" by itself does not have a positive connotation for either of them. M. Douglas Meeks focuses on the relationship between economics and our view of God ("The Holy Spirit and Human Needs," *ChrCris* 40 [1980]: 307-16; *God the Economist: The Doctrine of God and Political Economy* [Minneapolis: Fortress, 1989]). He criticizes the way in which God has been thought of in terms of mastery, leading to a corresponding view of human mastery and rulership in our market culture (*God the Economist*, p. 56).

demise is something that need not be lamented.[26] Before we open up our memories as widely as Schwartz wants us to, however, I suggest that we evaluate the potential of the alternative which she puts forward, that of polytheism.

From the One to the Many?

What about the other option: polytheism? Domestic violence, regional conflicts and international tensions seem to be on the rise in our postmodern world. Perhaps we should be careful, therefore, how we replace Blake's violent, male and solitary god. Should we shift from the one to the many, from monotheism to polytheism? Can we expect peace and harmony to result naturally from a pluriform concept of god? If there is a natural correlation between polytheism and the absence of violence, the track record should indicate this. Let us single out some of the gods of the ancient world for closer inspection. First, there is Inanna (or Ishtar), the goddess of the ancient Sumerians. Apparently, the Sumerians looked at their kings as gods, as sons of gods and goddesses and as husbands of the goddess Inanna.[27] Inanna was the goddess both of love and of war. Royal power, apparently, does not depend on monotheism to bolster its position. Royal power and violence may well ground themselves in the violent world of the many gods. One of the hymns of the Sumerians describes Inanna as follows:

> *That you totally destroy rebellious lands – be it known!*
> *That you roar at the land – be it known!*
> *That you kill – be it known!*
> *That like a dog you eat the corpses – be it known!*
> *That your glance is terrible – be it known!*
> *That you lift this terrible glance – be it known!*

---

[26] Christians, when faced with the chaos and violence of postmodernity, may be tempted to look back wistfully to modernism—and radical monotheism. With James B. Torrance, I believe that this would be a mistake: "What is the Christian answer? Is it to go back to Plato's *Republic*, as Allan Bloom suggests, to recover the objectivity of truth, beauty, goodness, justice? Is it to revive the older notions of natural law and moral law discerned by the kindly light of reason, with their concomitant individualism? Or is it not rather to return to "the forgotten Trinity ..." (*Worship, Community, and the Triune God of Grace* [Downers Grove: InterVarsity, 1996], p. 41). Torrance's last comment points to an alternative on which I will elaborate in the second half of this chapter.

[27] Tikva Frymer-Kensky, *In the Wake of the Goddesses: Women, Culture, and the Biblical Transformation of Pagan Myth* (New York: Free, 1992), p. 59.

That your glance flashes — be it known!
at those who do not obey — be it known!
That you attain victories — be it known![28]

At one point, as this goddess descends into the netherworld, she shouts: "I will smash the door, I will shatter the bolt, I will smash the doorpost, I will move the doors, I will raise up the dead, eating the living, so that the dead will outnumber the living."[29] Violence and domination may be a concern with Blake's god of radical monotheism, but they are a concern also in polytheism.

The pantheon of the Babylonian gods offers more of the same. The creation myth, *Enuma Elish*, tells the story of Apsu (the male, primeval sweet water ocean) and Tiamat (the female, primeval salt water ocean).[30] From the commingling of the two waters came divine offspring, who in turn gave birth to more generations of gods. The young gods, however, disturbed the peace of Tiamat and Apsu, who therefore decided to destroy the younger generation of gods. Apsu was killed before he could carry out his evil plans. Tiamat, enraged, planned evil against her offspring to avenge Apsu. The young gods then asked the young upstart, Marduk, to lead them in battle. Marduk agreed, defeated Tiamat's forces and sliced her carcass in two, creating from the one half the firmament of heaven and from the other half the foundation of the earth. Thus, Marduk created order out of the chaos of the waters. With the cosmos now in place, the gods started to complain to Marduk that they had too much work to do in the newly created universe. Marduk, therefore, created humans to do the work. He created the first human beings out of the blood of Kingu, Tiamat's second husband and captain of her army.

This story shows that in the Babylonian worldview there is no absolute preference for good over evil. Apsu and Tiamat already plan "evil" before the universe has come into being. It is a normal part of the universe, not a later, alien intrusion into a fundamentally good world. Power is the ultimate morality. It is only "by violence that the youngest

---

[28] Frymer-Kensky, *In the Wake*, pp. 64-65.

[29] Aida Besançon Spencer, et al., *The Goddess Revival* (Grand Rapids: Baker, 1995), p. 58.

[30] For a helpful comparison between *Enuma Elish* and the biblical story of creation, see J. Richard Middleton, "The Liberating Image? Interpreting the *Imago Dei* in Context," *CSR* 25 (1994): 8-25.

of the gods establishes order."[31] Moreover, the violence among the gods in turn justifies human violence. The Babylonian king receives his authority from the gods. Paul Ricoeur, in his analysis of the Babylonian creation myth, makes the point that the king represents the god who through violence has overcome chaos. This means that the king's enemy represents the forces of evil, the resurgence of chaos.[32] "Heavenly events are mirrored by earthly events, and what happens above happens below."[33] Polytheism here does not offer a solution to violence; rather, it covers the origin and life of both gods and humans with the blood of violence.

Does perhaps the Greek pantheon of gods offer more hope? The well-known father of gods and of humans, Zeus himself, was so known for his outrageous violence that he became an embarrassment to his worshippers. By cleverly disguising himself, he deceived and raped numerous women. Greek mythology tells the story of the beautiful princess, Antiope. Zeus, disguising himself in the form of a satyr (a creature partly human, partly animal), raped Antiope, who became pregnant and was therefore rejected by her own family. Antiope subsequently gave birth to twins. The result of Zeus's violence was a long litany of horrific experiences in the life of his victim, Antiope.[34] Similar stories about the gods of the Greeks abound. Passion and power were the two dominant characteristics of the Greek gods.[35] The many horror stories of violence among the gods so disgusted Socrates that he insisted that young people should be protected from them:

> Even if they [the Greek myths] were true I should not think that they ought to be thus lightly told to thoughtless young persons. But the best way would be to bury them in silence, and if there were some necessity for relating them, that only a very small audience should be admitted under pledge of secrecy and after sacrificing, not a pig, but some huge and unprocurable victim, to the end that as few as possible should have heard these tales.[36]

---

[31] Paul Ricoeur, *The Symbolism of Evil*, trans. Emerson Buchanan (Boston: Beacon, 1969), p.179.

[32] Ricoeur, *Symbolism*, p. 196.

[33] Wink, *Engaging*, p. 15.

[34] Cf. Spencer, *Goddess Revival*, pp. 65-74.

[35] William C. Placher, *Narratives of a Vulnerable God: Christ, Theology, and Scripture* (Louisville: Westminster, 1994), p. 4.

[36] Plato, *The Republic*, trans. Paul Shorey, Loeb Classical Lib. 1 (Cambridge: Harvard University Press; London: Heinemann, 1963), 2:378.

Socrates was obviously afraid of the impact that the stories of divine
violence would have on human relationships. The passion of the gods
was becoming an embarrassment to the Greeks. Some would argue that
if one's god(s) engage in warfare, their worshippers become warriors,
too. If this is true the picture does not look rosy for polytheism. Violence
can be associated with polytheism no less than with monotheism. After
all, "[t]he strongest gods get the greatest bribe."[37] We may conclude,
then, that polytheism is anything but an attractive alternative to Blake's
violent, solitary god.[38]

A Trinitarian Approach

If neither radical monotheism nor polytheism provides answers to the
issue of violence, the question needs to be asked if the Bible perhaps
presents us with an alternative to these two options. I do not mean to
suggest that we give up on the word "monotheism." Judging by its root
meaning alone, the word "monotheism" (one god) has strong biblical
backing. The monotheistic confession of Deuteronomy 6:4 lies at the
heart of the Christian faith: "Hear, O Israel: The LORD our God, the LORD
is one." Still, the biblical picture of God—and the biblical understanding
of monotheism—neither conforms to Schwartz's arbitrary despot, nor to
the radical monad of Arian theology. A look at a famous medieval icon,
"The Holy Trinity," drawn by the Russian Orthodox monk, Andrei
Rublev (d. 1430), may be helpful.[39] There are three elements in this icon

---

[37] Max L. Stackhouse, *Ethics and the Urban Ethos: An Essay in Social Theory and
Theological Reconstruction* (Boston: Beacon, 1972), p. 122.

[38] Because of the evidence of violence in ancient Near-Eastern polytheism, several
feminist theologians have borrowed H. Richard Niebuhr's phrase, "radical
monotheism" (H. Richard Niebuhr, *Radical Monotheism and Western Culture: With
Supplementary Essays* [Louisville: Westminster, 1993]), and have argued that it would
be the most adequate option as a basis for equality between the sexes (Frymer-
Kensky, *In the Wake*, pp. 217-20; Erhard S. Gerstenberger, *Yahweh the Patriarch: Ancient
Images of God and Feminist Theology*, trans. Frederick J. Gaiser. [Minneapolis: Fortress,
1996], p. 37).

[39] For a discussion of Rublev's icon, see Dan-Ilie Ciobotea and William H. Lazareth,
"The Triune God: The Supreme Source of Life: Thoughts Inspired by Rublev's Icon of
the Trinity," in *Icons: Windows on Eternity: Theology and Spirituality in Colour*, ed.
Gennadios Limouris (Geneva: WCC, 1990), pp. 202-04. The icon's central role in Iris
Murdoch's novel, *The Time of Angels* (1966), is discussed in David S. Cunningham,
David S. *These Three Are One: The Practice of Trinitarian Theology* (Malden: Blackwell,
1998), pp. 190-95.

of which we should take notice. First, Rublev's icon is based on the well-known story of Abraham's three visitors (Genesis 18). We see one of the trees of Mamre in the background. In other words, the starting-point of our understanding of God lies in human history. The underlying theological statement is that we can only understand who God is by the way in which he has revealed himself in history. More specifically, we know God in the life and death and in the words of Jesus Christ and through the power of the Holy Spirit. We should not turn the doctrine of the Trinity into an abstract and speculative theory. We may trust that the way God has shown himself in history is the way he really is. In other words, Rublev's God is a trustworthy, dependable God.

Second, Rublev's picture of Abraham's three visitors indicates that he does not hold to a solitary god. Rublev takes his starting-point not in the one-ness but in the three-ness of God. In other words, there is a strong emphasis on the communion between Father, Son and Holy Spirit. One author makes the point that "the most heartfelt idea that guided Rublev's brush as he painted his *Trinity*, was the belief in the need for and benefit of love, of a union based on the trust of one individual in another."[40] The God we have come to know in history is a relational God. It has been said that the middle figure represents the Son, who nods in agreement to the Father, voluntarily agreeing that he will take on human flesh and will suffer the curse of humankind on the cross. Although the Father and the Son are equal, the Son readily submits to the Father who sends his Son into the world.

Third, there is an open place at the table where the chalice stands. Human beings are invited to join in the communion of the divine Persons.[41] The icon invites us, as it were, to step into the picture from our finite perspective in order to join the widening, infinite perspective of the Trinity. In summary, Rublev's God is a dependable God known in history as three Persons in communion inviting us to participate in the unity of Father, Son and Spirit.

The Dance of God

Rublev's picture is radically different from that of William Blake. Blake's god, criticized sharply by Schwartz, is violent, male and solitary: a god with stomping boots. Rublev's God — and I believe the God who meets

---

[40] G.I. Vzdornov, *Troitsa Andreia Rubleva: Antologiia* (Moscow: Iskusstvo, 1981), p. 214.
[41] Jeff Imbach, *The Power Within: Loving God, Living Passionately* (Colorado Springs: NavPress, 1998), p. 241.

us on the pages of Scripture—is dependable, relational and inviting: a God wearing dancing shoes. The implications of this different view of God are huge. If God wears dancing shoes, then the best way to get to know him is by looking at him dance. I want to characterize the dance of God in four ways: (1) as a social dance, (2) as a grace-ful(l) dance, (3) as a passionate dance and (4) as an ecstatic dance.

(1) *God's dance is a social dance.* Over the ages, people have often tried to come up with something to which they might be able to compare the Trinity. Comparing God to anything created is naturally a risky business. It is easy to fall off the edge, to the one side or to the other. There are limits to any comparison between the Triune God and anything created. I see two limitations.[42] First, there is no exact identity between God and something in his creation. The creator remains distinct from the creature. This means that when we talk about God dancing, or God engaging in a social dance, we are not saying that he is dancing just as we are dancing. We are simply using a metaphor taken from our own, human experiences. In other words, we can do no more than draw analogies between the creator and the creature. So, when we talk about God being relational, being social, and when we talk about the Persons of the Trinity, then we are simply using analogies taken from our own experience. This is the only way in which we are able to talk about God. That does not mean that our talk about God, about the Persons of the Trinity, about God being a relational God, about God dancing, etc., does not correspond to a reality in God. It does. Without such correspondence, any language about God would become entirely impossible. When God reveals himself to us, he does so by means of images derived from the creaturely reality, and in a way that at the same time is faithful in communicating who God is.[43]

---

[42] Miroslav Volf, *After Our Likeness: The Church as the Image of the Trinity* (Grand Rapids: Eerdmans, 1999), pp. 198-200.

[43] There is always the danger of positing analogies between the human and the divine realms in the hope of proving something that we already hold on other grounds. For example, Stanley J. Grenz argues for interdependency and mutuality between male and female on the basis of the relationality within the social Trinity ("Theological Foundations for Male-Female Relationships," *JETS* 41 [1998]: 615-30.) It would be equally legitimate, however, to use the analogy of the Trinity to argue for a functional subordination of women to men. After all, the interdependency and mutuality among the divine Persons does not exclude a functional subordination of the Son (see Stephen D. Kovach and Peter R. Schemm, "A Defense of the Doctrine of the Eternal Subordination of the Son," *JETS* 42 [1999]: 461-76.) This means that the argument from a Trinitarian analogy may be used to defend two quite different positions. This is not

In addition to the creaturely limits, there are historical limits to the correspondence between Creator and creature.[44] The correspondence between God and ourselves is limited because we still live in an imperfect world in which we often find ourselves stumbling along in our efforts to reflect God and to participate in the dance of God. Our sins often make our dance less adequate than it might have been.

With these cautionary comments in mind, let us explore what it means that God's dance is a social dance, and what that means for us as we move around on the dance floor designed by the Master Dancer. The metaphor of the three divine Persons engaged in a dance is not the only way to picture the relationship between the Persons of the Trinity. Other images have also been used. Nonetheless, the picture of a dance, and particularly a social dance, is often used, and it is helpful.[45] One author puts it as follows:

> Choreography suggests the partnership of movement, symmetrical but not redundant, as each dancer expresses and at the same time fulfills him/herself towards the other. In interaction and inter-course, the dancers (and the observers) experience one fluid motion of encircling, encompassing, permeating, enveloping, outstretching. There are neither leaders nor followers in the divine dance, only an eternal movement of reciprocal giving and receiving, giving again and

---

to deny the analogy *per se*, only to caution against looking for support for our prior judgements in a social concept of the Trinity.

[44] While I am using Volf's terminology about historical limits, I would want to emphasize that these limits are not given with historicity as such, but with the entrance of sin in history. Placher, speaking about how we can find ourselves by making ourselves vulnerable to others, makes the concise comment: "There are limits to how much humans can do this sort of thing. We are sinners, and we have bodies—for the Christian tradition these are two quite different issues, but in different ways they both limit our capacity to find ourselves in losing ourselves" (Placher, *Narratives*, pp. 70-71).

[45] The metaphor is used in Nicholas Lash, *Theology on the Way to Emmaus* (London: SCM, 1986), p. 156; Gregory L. Jones, *Transformed Judgment: Toward a Trinitarian Account of the Moral Life* (Notre Dame: University of Notre Dame Press, 1990), pp. 94-95, 116; Catherine Mowry LaCugna, "The Baptismal Formula, Feminist Objections, and Trinitarian Theology," *JES* 26 (1989): 235-50; *God for Us: The Trinity and the Christian Life* (New York: HarperSanFrancisco, 1992), pp. 271-72; Clark H. Pinnock, *Flame of Love: A Theology of the Holy Spirit* (Downers Grove: InterVarsity, 1996), pp. 31, 37, 47-48; Volf, *Exclusion and Embrace*, pp. 129, 300; Cunningham, *These Three*, pp. 180-81. C. Baxter Kruger gives an exposition of the parable of the prodigal son in *Parable of the Dancing God* (Jackson: Perichoresis Press [!], 1994). Kruger makes the comment that heaven "is the excitement of God; it is the Father's dancing joy, exploding into the greatest party in history" (*Parable*, p. 8). I owe this reference to Professor J.B. Torrance.

receiving again.... The divine dance is fully personal and interpersonal,
expressing the essence and unity of God. The image of the dance
forbids us to think of God as solitary.[46]

To describe this social dance, the church—especially the Eastern
church—has traditionally used a technical theological term: *perichōrēsis*.[47]
If Rublev's picture of the Triune God might perhaps give the impression
that there are three gods, the notion of the social dance (*perichōrēsis*)
shows that this is not the case.[48] The divine family is such a close-knit
family that the various Persons find their identity not simply in
themselves, but in each other.[49] Jesus comments in the Gospel of John:
"[T]he Father is in me and I in the Father" (John 10:38; cf. 14:11; 17:21).
The Father does not just exist by himself, and is not a self-contained,
autonomous individual, but the Son and the Spirit move, as it were, into
the Father. In the same way, the Father and the Son exist in the Spirit,
while the Father and the Spirit live in the Son.

---

[46] Catherine Mowry LaCugna, "The Baptismal Formula, Feminist Objections, and
Trinitarian Theology," *JES* 26 (1989): 272. As I will indicate below, I have reservations
about LaCugna's pervasively egalitarian understanding of the Trinity.

[47] See G.L. Prestige, *God in Patristic Thought* (London: SPCK, 1952), pp. 282-301 for the
history of the notion of *perichōrēsis*. The Greek verb *perichoreo* (to go around) is related
to the word *perichoreuo* (to dance around) (LaCugna, *God for Us*, p. 312, n. 94).

[48] Social notions of the Trinity have often been charged with tritheism (e.g., Henri
Blocher, "Immanence and Transcendence in Trinitarian Theology," in *The Trinity in a
Pluralistic Age: Theological Essays on Culture and Religion*, ed. Kevin J. Vanhoozer
[Grand Rapids: Eerdmans, 1997], p. 107). Cunningham makes the comment: "When
picturing 'the triune dance,' it is hard not to think of *three people*" (Cunningham, *These
Three*, p. 180). Cornelius Plantinga gives a carefully argued defence against the charge
of tritheism when he says that God is one in three senses: (1) the Father is typically
referred to as God in the Bible; there is only one Father; (2) there is only one divine
essence, one generic divinity; and (3) there is only one Triune God, one divine family
("Social Trinity and Tritheism," in *Trinity, Incarnation and Atonement: Philosophical and
Theological Essays*, ed. Ronald J. Feenstra and Cornelius Plantinga [Notre Dame:
University of Notre Dame Press, 1989], pp. 31-32). The charge of tritheism can also be
successfully countered by keeping in mind the analogical character of Trinitarian
language (John L. Gresham, "The Social Model of the Trinity and Its Critics," *SJT* 46
[1993]: 330-31). At the same time, it seems to me that we need recourse not just to a
generic identity of the divine Persons, but also to a numerical identity, if we are to
successfully ward off the danger of tritheism. My notion of a dance of three divine
Persons is not meant to undermine this numerical identity of the Persons. (I owe this
cautionary qualification to personal discussion with Dr. Miroslav Volf.)

[49] For the family analogy, see Moltmann, *Trinity*, p. 199; Cornelius Plantinga, "The
Perfect Family: Our Model for Life Together Is Found in the Father, Son, and Holy
Spirit," *CT*, 4 March, 1988, 24-27; Plantinga, "Social Trinity and Tritheism."

This presence of the various Persons of the Trinity in each other is not something static. The unity of the three Persons is a unity of love, of purpose and of work. The biblical narrative repeatedly shows how the Father, the Son and the Spirit are united in their involvement with the world. To mention but one example, at the baptism of Jesus, the Spirit comes down like a dove, the Father speaks from heaven, and he declares his love for the Son (Matt 3:16-17). We noticed earlier as the first important lesson from Rublev's icon that the Triune God is a dependable God. He shows himself in history the way he really is. The unity of love, purpose and work shows how God truly is, in himself. This means that *perichōrēsis* is not like a one-time snapshot, but that there is movement in God: the movement of the perfect social dance. The Greek word *perichōrēsis* speaks about a going or moving from the one Person into the other. The communal character of the Trinity is one in which there is a constant making room for each other, a continuous back-and-forth flow of love. As Cornelius Plantinga puts it, "The Trinity is thus a zestful, wondrous communty of divine light, love, joy, mutuality, and verve."[50]

Looking at the Triune life as a social dance has its implications for our own little shuffles on the terrestrial dance floor.[51] It may be a little difficult for people with a modern mindset—used to Blake's understanding of the divine—to accept the idea that the notion of the Trinity could have any implications at all. We are often still entrenched in the modern Enlightenment worldview, which can be captured in the statement of Immanuel Kant (1724-1804) that "absolutely *nothing can be acquired for practical life* from the doctrine of the Trinity."[52] The last few decades, however, a great deal of material has been written in defence of the practical implications of the doctrine of the Trinity. The modern, scientific worldview is no longer as sure of itself as it has been in the past.

And rightly so. If God's dance is a social dance, a perichoretic dance, this means that human relationships are affected. The macho North-American, the autonomous individual, is forced to retreat—stomping boots and all—when faced with the dancing shoes of

---

[50] Cornelius Plantinga, "The Threeness/Oneness Problem of the Trinity," *CTJ* 23 (1988): 30.

[51] The implications of the notion of *perichōrēsis* for human relationships is noted in Moltmann, *Trinity*, pp. 174-76; Barbara Brown Zikmund, "The Trinity and Women's Experience," *ChrCent* 104 (1987): 356; Colin E. Gunton, *The One, the Three and the Many: God, Creation and the Culture of Modernity* (Cambridge: Cambridge University Press, 1993), pp. 163-66; Placher, *Narratives*, pp. 71-74; Volf, *After Our Likeness*, pp. 208-13.

[52] Volf, *After Our Likeness*, p. 198.

God. If on our dance floor here below we image the divine dance, this will mean that we take our steps depending on the steps of our dance partners. It will mean that our dance is shaped by the dance of others. And as we dance, our characters, our personalities, are being shaped by others, and theirs by us.[53] "Discipling through Community" is Trinity Western University's slogan this year. It is a slogan that turns into reality when we become disciples of the community of the Triune God. It is only in community that we truly become disciples. Miroslav Volf terms such a disciple, shaped by means of the social dance, a "catholic person": "Every person is a catholic person insofar as that person reflects in himself or herself in a unique way the entire, complex reality in which the person lives."[54] Becoming a "catholic person" means that we learn the steps of the social dance. When we stomp with violent boots on the dance floor, we inflict pain and violate other people's identities, in the meantime remaining isolated and lonely individuals ourselves. God's social dance is a call for us to replace our own stomping boots with dancing shoes.

(2) *God's dance is a grace-ful(l) dance.* When God dances he moves gracefully—full of grace. How can we be so sure? Again, the reason is that we get to know who God is in history, in concrete places, in particular circumstances. God has revealed himself in Jesus Christ through the Holy Spirit. That is the only way to answer the question what God is like. Maybe it sounds as though I am simply stating the obvious. The Christian tradition, particularly in the West, however, has not always been equally insistent on this point. The impression has often been given that behind the God whom we know in history, there is some unknown, hidden god, of whom we really can say nothing at all. The Western tradition has a long history of saying that behind the Triune God—Father, Son and Spirit—lurks another picture of God: the one God, as he really is, in himself.[55] It is almost as though the Western tradition,

---

[53] Taking his cue from John 15:9—"As the Father has loved me, so have I loved you. Now remain in my love"—J.B. Torrance extends the concept of perichoretic unity beyond the mutual indwelling among the Persons of the Trinity. Torrance sees a perichoretic unity (a) between Jesus and the Father in the Spirit, into which we are drawn to participate; (b) between Christ and his body in the communion of the Spirit; and (c) between the members of the body by life in the Spirit (Torrance, *Worship*, p. 38).

[54] Volf, *After Our Likeness*, p. 212; cf. *Exclusion and Embrace*, p. 51.

[55] Cf. Karl Rahner, *The Trinity*, trans. Joseph Donceel (New York: Seabury, 1974), pp. 15-21; Moltmann, *Trinity*, pp. 16-20.

going all the way back to Thomas Aquinas in the thirteenth century, has not been content with Andrei Rublev's icon of God, but has superimposed on it William Blake's engraving. What this has often boiled down to is that we thought we could know the one God by our own reason, and that subsequently we searched God's revelation in the Bible for the three Persons of the Trinity.[56]

The results of such a picture of God are, of course, dramatic. It is difficult to see Rublev's icon once Blake's engraving has been splashed over top of it. God, as he really is, thus turns into a god who is defined by Greek philosophical notions rather than by the way we have come to know him in history. Unfortunately, the god shaped by Greek philosophy is not nearly as graceful a dancer as the God of the Bible. The god shaped by Greek philosophy tends to wear stomping boots rather than dancing shoes. The longer we keep separating the notions of the one-ness and the three-ness of God, the longer we will be stuck with the picture of William Blake's god superimposed on Andrei Rublev's icon. It is really quite difficult to see the God of the grace-full dance when we are constantly faced with his stomping boots.

Is it true that in our worldview the one god with the stomping boots has obscured our appreciation for the grace-full dancer? This issue may be clarified by asking ourselves a question: Jesus of Nazareth, who lived in first-century Palestine, was he truly God? How are we going to answer this question? Many of us would likely answer, "Yes, he was truly God." What does this answer mean? Could it be that by giving this answer—"Yes, he was truly God"—we have taken the following steps?

a) We assume that there is some universal idea of "god-ness" out there.

b) We accept that Jesus fits the bill of this prior notion of God.

c) We therefore conclude that Jesus was God.

If this is the line of argument we tend to follow, this means that we have fallen into the age-old trap of dividing the one-ness of God (the god of philosophy) from the three-ness of God (God as he has shown himself to us in history). What is more, we have forced the Bible's picture of who God is into our own reasoned understanding of what God should be like.

What we need to do, instead, is start at the other end: with the Bible's picture of Jesus. If we were to do that, we would ask ourselves: if

---

[56] In the Belgic Confession (1561) the articles about the attributes of God (article 1) and the Trinity (article 8) are separated by articles about God's revelation (articles 2-7).

it is true that God comes to us in history, in Jesus of Nazareth, then what does this mean for our understanding of God? What is this God like? N.T. Wright, an influential evangelical New Testament scholar, makes the following comment on the question whether Jesus was God: "That's one of those trick questions that you can't answer straight on. It assumes that we know what 'God' means, and we're simply asking if Jesus is somehow identified with this 'God'. What we should say, instead, is: 'It all depends what you mean by "God."'"[57] When we look to Jesus to see what God's dancing shoes are like, we see a God who makes lepers clean; we see a God who drives out demonic powers; we see a God who has table fellowship with the wrong crowd: prostitutes and tax collectors; we see a God who unceremoniously runs out the door with his robe flapping in the wind to welcome his prodigal son (Luke 15:20); we see a God who as a mother hen longs to gather her chicks under her wings (Matt 23:37); in short, we see a God who plays the flute so that the people might dance (Matt 11:17). When we look to Jesus to see what God is like, we come to know the God of the grace-full dance.[58] Monotheism is only acceptable when it includes Jesus Christ in its definition of God.[59]

The Apostle Paul talks about the "wealth," the "abundance" and the "fullness" of the grace of the Triune God in the following way:

- 2 Corinthians 8:9 — " For you know the grace of our Lord Jesus Christ, that though he was rich, yet for your sakes he became poor, so that you through his poverty might become rich."
- 2 Corinthians 9:8 — "And God is able to make all grace abound to

---

[57] N.T. Wright, *Who Was Jesus?* (Grand Rapids: Eerdmans, 1992), p. 51.

[58] Cunningham makes the point that the concrete narratives of the Christian faith lay at the root of the development of Trinitarian doctrine, and that the neglect of these concrete narratives led to a neglect of the doctrine of the Trinity in the Enlightenment period, which in turn was the cause of modern atheism. Cunningham rightly applauds today's renewed emphasis on the narratives of God's history as enabling a renewed understanding of the doctrine of the Trinity (Cunningham, *These Three*, pp. 21-25). At the same time, this does not mean a strict identity between the economic and the immanent Trinity. Cf. Miroslav Volf, "'The Trinity Is Our Social Program': The Doctrine of the Trinity and the Shape of Social Engagement," *ModTh* 14 (1998): 407.

[59] In 1 Corinthians 8:6 Paul takes the monotheistic confession of Deuteronomy 6:4 and reinterprets it in such a way as to include Jesus Christ in his definition of God. Deuteronomy 6:4 states: "The LORD our God, the LORD is one." Similarly, Paul speaks about "one God" and "one Lord" in 1 Corinthians 8:6, taking the word LORD (or Lord) from Deuteronomy 6:4 as referring to Jesus. Cf. N.T. Wright, *The Climax of the Covenant: Christ and the Law in Pauline Theology* (Minneapolis: Fortress, 1991), pp. 125-32.

you, so that in all things at all times, having all that you need, you
will abound in every good work."

- Ephesians 3:18-19 — "I pray that you may ... have power ... to
  know this love [of Christ] that surpasses knowledge—that you
  may be filled to the measure of all the fullness of God."

God's grace in Jesus Christ and through the Spirit is one of plenty.
Schwartz may have a point that radical monotheism tends to be
characterized by the "principle of scarcity." The Trinitarian God who
comes to us in history, however, is characterized by the principle of
abundance. The Trinitarian God is full of grace; he is the God of the
grace-full dance.

It may not be easy to dance gracefully with people around you
stomping around in their boots. It is tempting at times to exchange our
dancing shoes for stomping boots. Our dance floor, we sometimes think,
seems more designed for stomping boots than for dancing shoes. Indeed,
our societal system is built on scarcity. M. Douglas Meeks mentions three
areas where modern society has artificially created scarcity.[60] We have
spiritualized—I would say, idolized—three areas of life:

- Work: we have allowed work to define who we are. Work has
  become an end in itself.
- Money: because the media and its commercials tell us that we
  never have enough, we want more and more, and we want it now.
  The result is that we are an economy that is deeply in debt.
- Sexuality: the constant barrage of sexual stimuli in the media
  makes people feel empty and constantly unsatisfied.

The principle of scarcity has led to violence everywhere: economic
violence, social violence, sexual violence; violence at home and violence
at work. There is only one way out of this spiral of violence, and that is
by becoming imitators of God (Eph 5:1)—of the Triune God. We need to
learn the steps of the grace-full dance, call into question our society's
"principle of scarcity" and replace it with the principle of abundance.[61]
Meeks puts it well: "The biblical traditions uncover God as the
Economist who constructs the household with a radically different

---

[60] M. Douglas Meeks, "The Holy Spirit and Human Needs," *ChCris* 40 (1980): 314-15.

[61] M. Douglas Meeks makes clear that he does not deny the reality of shortages and
insufficiencies. What he objects to is the modern economic definition of scarcity as the
driving force of our economy (*God the Economist: The Doctrine of God and Political
Economy* [Minneapolis: Fortress, 1989], pp. 171-72, 174). I would want to emphasize
that even in the midst of scarcity the abundance of God's grace provides for the true
needs of the Christian pilgrimage.

assumption: *If the righteousness of God is present, there is always enough to go around.* From the manna in the desert, to Jesus' feeding of the multitudes, to the Lord's Supper, the biblical traditions depict the superabundance (*plēroma*) of God's Spirit as the starting point of God's household and its practice of hospitality."[62]

(3) *God's dance is a passionate dance.* It has already become clear that the divine dance turns things topsy turvy. A dance floor accustomed to the violence of stomping boots is graced with God's fine dancing shoes. This role reversal is nowhere more evident than in the characterization of God's dance as a passionate dance. After all, God literally cares passionately for his creation. His care is such that it climaxed in the passion (the suffering) of his Son. If the cross of Jesus Christ truly shows what God is like, it is clear that the Triune God is a compassionate God, a God who suffers with (*com*-passion) the world in its suffering.

God's passionate dance, his suffering in Jesus Christ, does not mean an abdication of his power. God does not become powerless in the suffering of Jesus Christ.[63] In God, suffering and strength, passion and power, are not each other's opposites. Instead, his passion and his power mutually enrich each other's meaning. According to the Gospel of Mark, it is on the cross that Jesus becomes king.[64] In Paul's understanding, it is on the cross that Jesus disarmed the principalities and powers (Col 2:15).

---

[62] Meeks, *God the Economist*, p. 12.

[63] There is a growing unease in the last number of decades with the notions of divine impassibility and omnipotence. If traditionally theology has emphasized the power of God, today the emphasis is on the love of God. William C. Placher, for example, argues for a God who is "weak in power but strong in love" (*Narratives*, p. 21). I believe a more nuanced way of relating the two notions is required. When God undertakes to rescue Israel and the world, power becomes an expression of his love. In the passion of the cross, God showed his love ultimately in a powerful way, since the weakness of his suffering was still stronger than any human strength (1 Cor 1:25). At the same time, power is not an abstract or independent characteristic in the God who shows his identity on the cross, as it was among the Sumerian and Greek gods. God's power is a power defined by his love shown on the cross.

[64] Mark 15:2,18,26,32. Cf. Paul J. Achtemeier's comment that the disciples had been unable to recognize who Jesus was "simply because he could not be truly acknowledged as the king he is until he was enthroned — on the cross; he could not be confessed as king until he had been crowned — with death" ("Mark, Gospel of," *ABD*, ed. David Noel Freedman [New York: Doubleday, 1992], 4:553). Similarly, Richard B. Hays: "Because Jesus uses power to serve rather than to be served, authentic power is shown forth paradoxically in the cross" (*The Moral Vision of the New Testament: A Contemporary Introduction to New Testament Ethics* [New York: HarperSanFrancisco, 1996], p. 90).

And in John's visionary description, the royal Lamb, sovereignly opening the seals of the scroll of history, stands "looking as if it had been slain" (Rev 5:6); it is the Lamb who attains victory by means of his blood (12:11).[65]

In his passionate book, *Exclusion and Embrace*, Miroslav Volf argues this bold thesis: "A genuine Christian reflection on social issues must be rooted in the self-giving love of the divine Trinity as manifested on the cross of Christ; all the central themes of such reflection will have to be thought through from the perspective of the self-giving love of God."[66] In a society that is dominated by greed, these words are revolutionary. God's passionate, self-giving character comes to the fore at several of the most central pages of Scripture:

- John 3:16 — "For God so loved the world that he gave his one and only Son, that whoever believes in him shall not perish but have eternal life."
- Romans 8:32 — "He who did not spare his own Son, but gave him up for us all—how will he not also, along with him, give us all things?"
- Philippians 2:5-8 — "Your attitude should be the same as that of Christ Jesus: Who, being in very nature God, did not consider equality with God something to be grasped, but made himself nothing, taking the very nature of a servant, being made in human likeness. And being found in appearance as a man, he humbled himself and became obedient to death—even death on a cross!"

The Pauline hymn of Philippians 2 explicitly makes the humiliation of the Son a pattern for us to follow. The compassion of the Triune God, God's self-giving suffering with the world in the cross of the Son, is a model for us to follow: "The compassionate response of God to the world he has made provides for us the paradigm of what should characterize our cooperation with him in the completion of his program of the world."[67] I will not detail the implications of this, except to say that God's self-giving, passionate dance puts under judgement all

---

[65] Reflecting on the repeated use of the word *pantokrator* in Revelation, M. Eugene Boring comments that "for John 'almighty' was simply a part of his definition of 'God'; to try to conceive of God in less than omnipotent terms was for him the functional equivalent of abandoning faith in God" ("The Theology of Revelation: The Lord Our God the Almighty Reigns," *Int* 40 [1986]: 260).

[66] Volf, *Exclusion and Embrace*, p. 25; cf. p. 127.

[67] Stanley J. Grenz, *Theology for the Community of God* (Nashville: Broadman & Holman, 1994), p. 125.

domineering, self-serving attitudes in the church, all dictatorial or totalitarian structures in society and all empty boasting and self-glorification in the academy.

(4) *God's dance is an ecstatic dance.* God is not content simply with the heavenly divine dance. He wants to draw the world into his dance. God's dance has been carefully choreographed. It leads to a climax. And the climax is one of ecstasy. Clark Pinnock, in his book on the Holy Spirit, makes this comment: "I like the term *ecstasy* for the Spirit. It means 'standing ouside oneself,' which suggests that Spirit is the ecstasy that makes the triune life an open circle and a source of pure abundance."[68] The Triune God has freely chosen to open up the social dance among the three Persons of the Trinity to involve all of creation. This decision has made the dance grace-full, it has made it passionate, and it makes it ecstatic.

Since the Triune God has made us into partners of the divine dance, we are taken up in the movements that ultimately lead to the climax in which a great multitude, from all tribes and peoples and languages will be standing before the throne and before the Lamb. All the dancers will be robed in white, with palm branches in their hands, and they will all cry out: "Salvation belongs to our God who is seated on the throne, and to the Lamb!" (Rev 7:9-10) Then the guests invited to the wedding dance turn out to be the bride of the Lamb himself (19:7,9). The dance of God will reach its climax: an ecstatic dance in which God, through the Lamb, has gone outside himself (*ekstasis*); in which the bride, dancing arm in arm with the Lamb, has been taken up into the dance of God.

God and Stomping Boots

It is time to face the question head-on: are God's dancing shoes the only footwear he has? Is the dance that we have been exploring above the only way to characterize God? Or is there still something behind this dance of God? Is God ultimately an arbitrary God who capriciously kicks the one with his boots and warmly embraces the other in a passionate dance? Does God have his stomping boots hidden away behind his back

---

[68] Pinnock, *Flame of Love*, p. 38. Similarly, James B. Torrance comments: "The Father has given to us the Son and the Spirit to draw us into a life of shared communion—of participating through the Spirit in the Son's communion with the Father—that we might be drawn in love into the very trinitarian life of God himself" (*Worship*, p. 36; cf. p. 32).

as he meets us on the dance floor? Should we, along with Regina Schwarz, be exasperated about a God who favours Abel over Cain? Should we, along with Gilles Deleuze, denounce the Lamb in the book of Revelation as a "carnivorous" monstrosity? Is the Bible a book of violence from beginning to end, after all? Does this ultimately mean that, in imitation of such an unpredictable god, humanity has no option but to be devoted to the violent god of modernism, to the god of William Blake?

I believe that the biblical answer to these questions must be that God has only one set of shoes, and that they are dancing shoes. When we look at God's social, grace-full, passionate and ecstatic dance, we see God as he really and ultimately is. What, then, about the objections that Schwartz and Deleuze might want to lodge against our understanding of God? Let me just offer a couple of considerations. The Cain and Abel story hardly offers us the arbitrary god of monotheism suggested by Schwartz. Instead, the story offers a weak Abel, whose name means "vapour" or "nothingness," and who is willing to give the "fat portions" of the "firstlings" of his flock (Gen 4:4). The story offers a jealous and defiant Cain who refuses to listen to God's warning (4:8) and who instead murders his brother and denies responsibility (4:9). The story offers a God who not only graciously warns Cain (4:6-7) before the act of murder, but who also graciously places a mark on Cain to prevent others from taking vengeance on Cain (4:15). In Volf's words: "God did not abandon Cain to the cycle of exclusions he himself has set in motion. Labeled by the mark of God, Cain belonged to God and was protected by God even as he settled away 'from the presence of the Lord' (v. 16)."[69] There are stomping boots in this story, but they are not the boots of the God of biblical monotheism. They are, sadly enough, the boots of Cain himself. There are also dancing shoes in this story. They are the grace-full dancing shoes of the Triune God made known in Jesus Christ.

It is true, Revelation describes the Lamb in the centre of the throne also as "the Lion of the tribe of Judah" (Rev 5:6). It is a Lamb with seven horns (5:6), whose wrath makes the powerful of this world cringe with

---

[69] Volf, *Exclusion and Embrace*, p. 98. Cf. James G. Williams's comment: "The difference between this text and ordinary mythical texts is that the latter typically justify the murder, presupposing the existence of the community that must not let itself be subverted by taking the side of the victim. Nothing like an altar appears in the Cain story — but the *sign or mark on Cain functions as a prohibition*: 'so that no one who came upon him would kill him' (Gen 4:15)" (*The Bible and the Sacred: Liberation from the Myth of Sanctioned Violence* [New York: HarperSanFrancisco, 1991], p. 34).

fear (6:16-17), in whose presence the worshippers of the beast will be "tormented with fire and sulfur" (14:10). God comes with power, even with violence, in the last book of the Bible.[70] But this does not mean that God's feet are shod with two different pairs of footwear after all: stomping boots in addition to dancing shoes. Rather, it means that God's dancing shoes are more versatile than human dancing shoes. If need be, he will use them to violently remove those from the dance floor who consistently refuse to join in the divine dance and who continue to violently stomp across the floor.[71] God's last word, however, remains a word of love, and his ultimate step a dance step. The Bible says that God is love (1 John 4:8, 16), not that God is wrath. God's anger, his wrath, is simply an expression of his love when it is rejected. God's only shoes are dancing shoes.

In this chapter I have tried to show something of what the divine dance looks like. Of course, it is only possible to see the dance when proper lighting shows up the movements. The apostle Paul cautions us that we still only see in in a mirror, dimly (1 Cor 13:12). We still only have a limited appreciation of the astonishing dance of the Triune God. Nonetheless, already today the Lamb is the light of the world. As Geneva Society, we want to do our work, already today, in the LambLight. I am thankful to the Geneva Society, and also to Trinity Western University, for the confidence they have in me that I will do my work in that Light. It is my prayer that through Geneva's presence at Trinity Western many may be encouraged to explore how to dance in

---

[70] At the same time, it should be obvious from the imagery of the Lamb as a sacrificial lamb that the blood of the Lamb is not the blood of its enemies (pace Lawrence, Apocalypse, pp. 50-51). Cf. Donald Guthrie's comment: "Clearly the writer is not intending to portray Christ in an overmastering fashion. The Lamb is essentially a sacrificial symbol, as is seen from the description of its 'looking as if it had been slain' (5:6). Since this description occurs in a section in which the Lamb is said to have purchased men and women for God through his blood it can hardly be denied that the Lamb is here sacrificial (cf. 7:14)" ("The Christology of Revelation," in Jesus of Nazareth: Lord and Christ – Essays on the Historical Jesus and New Testament Christology, ed. Joel B. Green and Max Turner [Grand Rapids: Eerdmans; Carlisle: Paternoster, 1994], p. 400).

[71] Volf speaks of God's "monopoly on violence" when he comments: "The divine system of judgment is not the flip side of the human reign of terror, but a necessary correlate of human nonviolence" (Exclusion and Embrace, p. 302). For discussions of Volf's approach, see Joe L. Coker, "Peace and the Apocalypse: Stanley Hauerwas and Miroslav Volf on the Eschatological Basis for Christian Nonviolence," EvQ 71 (1999): 261-68; and CGRev 18.3 (2000), a special issue dealing with Volf's theology (with thanks to Dr. Mark Charlton for alerting me to this issue).

step with the social, grace-full, passionate, and ecstatic dance of the Triune God.

Chapter 5

Death of the Watchmaker:

Modern Science and the Providence of God[1]

Arnold E. Sikkema

Let me begin by quoting John Polkinghorne, theoretical physicist and Anglican priest, as he addresses the nature of this presentation. "Interdisciplinary work is both essential (for, in the end, knowledge is one) and risky (for we must all venture to speak on topics of which we are not wholly the master)."[2] A key phrase affirmed by Reformational thinking which upholds a high view of creation is that "knowledge is one"; we believe that "in [Christ] *all things* hold together" (Col 1:17). I had the pleasure of spending five weeks in the summer of 1998 at Calvin College with Polkinghorne and a dozen other physicists, philosophers, and theologians, and much of what I have to say tonight is influenced by that experience.

The doctrine of the providence of God is one of the most cherished truths of Christianity. Article 13 of the Belgic Confession (1561) states that God, having created all things, does not forsake them, but rules and governs them. Chapter V of the Westminster Confession (1648) goes on

[1] This paper was made possible in part through support of The Pew Charitable Trusts and the Seminars in Christian Scholarship program at Calvin College.
[2] John C. Polkinghorne, *Belief in God in an Age of Science* (New Haven: Yale University Press, 1998), p. 83.

to say that he uses "means" to "govern all creatures, actions, and things." In this presentation, I wish to explore what modern science has to offer to flesh out an understanding of the means by which God rules and governs his creation.

In the centuries before what is commonly called the scientific revolution, the working of the world was seen as essentially deeply spiritual. Those who believed in God trusted that it was his hand that made things happen. They would say he ends the night by bringing sunshine in the morning, sends rain for the fields, brings babies to birth. And we who believe in God have this same trust. While labelling that time period as the Dark Ages gives the impression that processes were seen as entirely mysterious or random, there was clear understanding of cause and effect. If a large dark cloud approached, everyone knew it might very well rain. God sent the rain *by* dispatching the cloud. God uses means to provide for his creation, and to provide for his people.

The scientific revolution brought more detail and sophistication to our understanding of the way in which God uses means. Rain comes because water vapour condenses when it cools and the droplets get too large to remain suspended. But it is God who condenses the water vapour and who puts tiny droplets together to make larger ones.

Newton: Dualism Overturned

Foundational to this scientific revolution in physics were ideas formulated by Galileo Galilei (1564-1642) and Johannes Kepler (1571-1630) at the turn of the sixteenth century. They developed the mathematical description of the motion of balls rolling down inclined planes as well as of planetary motion. Born in the year Galileo died, Isaac Newton (1642-1727) completed their program by providing a very general and accurate description of motion in terms of the forces involved. One of the most important (and shocking!) things Newton did was to shatter a strong Greek dualism which had been incorporated into Christian philosophy by Thomas Aquinas (1225-1274) and the scholastics several centuries before. Scholastic physics represented a three-way synthesis of Aristotle's (384-322 BC) beliefs about the nature of things, Christian doctrine, and astronomy. It taught that here on the earth, everything was composed of a mixture of four basic substances: earth, water, air, and fire. Motion is mainly due to the tendency of things to separate into the four substances, with each substance proceeding to its so-called natural place. Ideally, earth (solids) would be at the centre of the universe; next there would be a layer of water; then the air; and finally fire reaching up to the heavens. The churning of the heavens above kept things from reaching this ideal state. So, heavy things, such as rocks and apples, fall down because they are made of earth. Smoke is made of fire and air which tends to rise toward the heavens. In the perfection of the heavens, sun and moon, planets and stars, were made of a fifth essence, *quintessence*, entirely different in nature from things on earth. These inhabitants of the heavenly realm move with perfection among the crystal spheres.

But Newton, over against this Aristotelian dualism, demonstrated that the motion of the moon around the earth and the motion of an apple falling off a tree have exactly the same cause: gravity. It is just a matter of scale: an apple falls five metres from rest in one second, the moon one and one third millimetres. Most of us will have been faced with Newton's three laws of motion and his law of universal gravitation in high school or university. Since these laws can be expressed mathematically, you can accurately predict the time it will take for a ball to roll down an inclined plane if you know the angle and length of the slope. You can figure out how much longer to make the pendulum of a grandfather clock to make it tick off one second less in a day. And we've used Newtonian mechanics to put a man on the moon. All of this works because if you know what forces are acting on an object (like a ball, a pendulum bob, a rocket), you can predict its resulting motion, and this works with remarkable precision.

Newton, being a believer in God, was concerned that his understanding of the universe seemed too mechanistic. So he found four ways to fit God into this world operating as a machine. (1) God is the one who designed it intelligently. (2) His omnipresence and eternity are what give expression to the infinite space and time of the cosmos. (3) He is the one who provides action at a distance (like the force of gravity between earth and moon). And (4) he intervenes from time to time to stabilize processes. This last idea, the stabilization of processes, Newton thought was necessary to understand planetary motion. While a single planet orbiting around the sun is quite straightforward to analyse, things get complicated when there are several planets, each affecting the other. Newton thought the resulting irregularities could eventually magnify and destabilize the entire solar system; God had to do the job of making minor adjustments directly when necessary. But within two generations, Pierre Simon de Laplace (1749-1827) showed that the orbits' irregularities are actually self-correcting—so God is no longer needed for that. All God was required for was to design the watch and wind it up. The idea was that, once started, the subsequent motion of all the little bits of the world would be fully determined. The world is a machine, a nicely ticking watch. While Newton would not necessarily have approved, this Newtonian mechanical worldview with God as the watchmaker became firmly embedded in culture.

Newtonianism: Dualism Re-established

So firmly embedded, in fact, that the majority of Christians also believe it, and many have, perhaps unwittingly, adopted it into their framework of Christian beliefs. However, this is not simply a typical Christianization of secular philosophy, such as was completed by Thomas Aquinas's assimilation of Aristotelianism into Christianity. Newtonian mechanistic beliefs in large part originated in the Christian belief that the faithfulness of the Creator should be evident in the process of the world. Then they were secularized as the "necessity of God" was removed. And finally Newtonian beliefs were re-Christianized into the notion of God operating in the world simply by maintaining the laws which govern the processes in the world. Christians take the liberty of including occasional miracles in which God temporarily acts differently from the way he regularly does. But for the most part, things carry on as they should. After all, the individual particles that make up the universe, including those at the smallest level, are simply bouncing off each other in ways easily understood and in principle fully predictable.

So, summarizing the Christianized view of the "Newtonian world as machine" idea, God acts in the world in two ways: the regular way (maintaining the laws) and via miracles. Given this, what do we expect when we offer prayers to God, particularly petitionary prayers? I don't take seriously the idea that we pray *simply* because God wants us to; I think Scripture describes prayer as being genuine communication. Suppose we hold a Christianized Newtonian understanding of the universe as being, for the most part, a deterministic mechanism. Consequently, *either* we express the desire, hope, or wish that things have already been set up to proceed in the direction we are asking, *or* that God will intervene and go against the regular laws he has instituted. It is this dualistic understanding that I think needs to be corrected, and it seems to me that modern physics can be instructive to this end. For the Christianization of Newtonian ideas must be tempered by the fact that

Newton's laws have seen substantial revision in this century. In fact, the notion of God as watchmaker has been dealt a fatal blow by twentieth-century discoveries in physics. If God is a watchmaker, then he is dead.

Modern Physics: What's an Electron?
Two things killed the watchmaker picture: quantum mechanics and chaos theory. Quantum mechanics says that, for example, it is intrinsically impossible to say when a particular atom is going to undergo radioactive decay. For when we consider the smallest processes, it is fundamentally impossible to make specific predictions apart from statistical ones. And chaos theory says that we cannot make even very general predictions about large-scale systems (such as the air in a room, or the entire atmosphere) without having literally universal knowledge. For example, in what is known as *the butterfly effect*, the precise way a butterfly flapped its wings in Tokyo in early September may have been what made Hurricane Mitch pound Central America in late October instead of fizzling at sea. There are currently a number of scientists and theologians working on using the openness afforded by quantum mechanics and chaos to approach a cohesive understanding of how God acts in the world in such a way as to both truly answer prayer and be fully faithful to his covenant with creation. John Polkinghorne, for example, believes that the way God works in the world is by using universal knowledge to direct "active information" in a top-down holistic way.

What does all this have to do with the development of a Reformational world- and life-view? In addition to informing our approach to petitionary prayer, there is a particularly interesting idea about the lawfulness of creation that modern physics proffers. A Reformational worldview understands creation to be governed by God by means of laws, or norms. All things owe their existence directly to God, and all things function in reference to laws governing the various aspects of existence. God gives creation inherent laws which allow sense to be made of things and meaning to be attached to things. This structure—God, law, thing—seems to require three parts: (1) *God* institutes a set of (2) *laws* to govern each (3) *thing*.

But what is a *thing*? I believe that modern physics tells us that thing-ness must be defined very carefully. Earlier I mentioned that quantum mechanics has implications for the very small. I don't mean the size of a dust particle, but the sizes of atoms, nuclei, protons, electrons.

But what is an electron? Ignoring the wave/particle question, the usual answer is that an electron is an entity with a certain mass, charge, spin, etc. Each of these properties of the electron is responsible for its reaction to the relevant type of environmental disturbance, such as applied force or gravitational field, electric field, magnetic field, etc. So an electron is an object which is subject to certain laws, just like every other object in the universe. But modern physics, in particular quantum field theory, reveals that this picture is far too naive. For even in the absence of any kind of external influence, all of these electron's properties are at play. We have discovered that the electron is far from being a bit of matter subject to certain laws: no quiet little electron sitting there waiting for something to react to, no simple objective existence here. Instead, what we call an electron is actually an extremely complicated "mess" of astonishingly rapid emission and reabsorption of photons (particles of light), and of every other sort of particle in fact! (See figure.)

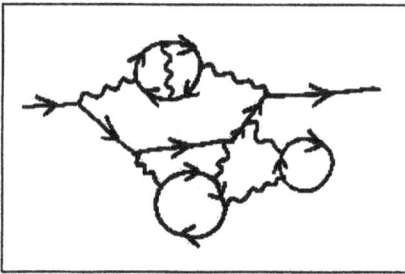

Figure 1: a Feynman diagram indicating a set of possible ways in which an electron (solid lines with arrows) is a seething mass of emission and reabsorptions of virtual photons (wavy lines).

And each thing that is emitted and absorbed is itself a seething mass of emission and reabsorption, a bit like fractal images. But each emission and reabsorption demonstrates intricate concern for detail with regard to very general conservation principles. So there is never actually just a "thing" which we call an electron sitting there, for its lawfulness is built inextricably into its thingness.

Let there be...

I believe this is an example of a more general principle. God doesn't just create things and then institute laws to govern them. He gives them being, building lawfulness inextricably into thingness. This may be understood with reference to God's recurring command in Genesis 1, "Let there be." God isn't just saying, "Make light," and then proceeding to govern it once made; no, he *allows light to have an existence.* And part of this existence is that light goes ahead and behaves like light does, especially in its quantum field theoretical sense of being a seething and indeterminate mass of particle creation, annihilation, emission, and absorption. God could make light do whatever he wants it to do, but he has *let it be* light; therefore he chooses to restrict his operation in the universe in a manner which is consistent with his allowing it to be.

This does not mean that I am suggesting that light, or anything else for that matter, can have any properties in and of itself. All created things depend for their continued existence directly upon the Creator as much as they do for their original (created) existence. I am, however, suggesting that light, and indeed all things, actually have properties: properties which affect their behaviour. The having of properties is entailed by God's "Let there be" imperative, and is not merely illusory. Things having properties is what makes cause and effect real in the universe.

Cause and Effect: Illusion or Real?

But is cause-and-effect real? Consider what happens when a video game is being played on a TV screen. You see balls getting hit by bats, but what's really happening is that the electrons being shot from the back of the TV tube are turned on and off in complicated patterns as they sweep over the screen, so that images are formed. An image of a ball traveling to the left getting hit by the image of a bat traveling to the right cannot actually make the image of the ball end up traveling to the right! What we think of as cause-and-effect (the bat hitting the ball) is purely contained within the programming—none of it resides on the screen. The notion of cause-and-effect we see on the screen is merely an illusion, and must be credited to the program. So it is in the universe, says Donald MacKay, a Scottish theologian writing about God and science.[3] He believes the sovereignty of God requires that God arranged the world so that it has the *appearance* of cause and effect. A universe which was completely unpredictable (*e.g.,* in which releasing a ball in the air would not be followed by the ball falling down), would be one with no apparent cause and effect, and certainly would be displaying a different kind of a god. The fact that it appears to have cause and effect is a reflection of God's goodness and omniscience, his power and wisdom,

---

[3] Donald M. MacKay, *Science, Chance, and Providence* (Oxford: Oxford University Press, 1978), pp. 18ff.

and reveals a God who is concerned about and for his creation and especially his human creatures.

While I affirm some of what MacKay says about God being revealed in the way things happen, I would contend that a Reformational worldview takes creation much more seriously than his video game analogy does. God has actually endowed his creation with cause and effect relationships as part of the divine fiat "Let there be." While agreeing with MacKay's assertions about the video game itself, I am sure that a bat hitting a ball actually does something—of course not outside of the purview of God's sovereignty, but God has given bats and balls the properties they and their fundamental constituents have, so that when bat impacts ball, the bat and ball are actually interacting. Properties are not mere illusions. A world with no real cause and effect is a world in which there are no real properties and is therefore in effect a world in which no "Let there be" has been spoken and is not the world whose creation is depicted in Genesis 1.

The reader may have noticed that I have been using the word "real" a few times in the last few paragraphs. What is the alternative to "real"? And why insist on reality? Talking about things like properties and interactions being real is an aspect of realism, the philosophy of science which most physicists operate under but few philosophers hold. Basic to realism is its insistence that "what we can know ... is a reliable guide to what is the case."[4] The development of scientific theories, being rooted in the real world, is an approach to an understanding of the way the world *is*, not just the way the world *appears*. God, having created us in his image, equips us to fulfill the creational cultural mandate, so we may be confident that the world has an underlying existence which we are able to some extent to grasp.

Revelation: Covenant Faithfulness

Now, we do not have to rely solely on our scientific expertise, or even our experience with the world, to figure things out. God has also revealed in Scripture some important aspects of the way he works in and with the world. Foundational is God's covenantal relationship with his creation. In Genesis 8:22 we read, "As long as the earth endures, / seedtime and harvest, / cold and heat, / summer and winter, / day and night / will never cease." The fact that the daily and seasonal cycles

---

[4] John Polkinghorne, *Faith of a Physicist* (Princeton: Princeton University Press, 1994), p. 156.

continue is a direct result of God's covenant faithfulness. God has made a commitment to us and to his creation that this will be so until the earth remains no more. Every person who sets his alarm clock affirms and expects God's covenant faithfulness, whether he acknowledges it or not. For there is no other way that we can know for certain that the sun will not suddenly rise in the west at midnight. One of my worst nightmares was a dream in which the sun and moon were bouncing off the horizon; it wasn't until I saw the Genesis 8:22 connection between God's covenant faithfulness and the cycle of morning and evening that I realized the true depth of horror I was experiencing.

There are other indications in Scripture that God governs the physical aspect of his creation by means of law. In Job 38:33, God asks Job if he knows the "ordinances of the heavens, [o]r fix[es] their rule over the earth." Psalm 148:6 says, "He set them in place [things in creation] for ever and ever; he gave a decree that will never pass away." Jeremiah 31:36: "Only if these decrees [of sun, moon, stars, and sea] vanish from my sight," / declares the LORD, / "will the descendents of Israel ever cease / to be a nation before Me." Jeremiah 33:20-26 repeatedly emphasizes covenantal language: "This is what the LORD says; 'If you can break my covenant with the day and my covenant with the night, so that day and night no longer come at their appointed time, then my covenant with David my servant ... can be broken and David will no longer have a descendant to reign on his throne.' ... This is what the LORD says, 'If I have not established my covenant with day and night and the fixed laws of heaven and earth, then I will reject the descendants of Jacob and David my servant and will not choose one of his sons to rule over the descendants of Abraham, Isaac and Jacob. For I will restore their fortunes and have compassion on them'"

To summarize what these and other passages teach, God's laws (also called ordinances, rules, boundaries, decrees) for the physical aspect of creation are normative and covenantal, but these are incompletely knowable by man; they serve not only to regulate the creation, but also to reveal to humanity God's character, faithfulness, omnipotence, omniscience, wisdom.

Eighteenth-century philosopher David Hume claims there is no logical way that *we* can figure out laws concerning future events strictly from regularities observed in the past. Hume is in effect affirming God's humbling of Job when he asked, "Do you know the ordinances of the heavens?" But does that mean that science has no hope of figuring anything out, or that when we do, it only relates to our perception and not to the way things really are? This problem is never satisfactorily addressed by unbelieving scientists, but Christians (and Jews) have reason to believe the possibility of discovering laws: a grounded belief that reality is lawful together with faith in God who in his covenant faithfulness maintains his laws.

A Caveat

God governs the behavior of the universe via laws of which we can at best hope to attain partial understanding. And while it is true that because God is faithful to his creation, and that he faithfully maintains his laws, we must be careful not to tie faithfulness too closely to our *limited* and *current* understandings of regularity. To be sure, God has revealed that certain regularities can be absolutely depended upon in connection with his covenant faithfulness, namely those of days and seasons (Gen 8:22; Ps 74:17; Jer 33:20). But going beyond this one must avoid any absolute certainty that it is God's establishment of regularity we are dealing with. For example, we now recognize that expecting the interior angles of a triangle to always add up to 180° (or, equivalently, that $a^2 + b^2 = c^2$ in a right-angled triangle) because of God's faithfulness fails when considering the real world. The so-called fact that a triangle's angles add up to 180° is only *precisely* true in the abstract: in Euclidean geometry. Experience and observation show that this is only *approximately* true (indeed, to a *very* high degree of precision). The real world is not exactly Euclidean; measurements show that the sum of the angles is actually always ever-so-slightly greater than 180°. The amount by which it is greater depends on the area of the triangle and the strength of the gravitational field in its interior! This is just one example indicating that, in general, currently perceived regularities are only approximate and potentially subject to more accurate description. We must be very careful to give credit to God's faithfulness and dependability for our current understanding of regularity, for this understanding is limited and subject to revision.

God's faithfulness allows for the intelligibility of the universe. We can rely on this to come to a greater appreciation of and insight into the regularities of the world. It is within the context of these regularities that we work and develop fruitful theoretical understanding. To do this, a scientist must either trust in God's faithfulness, or believe that there is some other self-existing governing entity.

The Governor of the Universe

The scientific enterprise is, of course, engaged in an effort to understand the world in terms of scientific laws. Steven Weinberg, a Nobel prize-winning theoretical physicist, talks about the discovery that "nature is strictly governed by impersonal mathematical laws."[5] You may notice the metaphysical assertions contained in every single word of that claim, and that this understanding is a discovery. Fortunately he is considered extreme in his position, even among unbelieving scientists. Physicists generally believe there is some set of fundamental laws which in some sense *govern* what happens, and that our laws of physics are mathematical expressions which *describe* what happens. There seems to be good reason to believe that, in the course of scientific advance, the descriptive laws of physics are improving as approximations to the fundamental governing laws with greater degrees of accuracy. Few physicists actually think that Einstein's gravitational theory, general relativity, is *responsible* for keeping the solar system from flying apart, although it is an undeniable fact that such language is very commonly employed or approved of, especially in teaching, popular writing, and the media. General relativity is only a theoretical description of a deeper, more mysterious, *working* of the universe. Theories and principles simply cannot govern. The physicist believes that something underlies these laws and is able to govern, and the theist identifies that with God (although he is much more than that), even if a so-called "theory of everything" is found.

It *is* our God who governs the universe in his providence. He has created all things, endowing them with real properties. He continually upholds these properties in his covenant faithfulness and allows these properties to contribute to the course of events in a true cause-and-effect manner. One of the characteristics of physical processes is their openness to future development in ways which are not determined by their present state. God, having truly *let* these properties *be*, continually works within the created structure to direct the course of events to the fulfillment of his plan, retaining the integrity of the created order. But there is more to reality than simply the physical. There is life, there is human consciousness, there is art, there is faith. How God works within the context of the human will is far less scientifically understood.

Adam and Eve were created in the image of God. After their rebellion, God in his mercy promised to provide a Redeemer. Through

---

[5] *NYRB*, 8 August 1996, 12, 15.

the course of the Old Testament, we see how God focused his plan on the people of Israel, by whom all nations would be blessed. Luke 2 shows how detailed that plan was, involving what would at first appear to be insignificant details. It all comes together in Jesus Christ, born in Bethlehem, and it all proceeds from him in the propagation of the gospel.[6] He is Lord of all. In him *all things* hold together. To God alone be all praise and all glory.

---

[6] Editorial comment: this LambLight Lecture was presented just before Christmas, 1998.

Chapter 6

Is God Our Mother?
The Bible and Inclusive
Language for God

John Cooper

Surely the most influential development in mainline North American Christianity during the last quarter century has been feminist theology and its campaign to reshape the church according to the principle of gender equality. Of course the movement demands equal rights for women in academic theology and in the official leadership of the church. But many Christian feminists are not satisfied with gender equality on the human level. They also insist that our language and ideas of God be gender-inclusive. They urge that the liturgy, prayers, and hymns of Christian worship as well as the creeds and even the Bible itself be modified accordingly. Perhaps the greatest public manifestation of this movement was the Re-Imagining God Conference held in Minneapolis in 1993, sponsored by several major American denominations and covered widely by the media. Gender inclusivism is also a force in major Canadian denominations. It is common in the progressive part of the United Church. Anglicans are considering a new version of the Book of Common Prayer. The Presbyterian Church has considered and taken distance from full-scale inclusive language for God.

What exactly is inclusive language for God? Its rules are exactly the same as the rules of inclusive language for humans. One must either use feminine terms just as often and just as significantly as masculine terms or else avoid gender words altogether. It is no longer culturally acceptable, for example, in speaking of people generically to use the noun "man" and pronoun "he." One must now say "men and women" and "he or she" or otherwise "chairperson" instead of "chairman," either referring to both genders or neither. In the same way God must be called Mother as well as Father, she as well as he, or otherwise Parent instead of Father, Monarch instead of King, and the pronoun "he" simply avoided. Accordingly, the Inclusive Language Lectionary of the National Council of Churches in the United States renders John 3:16: "For God so loved the world that God gave God's only Child." Jesus' Great Commission in Matthew 28:19 comes out like this in *The Gospels and Letters of Paul,* published by The United Church of Christ: "Go therefore and make disciples of all nations, baptizing them in the name of God the Father and Mother and of Jesus Christ the Beloved Child and of the Holy Spirit." The Lord's Prayer now begins, "Our Father-Mother in heaven." In 1995 Oxford University published the *New Testament and Psalms* in completely inclusive language. Beyond Scripture, the UCC's *New Century Hymnal* contains a version of the Apostles' and Nicene Creeds that renders the Triune name of God "the Father-Mother, the Child, and the Holy Spirit." Its hymns too have been politically corrected. Progressive congregations now sing "This is our Parent's World" and "Come Now Almighty God" instead of "Come Thou Almighty King." Either both genders or neither: masculine and feminine must be equal. Inclusive language for God is not just a passing theological fad. It is a significant movement for permanent change in the doctrine and worship of many mainline churches, recasting the faith of ordinary believers.

Conservative Christians may be tempted simply to dismiss this development as the influence of worldly feminism facilitated by liberal theology and a higher critical approach to the Bible. Undoubtedly these influences are powerful ingredients of much feminist theology. But inclusivists also offer theological and pastoral arguments in support of their position that cannot so easily be ignored by biblical Christians. They charge that using only masculine language for God actually distorts or undermines biblical faith in several ways. First, it leads many people to assume uncritically that God is somehow male, whereas Christian theologians have always taught that the God of the Bible is beyond gender, neither male nor female. Second, they point out that using exclusively masculine language leaves the impression that human males are more like God than females are, whereas Scripture teaches that both genders are made in God's image. Inclusivists believe that this impression has reinforced sexism in society and left women feeling inferior and resentful toward men. Furthermore, inclusivists point out that there are people, both men and women, who have been so abused by their fathers or other men that they find it difficult to relate to a God who is presented in exclusively masculine terms. Those of us who defend the biblical tradition's language for God should be able to answer these charges and address these pastoral problems.

When traditional Christians point out that inclusive language changes the way the Bible speaks of God, inclusivists respond that the Christian tradition has adopted many terms for God not explicitly found in Scripture. The theological terms "Trinity" and "First Person" are examples. So are the philosophical labels "Great Designer" and "Absolute Being." Contemporary preachers have likened God to a computer programmer and an air traffic controller. Francis Thompson's poem calls him "the Hound of Heaven." (God a dog?) Inclusivists claim to be doing no more than what has always been acceptable in the Christian tradition: adding new terms to the rich vocabulary of biblical faith. How do we respond to this argument?

The greatest challenge of inclusivism, however, is its claim to be based in Scripture. This appeal comes as a surprise, because inclusive language seems significantly different than biblical language for God. Inclusivists argue that this difference is only one of quantity, not quality or meaning. They acknowledge that biblical language for God is overwhelmingly masculine, but immediately point out that Scripture also contains feminine and gender-neutral references to God. God likens himself to a mother in Isaiah 66:13, for example, when he says to the people of Jerusalem, "As a mother comforts her child, so will I comfort you." And God is called a rock, a genderless, inanimate object in Psalm 18:2: "The LORD is my rock, my fortress and my deliverer; my God is my rock in whom I take refuge." Since the Bible itself speaks of God with feminine and gender-neutral language, inclusivists argue, it cannot be wrong to do so. The only difference between inclusive language and biblical language is proportion. Whereas the Bible is heavily masculine, inclusive language balances the frequency of masculine, feminine, and neuter language for God. In this way inclusivists attempt to invoke the authority of Scripture for their project. Christians who acknowledge the Bible as the inspired Word of God, the final norm for faith and practice, should be able to respond to this appeal to Scripture if we believe that inclusive language for God is unbiblical.

The main part of my contribution is to challenge the biblical and theological arguments for inclusive language for God. I do not believe that the new way of speaking is compatible with biblical and historic Christianity. At the same time I admit that there are elements of truth in some inclusivists' assertions and validity to some of their concerns. There are feminine references to God in Scripture. There are Christians who think that God is male, even referring to him as "The Man Upstairs." And there are sincere believers who find it emotionally difficult to pray to God as Father because they have been abused by their own fathers. I know some of them. So the final part of my presentation will call for Christians to use the Bible's feminine imagery for God and to address the legitimate concerns of inclusivism without endorsing gender-inclusive language for God.

The Doctrine of Revelation: The Finality of Scripture

I must begin my response to inclusivism with a brief statement about revelation. For we humans can truly know and speak of God only as he has revealed himself. Differing doctrines of revelation lie just beneath the surface of the debate about language for God. Historic biblical Christianity recognizes that God has revealed himself in a variety of ways. He has revealed himself in creating and sustaining nature and especially in humanity, the very image of God. Biblical faith recognizes that God has revealed himself in the history of his relationship with his people in Old Testament times and in his continuing presence in the church and hearts of believers since Pentecost. Biblical Christianity confesses that Jesus Christ, the incarnation of God the Son, the very image of the invisible God, is the fullest revelation of God himself in history. And it recognizes that God has and continues to reveal himself in Holy Scripture, his Word written by humans inspired by the Holy Spirit. Although Scripture is chronologically secondary to the other modes of revelation, it has primacy in the historic Christian church as the only infallible account of God's revelation in creation, in history, and in Jesus Christ. It is the final norm for the faith and practice of Christians until Christ returns.

Many of those who advocate inclusive language for God do so because they do not acknowledge the final authority of Holy Scripture. Some believe that God's revelation in creation and in world history tells us as much about God as the Bible does. Usually this is because they view the Bible not as the inspired Word of God for all times and places but as a collection of merely human writings expressing culture-bound male experiences of God. Given this view of Scripture, many also believe that the religious experiences of Christians after the New Testament are equally Spirit-inspired and continue to reveal God. Thus they regard recent feminist spirituality and theology as adding to or even superseding the Bible.

I will not debate the doctrine of revelation. I will simply assert that for historic Christianity the Bible is the final authority for our beliefs and language about God. It should be no surprise that most proponents of inclusive language do not accept that position. Nonetheless, virtually all inclusivists make the claim that, since the Bible contains feminine references to God, calling God "our Mother" as we do "our Father" is consistent with Scripture. There are even a few evangelicals who actually seek to ground inclusive language for God in a high view of Scripture. For this reason the most important step in our response to inclusivism is to evaluate this appeal.

The Incompatibility of Biblical and Inclusive Language for God

Let's begin with the Bible's feminine references to God. Inclusivists sometimes suggest that there are many of these in Scripture and that they have been lost in translation or suppressed by the patriarchal tradition. After extensive study of all such alleged references I have concluded that many are dubious or mistaken. It simply cannot be maintained, for example, that El Shaddai means "the God with breasts" or that God's Spirit is feminine because the Hebrew word *ruach* is grammatically feminine. It is certainly false that Paul's quote to the Athenian philosophers on Mars Hill, "in him we live and move and have our being," is a maternal womb metaphor for God. The line is from a poem about Zeus. Many other alleged feminine references to God likewise evaporate in the light of careful exegesis.

There are, however, about twenty instances where we can be reasonably sure that Scripture does speak of God with feminine language. I have already mentioned Isaiah 66:13: "As a mother comforts her child, so will I comfort you." And in Isaiah 42:14b God says: "Now like a woman in childbirth, I cry out, I gasp and pant." In Isaiah 49:15 the Lord asks: "Can a mother forget the baby at her breast and have no compassion on the child she has borne? Though she may forget, I will not forget you." Here God compares himself to a nursing mother. Psalm 123:2 contains parallel masculine and a feminine allusions to God: "As the eyes of slaves look to the hand of their master, as the eyes of a maid look to the hand of her mistress, so our eyes look to the LORD our God." In Deuteronomy 32:18 Israel is reminded of "the God who gave you birth." The Hebrew verb here is the word used for a woman giving birth. Sometimes God's creation of the world is also likened to giving birth, as in Psalm 90:2: "Before the mountains were born or you brought forth the earth and the world, from everlasting to everlasting you are God." Another example is Job 38:29: "From whose womb comes the ice? Who gives birth to the frost from the heavens…?" God is also likened to non-human females: a mother bear in Hosea 13:8 and mother birds in Isaiah 31:5. Best-known of all, in John 3 Jesus himself compares the work of the Holy Spirit in our regeneration to birth from our human mothers. These and a number of other examples are genuine cases of feminine references to God in Scripture.[1]

But now another question arises: what sorts of linguistic reference are these? Are they basic names and titles of God, as "Lord" and "Father" are? This issue is crucial, for the principle of gender equality requires that feminine terms be used just as frequently and in the same ways as masculine terms. If God has masculine names and titles, he must also have feminine names and titles. Inclusivism insists that we call God "Mother" just as prominently as we call him "Father." Here is exactly where the problem arises, where the fatal flaw in the biblical case for inclusive language occurs. "Father" is a basic and very personal title for God, perhaps even a name. But all the feminine references to God in Scripture are imagery, that is, figures of speech—what English teachers classify as similes, metaphors, analogies, and personification. In order to claim the feminine and maternal imagery as justification for calling God Mother the same as we call him Father, inclusivists must ignore the great differences between figures of speech and terms of proper identification, such as titles and names. This is a category mistake, a logical fallacy. It is not in the first place faulty theology but an error of elementary linguistics. Let me explain.

---

[1] The others are Num 11:12; Ps 123:2; Prov 8:22-25; Isa 45:10; Matt 23:37; Luke 13:34; 15:8-10; and 1 Pet 2:2-3. Possible but more debatable cases are the hovering (maternal?) wings in Gen 1:2; Ruth 2:12; Ps 17:8; Ps 91:4; and the maternal or midwife imagery in Ps 22:9-10; Isa. 46:3; and Isa. 66:7-9.

Figures of speech—similes and metaphors—are not literal identifications of things but are non-literal images, illustrations, or descriptions. Similes state figuratively what God's relation to us is like by comparing two explicitly different things: his effort to save Israel is like a woman giving birth; his faithfulness is like that of a nursing mother; his wrath is like a mother bear's. Metaphors assert figurative depictions more directly: "God is a rock and a fortress"; "God gave birth to the mountains." All of the feminine references to God in the Bible are figures of speech. Linguistically they depict what God's relation to us is like, but do not identify who he is.

In contrast, all the identifying terms, names, and titles of God in Scripture are masculine both in grammatical and personal gender. The Hebrew word *elohim* is a masculine plural noun that functions as masculine singular when it means "God." *El* is a proper name of God in Hebrew and is the high father god in other ancient Near Eastern languages. The Greek word for God is *theos*, a masculine term which has a feminine form that is used in Acts for the goddess Diana, but never of God. The special name of God revealed to Moses is *Yahweh*, a masculine form that almost surely means "He Who Is." The English title "Lord" either stands for the name *Yahweh* or translates the Hebrew word *Adonai*, which is also masculine. The Greek word for Lord is *Kurios*, which again is masculine. All the nouns that name God in the original languages are masculine. So are God's titles. A title indicates one's position or status. Chrétien's title is Prime Minister. Elizabeth's is Queen. In the Old Testament God's basic title is King: the Lord is King (Pss 24, 98, 145 and many others; Isa 6). In the New Testament his basic title is Father. In 1 Corinthians 8:6 Paul writes, "there is but one God, the Father." When Jesus addresses God as "Father," the term functions as a personal name just as "Daddy" does for a child. In Matthew 28:19, "Father" is the name of the first person of the Trinity. The connection between God as King and Father is the Messiah. God promised David in 2 Samuel 7 that one of his sons would be king of God's people forever and that God would be his Father. This came true in Jesus Christ, who is David's son, God's Son, and the King of kings forever and ever.

So all the feminine references to God are figures of speech, and all of God's names and titles are masculine. When the inclusive language movement makes them equivalent, it elevates figures of speech into titles and names, or it reduces all God's names and titles to figures of speech. ("'Father' is a metaphor.") It treats Isaiah's presentation of God as being like a mother equal to Jesus' addressing God as Father. There are two significant reasons why this equivocation is an illegitimate treatment of the biblical material. The first is that it violates standard linguistics. The second is that it is contradicted by the feminine images themselves.

It violates standard linguistics, because figures of speech do not imply or warrant titles or names. My students may say that I am bull-headed, as stubborn as a mule, or as grumpy as a bear. But these figures of speech do not mean to claim that I am in fact an animal or entitle students to call me "Professor Bear" or "Yogi." We may say that Mozart conceived a tune and gave birth to a symphony, but that does not literally make him a mother. During the Gulf War Saddam Hussein's own expression was parodied by calling him "the mother of all dictators," but no one was inclined to refer to him as "she." The reason is that in languages generally figures of speech are not names or titles and do not imply them. Therefore Isaiah's imagery of God as a mother does not of itself warrant calling God "Mother" or "she" any more than Moses' imagery of God as an eagle warrants calling him "Big Bird." This is simply a matter of linguistics, not yet an issue of theology or piety.

The second reason why using maternal imagery to name God "Mother" or use the pronoun "she" is inconsistent with Scripture is found within the very maternal images themselves. The grammatical subject of every one of them, either explicitly or antecedently, is a masculine term for God. The feminine images are not independent of the Bible's masculine language for God, a separate group of texts that might suggest a (divine) feminine subject. Each one is predicated of an explicitly masculine subject. In Isaiah 66, for example, where God says, "I will comfort you as a mother comforts her child," the one who is speaking is explicitly *Yahweh the King*, not a being who might be feminine. When the Psalmist writes that the Lord brought forth the mountains, the subject is the Lord, *Yahweh*, a masculine term, and the form of the Hebrew verb is masculine even though it means "to give birth." The one who gives birth is *Yahweh*, "He Who Is." It is simply impossible in the original text to suppose that God is somehow Mother because he figuratively gives birth.

What we have here is called "cross-gender imagery" by literary scholars. (I owe this insight to Prof. Al Wolters of Redeemer College in Ontario.) Cross-gender imagery predicates a characteristic of one gender of a subject of the other gender. "She is bull-headed" and "he is a real *prima donna*" are examples. Biblical instances of cross-gender imagery for humans are Isaiah's promise, "you shall nurse at the breasts of kings" (Isa 60:16; NRSV) and Paul's claim to be labouring as in childbirth with the Galatians (Gal 4:19). In spite of this maternal imagery, there is no question about the gender of the kings or of Paul. In just the same way, all the feminine images for God are predicated of a masculine subject. "Mother" and "she" are unequivocally ruled out as implied references to God.

Of course I hasten to emphasize with the theological tradition that the masculine language does not mean that God in himself is male or masculine. Baal and Asherah and Zeus and Artemis are gendered beings. The God of the Bible is not like them. The One who created both male and female in his image is neither male nor female, not both male and female. Genesis 1 implies that the image of God does not include gender, because animals are male and female while they are not the image of God. Furthermore, maleness and femaleness are partial and correlative characteristics, whereas God's attributes are all perfect and absolute. So theologically we conclude that gender is not a divine attribute. The masculine language for God in Scripture must therefore be treated like all human language for God, as limited and incapable of describing God literally because it speaks of the transcendent God in creaturely categories. In this sense all language for God is analogical or metaphorical, that is, non-literal. But this general non-literal quality does not imply that God's names and titles are merely figures of speech like the feminine references to God. Although all human language for God is non-literal, titles are still titles and imagery is still imagery. The inclusivist demand that we treat masculine and feminine terms for God equally ignores or confuses this basic distinction.

Spiritual and Theological Problems with Inclusive Language for God

Inclusive language for God is not merely linguistically incompatible with the Bible. It also suffers from profound spiritual and theological problems. Spiritually, it inevitably assumes a prideful, potentially blasphemous stance toward the God of the Bible. I make this judgment cautiously but intentionally. Inclusive language is arrogant because it presumes that humans have the ability and the right to name God almost as they name their own children. But according to the record of Scripture, when God revealed himself to his people he gave them his names. They did not have to guess at his name or name an unknown God, like the philosophers of Athens. In Exodus 3 the Lord introduced himself to Moses as *Yahweh*. God himself gave the names "Jesus" and "Immanuel" to his Son. Furthermore, the act of naming in the culture of the Bible assumes a relationship of authority. God renames Abram and Sarai. Nebuchadnezzar renames Daniel and his three friends. Jesus renames Simon as Peter. But we humans do not have authority over God to name him. To adopt inclusive language for God amounts to giving God basic names and titles and thus asserting authority over him. This reverses the divine-human relationship. Even in human relationships, we respect and use the names and titles by which people introduce themselves to us. We name our children, but not adults who already have titles and names. How much more so with God. In fact we are commanded to hallow God's name by the third commandment: We humans are not to take it in vain but to honour it as holy. Criticizing the revealed names of God in Scripture as patriarchal and sexist and then attempting to politically correct them both violates the commandment and attempts to dominate God. Inclusive language for God cannot be reconciled with biblical piety and spiritual humility.

In addition to spiritual dangers, inclusive language for God also promotes doctrinal confusion or falsehood. One crucial topic is God's relation to the world, the Creator-creature relation. Biblical Christianity affirms that, although God is omnipresent and always intimately involved with his creation as Sustainer, Redeemer, and Judge, he is in no sense part of the world, nor is the world part of him or continuous with him. When inclusive language speaks of God as both Father and Mother, it suggests a different image of the God-cosmos relation. Throughout the world religions mother-goddesses are typically understood as immanent in creation. There is some continuity of being between the fertile womb of the goddess and the life-force in the world. The ancient religious image of Mother Nature captures this notion. Here is the connection between feminist spirituality, Wicca, neo-paganism, and New Age religion. When inclusivists speak of God as Father and Mother, they suggest a theology called "panentheism," which is between theism and pantheism: God becomes part of the world and the world is part of God. God is incomplete without the world and needs it to be God. Some inclusivists seem unaware of this implication, but leading feminist theologians, such as Rosemary Ruether and Sally McFague, promote panentheism quite self-consciously and intentionally.

Confusion also arises in the doctrine of the Trinity. The triune name of the one God, given by Jesus himself in Matthew 28:19, is

"Father, Son, and Holy Spirit." Inclusivists suggest replacing the Triune name with such alternatives as "Father-Mother, Child, and Holy Spirit" or "Creator, Redeemer, and Comforter." But none of these substitutions is equivalent to the Triune name. In fact they either undermine or subtly alter what is stated in the Bible and summarized in the Nicene Creed about the one three-Personed God. The replacements either suggest one Person with three activities (creating, redeeming, comforting), which represents the heresies of unitarianism and modalism; or they imply four Persons (the Father, Mother, Child, and Spirit); or they imply three Persons with a procreational relationship among them, the Child apparently the offspring of the self-reproductive Father-Mother, which combines the ancient heresies of Gnosticism and Arianism. It is striking how many heretical movements have viewed God as both Father and Mother. The ancient Gnostics did so, and were followed more recently by the Shakers and Mary Baker Eddy, founder of Christian Science. The Mormons believe that God the Heavenly Father has a wife, the Heavenly Mother. Jesus Christ, the Holy Ghost, Lucifer, and we humans are their spirit children. The Unification Church of the Rev. Sun Myung Moon, the so-called Moonies, also teach that the divine nature is both masculine and feminine. Departure from biblical language for God often accompanies departure from the orthodox Christian faith.

The only way for inclusivists to preserve the historic doctrine of the Trinity is to acknowledge the definitive status of the biblical revelation of God as "Father, Son, and Holy Spirit" and to stipulate that the new inclusive-language substitutes continue to mean exactly what the biblical-creedal language of the Church has always meant. But this concession would require inclusivists to violate their own basic principle of gender equality. For feminine language would then be dependent upon and defined by the masculine language of the biblical tradition, an unequal status that no consistent inclusivist could tolerate. Inclusivism is between the rock of orthodoxy and the hard place of gender equality. It turns out that "inclusivist orthodox Christianity" is an oxymoron.

Furthermore, an inclusive language Bible is both untrue and unethical. It is untrue, to give just one example, simply because as a matter of historical fact Jesus did not teach us to pray to our Father-Mother or our Parent in heaven. Jesus did not command the disciples to baptize in the name of the Father-Mother, Child, and Spirit. A Bible that states otherwise is simply false. And so is any liturgy that intends to repeat the truth of the Gospel as historically revealed. As for ethics, if anyone would try to rewrite Shakespeare in inclusive language or edit the writings of Gloria Steinam in exclusively masculine language, cries of protest would rise to heaven itself. The rights of the author and integrity of the text would be violated. Why does the same principle not apply to the Bible?

To summarize the argument so far, we humans should continue to speak the Bible's language for God simply because Scripture is the most reliable and definitive form of revelation that we have in history. The Bible speaks of God exclusively as though he is a masculine being, while at the same time implying that God in himself is not masculine. It is not linguistically legitimate to turn the Bible's maternal imagery for God into names and titles for God equivalent to the standard masculine terms for God. Inclusive language for God cannot be derived from the Bible and thus cannot appeal to Scripture for its justification. Furthermore, the use of inclusive language for God is an arrogant and potentially blasphemous attempt to redefine how God has revealed and named himself. Finally, adopting inclusive language compromises basic biblical doctrines of God. For all these reasons, Christians who affirm the biblical tradition ought to reject it.

The Legitimate Use of Feminine Language for God

Having outlined the fatal flaws in inclusive language for God, I now wish to make the case for using feminine language for God properly, according to the biblical pattern. In so doing I will acknowledge the elements of truth in inclusivism and address its valid concerns.

In the first place I wish to strongly endorse the use of the Bible's feminine language for God: not inclusive language, not calling God our Mother, but maternal imagery following the biblical pattern. I stand on solid ground here. If we are to live by every word that proceeds from the mouth of the Lord, if we truly do endorse the principle of *tota scriptura*, the whole of Scripture, then using those passages where God is represented as being like a mother to us is not only permissible, it is required.

Feminists may have a point when they charge that the Christian tradition has largely overlooked these passages. I have been a believer all my life, reading Scripture and attending church faithfully. But I cannot recall ever noticing these images until I began reading about feminist theology. I surely never heard a sermon on any of these texts, not even on Mothers' Day. There is a verse of the hymn, "My God how wonderful thou art," that goes: "No earthly father loves like thee, no mother half so mild." But that is a rarity in a traditional hymnbook. Christians faithful to Scripture could do a lot more than we have to attend to these texts in personal devotions, the reading of Scripture in public worship, preaching, prayer, and in hymnody. Surely it is biblical to pray "O God who loves us like a mother" or "Father, we thank you for your motherly care." Surely it is necessary to use physical birth in a sermon on John 3 to illustrate how the Holy Spirit regenerates our hearts. I am not calling for primary or frequent focus on feminine imagery for God, which admittedly is a minor theme in Scripture. I am conceding nothing to inclusivism or political correctness. I am claiming that occasional but regular use is appropriate both because this imagery is part of God's revelation and because of its power for edification and healing in a culture where the matter of gender relations has become so prominent. In sum, although the Bible does not justify gender-inclusive language for God, inclusivists are right in exhorting us to use the feminine imagery that Scripture does contain.

But now we must address another issue inclusivists raise: the Bible is not the only source of Christian language for God. The Christian tradition has adopted many ways of referring to God that are not explicitly found in Scripture, terms such as "Trinity," "Great Designer," and "Hound of Heaven." If it is legitimate to use "Trinity to capture the biblical revelation of God as Father, Son, and Holy Spirit, why is it wrong to call God "Mother" to capture the maternal biblical imagery?

Perhaps we should not exclude "Mother" altogether. In fact there is precedent in Christian tradition. I leave aside the ancient church fathers who used it and Julian of Norwich, a fourteenth-century English prioress, who spoke figuratively of God and especially of Jesus as "Mother." John Calvin, in his commentary on Isaiah 46:3, which he interprets as a maternal metaphor, writes: "It is the intention of the Prophet to show ... the Jews ... that God, who has manifested himself to be both their Father and their Mother, will always assist them." In this unusual instance Calvin not only refers to God as "Mother" but does so in parallel with "Father." Was John Calvin wrong to speak of God in this way? Was he already on the slippery slope toward inclusivism?

Calvin's comment does not remotely resemble anything like inclusive language for God, which requires equality both in frequency and status of gender terms. He does not use "Mother" as frequently as "Father." In fact this instance is rare, if not unique. And he does not confuse figures of speech with names or titles. His analysis of Isaiah 46:3 makes clear that "Mother" is a figure of speech whereas he regards "Father" as a divine title. Calvin would be horrified by the idea of rewriting the entire Bible in inclusive language. He never dreamt of incorporating "Mother" as a term for God into the language of the creeds or worship of the church.

We can understand the legitimacy as well as the limitations of Calvin's use of "Mother" if we return to the doctrine of revelation. At the outset we noted that although Scripture is the final norm for our faith and practice, it is not the only means by which God has revealed himself. God first revealed himself in nature and especially human beings, who bear his image. Thus human females and animals reflect the nature of their creator. That is why Bible writers can liken God to a woman, a mother bear, and a nesting bird. That is also why a poet like Francis Thompson can call God "the Hound of Heaven," poetically imaging him as an English hunting dog in his relentless pursuit of the wayward sinner. Terms derived from nature by the human religious imagination or by philosophical reflection are legitimately used of God provided that they meet several conditions: they must be consistent with Scripture. They remain secondary to Scripture. They must in no way challenge the definitive status of the language of Scripture. And they must be interpreted according to the clearer, more definitive revelation of Scripture. If the term "Mother" is used according to these conditions the way "Trinity," "Great Designer," and "Hound of Heaven" have been used to refer to God, I have no objection to it in principle. But notice that these terms have never been regarded by the church as equal to or as able to supplant biblical language for God. The theological term "Trinity" is not substituted for "Father, Son, and Holy Spirit" in translating Matthew 28:19 or in the sacrament of baptism. We do not use the philosophical term "Great Designer" in the creeds or liturgy of the church. "Hound of Heaven" is a powerful poetic image that could be used in a hymn, but it would never become a standard term for God. In the same way, "Mother" as a non-biblical, general-revelation based reference to God would never be inserted into the Bible or become a regular part of the Christian vocabulary. Its occurrence would be much less frequent than the church's use of the Bible's feminine imagery for God, very far from the egalitarian requirement of inclusive language. But under these conditions its use is legitimate in principle.

The Benefits of Using Legitimate Feminine Language for God

Using feminine imagery for God is not only biblically warranted, it is also spiritually uplifting and healing for all of us, both male and female. Although I reject gender stereotypes, I do think that there are general differences between men and women. We humans, whether male or female, need both human parents. I was blessed to have two loving Christian parents. My father's love is strong, affirming, and genuine. But there are profound things about my mother's love that nourished my young soul in ways that my father's did not. It still warms me to the bottom of my heart to hear the Lord say in Isaiah, "I will comfort you as a mother comforts her child." I know what God's love is like because of my mother's love. All of us as God's children need to know that his love is not only like a father's love, it is also like a mother's. We all need the motherly love of our heavenly Father. We cut ourselves off from this blessing if we ignore the Bible's maternal imagery for God.

Some of us may have special emotional and spiritual needs. Perhaps we did not experience the love of human parents. Parental abuse is epidemic in our society, whether emotional, physical, or even sexual abuse. The opposite sin, parental neglect, is almost as bad. Statistically fathers are more likely to be guilty of these sins, but mothers also commit them regularly. Many children don't receive healthy love from one or both parents. Spiritual damage can take various forms.

People abused by fathers or other males may have a difficult time relating positively to God because the Bible does present him with masculine language. Genuine healing is achieved only when such persons are again able to pray to God as their heavenly Father, knowing that his love for them, unlike their human father's, is both wholesome and unfailing. Emotional therapy and pastoral counselling that is Christian will aim at this kind of healing. But it can be especially meaningful for such people, if they have had a good relationship with their mother, to focus on the Bible's maternal imagery for God until they are able to experience God as loving Father. It is also helpful to people who have not had a mother's love either because of neglect or abandonment to know that the emptiness they feel can be more than filled by God, who loves even more faithfully than a nursing mother. I have heard sincere biblical Christians who completely reject inclusive language for God testify about the healing that can come through focusing on the motherly love of God. Evangelism that presents God's love as a mother's love might also be more effective with people who have had difficult relations with human fathers or are bothered by sexism.

Using the Bible's feminine imagery for God will also blunt the attack of those who caricature and reject Christianity as essentially and irremediably patriarchal. Mary Daly, a feminist philosopher who abandoned the faith, makes the charge that in Christianity "God is male; therefore the male is god." This accusation tarnishes the reputation of the Gospel not only with feminists, but with many people in a society that affirms gender equality. We must patiently explain that Scripture neither teaches that God is male nor that men are superior to women. Although the Bible reveals God as Lord, King, and Father, it also shows that he is like a mother. Sound theological reflection on Scripture concludes that the divine nature itself is neither male nor female, neither masculine nor feminine, but beyond and greater than both.

We must also show our culture that the biblical view of women is as high as in any worldview. However we understand God's will for marriage and the role of women in the church, it is clear from the Bible that men and women are fundamentally equal. In Scripture, women are equal to men as created in the image of God, as fallen into sin, as objects of God's redemptive love in Jesus Christ, and as indwelt and gifted by the Holy Spirit to be prophets, priests, and kings. In Christianity women are not only equal to men, they are created and redeemed in the very image of God himself. This is a vastly higher view of women than the one presented in secular femininism. The God who confers this status on women is the Father, Son, and Holy Spirit. Biblical Christianity therefore refutes the basic assumption behind inclusive language for God: that a gender-inclusive view of humans requires a gender-inclusive view of God. The God who has revealed himself in masculine language has created and redeemed women and men equally, whatever their differences. Faithful presentation of the biblical teaching about God, men, and women will make clear that Mary Daly's charge against Christianity is false, that it deals with a caricature.

I am under no illusion, however, that the biblical view of God, men, and women can be made acceptable to contemporary culture, and I am not suggesting that we should try. The gospel itself is a scandal to those who don't believe. In a culture that wants to include and affirm the equality and goodness of everyone, in a society that downplays retribution and rejects capital punishment, it is outrageous to claim that all humans have sinned against God and are worthy of punishment, that all need to be reconciled to him, and that Jesus Christ, because of his atoning death and resurrection, is the only way to the Father. Similarly, Christian views about sexual ethics and the sanctity of human life are regarded by secular culture as oppressively narrow-minded. And so it is with significant features of the biblical view of God, men, and women. Making Christianity palatable to secular culture would require adopting inclusive language for God and affirming the absolute egalitarianism it presupposes. But I have argued that "inclusive language Christianity" is really an oxymoron. I trust that I have shown you a better way: let us embrace and apply Scripture fully. Let us use its feminine imagery as well as its masculine terms for God. And let us relate to each other, whether male or female, as one in Christ.

Part III

Relating to Our World

Chapter 7

On the Edge of the Millennium:

Making Sense of Genesis 1

Rikki E. Watts

Interpreting Genesis 1 continues to be a controversial issue—and for all sorts of people. This is hardly surprising for at least two reasons. On one level, how one reads Genesis 1 has in some circles become a litmus test of Christian orthodoxy, whether conservative or liberal. Hold the "wrong" view and one is either a dupe of secular critical theory or a troglodyte literalist. This hardly bodes well for the unity of that new humanity that God is forming in Christ. On another level, the importance of stories of origins cannot be overestimated. They define us.[1] They tell us who we are and what it means to be human. In terms of our topic, whatever the technical merits or otherwise of Darwin's theory of biological evolution, its widespread acceptance has gone a long way toward discrediting a "literal" reading of Genesis 1 and with it the standing of Christianity and its vision of humanity. Consequently, and rather more provocatively, it is hard to imagine the modern North-American trade in aborted baby body parts or the horrors of Holocaust and Gulag were it not for the stark materialism of, and the eugenic theory inherent in, the more imperialist and triumphalist forms of

---

[1] See Jacques Ellul, "Le rôle médiateur de l'idéologie," in *Demythisation et idéologie*, ed. Enrico Castelli (Paris: Aubier, 1973), pp. 335-54; and Paul Ricoeur, "The Function of Fiction in Shaping Reality," *Man and World* 12 (1979): 123-41; and in terms of the aims of the biblical authors, J. van Seters, *In Search of History: Historiography in the Ancient World and Origins of Biblical History* (New Haven: Yale University Press, 1983).

twentieth-century Darwinism. However, it must be recognized that it will be difficult if not impossible to reverse these trends if resistance is not undergirded by a more convincing and coherent alternative view of human origins than Darwinism can offer. And this in terms of both the objective—what happened—and the subjective—what it means. For Christians such an alternative must include Genesis 1 and that necessarily involves the question of how it is to be read. If in the end we find that Genesis 1 ought to be read "literally," then so be it. On the other hand, the more work I do on the world out of which this account emerged, the more I am led to question whether the "literalist" reading is in fact truly faithful to the text.

In my experience most Christians and readers of the Bible come to Genesis 1 with many of their beliefs already in hand. This is not to be dismissed as a typical example of blind private faith versus well-attested public fact, as Bertrand Russell so gloriously misconstrued things. It is an inescapable part of being human. Michael Polanyi reminded us that taking a great many things on trust is the essential first step to knowledge, even and perhaps especially in that highest and holiest of all modern callings, science. All of us, Christians and scientists together, simply have to take a great deal on trust, to assume much, if we are ever to get started on the path to knowing. The saying is sure, without assuming something no one shall know anything. But having said that, it is important regularly to reassess those assumptions in the light of our growing knowledge and in doing so to recognize that truth in this kind of historical and literary endeavour is much more a matter of coherence than of certainty. Bernard Lonergan rightly understood that the first step in knowing was to pay attention to all of the data, then to apply our intelligence in seeking to understand, and finally to use our reason to judge between hypotheses. This is the advice, which, to the best of my ability, I intend to take here.

Reading Ancient Documents

Our problems begin in that most of us read Genesis 1 in our mother tongue, and that tongue is not Hebrew. This is both helpful and potentially misleading. The help is obvious, the potential harm less so. The fact remains that this story was originally written in another language, a very long time ago, and in a culture whose world, while not totally other than ours, was both different and very differently understood. In one sense they no doubt looked out on the same physically constituted landscape, but as Lonergan also reminded us: seeing is not the same as knowing. The assumptions that they once brought and we now bring to the text—Gadamer's horizons—are very likely to be rather different. That this is so can hardly be contested as the divergent interpretations of Genesis 1 even in our own day bear witness. The same ink spots generate some very different understandings. The upshot is that if we are not attentive, the fact that Genesis 1 is in our own language can lull us into assuming that familiar words and phrases are intended to invoke the understandings and assumptions of our twenty-first-century world. This is, of course, just as much a mistake as reading Shakespeare as though he was writing in twenty-first-century Vancouver or Hong Kong. Not surprisingly, the less we "modernize" Shakespeare the more foreign he appears and the less likely the error of anachronism. It is useful, then, to remember that Genesis 1 was originally written in Hebrew, and even better to read it in the same.

The question arises: but even so, whose understanding is correct? Do not our individual perspectives mire us in a hopeless relativism? Not at all. These ink spots are not merely signs. They are particular signs in a particular order. They are the readers' "marching orders," designed by the writer to communicate what he intended to the competent reader.[2] The terms of those marching orders are indicated by the genre, the contract made between writer and reader as to how the signs are to be read. This is really nothing new since we all get along very well every day on this basis, almost unconsciously using genre to distinguish between the truth claims of Peanuts (no, there is not in fact a canine whose philosophizing rivals Plato) and *The Vancouver Sun* (but how we wish that some of our politicians were more like Snoopy!).

The trick is to do as much work as we can in determining the genre and in seeking to understand the worldview out of which Genesis 1 emerged. This will involve not only looking at Genesis 1 in detail but also paying attention to similar stories elsewhere in order to get a feel for the kinds of issues the ancients were concerned with and the language they used in dealing with them. The last sentence might generate some anxiety. There is no need. When a good preacher or exegete does word studies he or she is not confined only to the biblical texts as though they were written in a hermetically sealed environment. They also consider how the language functioned in the broader cultural context of the day.

---

[2] See Ben F. Meyer, *Reality and Illusion in New Testament Scholarship: A Primer in Critical Realist Hermeneutics* (Collegeville, Minn.: Liturgical, 1994), pp. 2-3.

The same surely applies here. But bear in mind the distinction: we are not talking about borrowing or dependence but rather about the use of common motifs and ideas to deal with common concerns. The central truth claims of Genesis 1 can be very different from the origins stories of the surrounding cultures even if it uses, as we would expect it to, the language and imagery of the day.

Genre as Reading Contract: Form and Content

Literary genre is communicated to the reader through form and content. Consider *The Simpsons*. First, we notice the form. It is a cartoon, replete with exaggerated colour and character features. The Simpson family seems to be suffering from a very serious kidney or liver problem, while Marg's blue haystack is beyond wonder. Second, the content. Ned Flanders can hardly be real, can he? Is anyone's life really this crazy and dysfunctional? Further, we have seen other such cartoons and know that they are not "real." The form and content together combine to inform us, as competent viewers, that this is not to be taken as an accurate historical account. But does this mean that "The Simpsons" is not true? Of course not. One of the reasons for its on-going popularity is its caustic wit and perceptive social satire.

William Blake's famous couplet, "Tiger, tiger, burning bright, in the forests of the night," is another case in point. It is true? Not if one reads it "literally" as a description of the propensity of feral cats to ignite spontaneously during their nocturnal wanderings. And protesting with increasingly agitated vigor "Blake says it, I believe it, and that settles it" does not help much. What Blake actually says is a matter of genre, that is, of form and content. We recognize the form: poetry. That means we need to be alert to metaphor, image, and poetic license, whether simplification or hyperbole. It would be folly, if not downright and culpable stupidity, to demand technical precision from poetry. We also consider the content. Tigers do not in our experience habitually explode whilst wandering in dark forests. These two considerations—form and content—help us understand what it is that Blake is trying to say. So is his description true? In one very real sense, yes. Ask yourself, what gives a better understanding of the essence of tigerness: Blake's simple and stylized couplet or a fifty-five-volume DNA map of tiger genes?

Two important considerations emerge. First, in our scientific world it is easy to forget that there are ways of telling the truth other than algebraic formulae or Western-style history. Furthermore, some of the most important and meaningful things in our lives are best shared using metaphor and poetic image. Listen to the top 40 and see how often lyrics such as E=mc² dominate the charts. The same applies to the biblical text, large slabs of which are not in plodding prose. Most of the prophets preferred poetry. This does not mean that what they say is not true. But in order to make their message more memorable and compelling, they use a genre best suited to that task. Now, I am not attempting to stack the deck for a particular reading of Genesis 1. I am only trying to establish the fact that some of us have a subconscious suspicion of anything other than one particular kind of truth-telling genre to which certain parts of our culture or our upbringing have accustomed us.

In my experience this immediately gives rise to a second question: but if we read Genesis 1 like this, where will it all end? What is to prevent everything solid from wilting into some kind of metaphorical jelly? The answer is again genre. Take, for instance, Jesus' walking on the water. Bultmann, like Schweitzer before him, regarded these stories as myths, largely on the grounds that people do not do this kind of thing. And they are, in part, right. We have never seen such things and we ought to be amazed and skeptical. But remember, content is only half the story. There is also form. Although there is some debate, it seems clear to me that the form of the gospels will not allow myth, fairy tale, novel, or legend as viable genre options. At this point, form overrides the content consideration. Whatever else the gospel writers were trying to do, to the best of our present knowledge the form of their stories indicates that they are convinced that these things really happened.

So with all this in view, what can we say about the genre and consequently the truth claims of Genesis 1?

Genesis 1: Form and Content

Turning first to the form, even a cursory reading of Genesis 1 reveals a great deal of repetition: "and God said" (vv. 3, 6, 9, 11, 14, 20, 24, 26, 28, 29), "let there be" (or some form thereof; vv. 3, 6, 9, 11, 14, 20, 24, 26), "and it was so" (vv. 3, 7, 9, 11, 15, 24, 30), "and God made" (or similar action; vv. 4, 7, 12, 16, 21, 25, 27), "and God saw that 'x' was good" (vv. 4, 10, 12, 18, 21, 25, 31), some form of naming or blessing (vv. 5, 8, 10, 22, 28), "there was evening and there was morning" (vv. 5, 8, 13, 19, 23, 31), and then a designation of the day as first, second, etc. (vv. 5, 8, 13, 19, 23, 31; 2:2), with most of these occurring seven times. Usually we associate this kind of repetition with poetry.[3] But we have examples of ancient Hebrew poetry (e.g., Exod 15; Num 23-24; Deut 33; Judg 5), and Genesis 1 is clearly not the same thing. But equally, if not more so, neither is this repetition characteristic of straight narrative, as a quick glance at even Genesis 2 or 1 Samuel will reveal. That modern translators and the vast majority of commentators recognize the poetic *character* of Genesis 1 is indicated by the printed format used in nearly all modern versions of the Bible.

There are other indications that this text is highly stylized. In ancient writing it is not uncommon to find the opening sentences offering clues to the structure of what follows—something like their version of a table of contents. Genesis 1:2 tells us that the earth was without structure (formless) and empty. With this in mind, it has long been recognized that days 1-3 and 4-6 are correlated with days 1 and 4, 2 and 5, and 3 and 6 concerning the same elements of creation:[4]

Day	Structuring	Filling	Day
3	water / land	land animals / humans	6
2	waters above (sky) / waters below	birds / fish	5
1	day / night	sun / moon and stars	4

[3] Or genealogies. This is interesting in the light of Gen 2:4, which may be read as referring to what has just preceded.

[4] This approach is known as the framework view and its primary literary feature has been recognized since Herder (c. 1750). See Henri Blocher, *In the Beginning*, trans. David G. Preston (Leicester: InterVarsity, 1984), pp. 49-59. Scholars such as N.H. Ridderbos, Bernard Ramm, Meredith G. Kline, D.F. Payne and J.A. Thompson hold this view; cf. also R. Youngblood. It has been challenged, unsuccessfully in my view, by Wayne Grudem, *Systematic Theology: An Introduction to Biblical Doctrine* (Grand Rapids: Zondervan; Leicester: InterVarsity, 1994), pp. 300-04. The primary weaknesses of his critique are a singular and inexplicable failure to address the issue of literary genre as it concerns form and content and an equally inexplicable assumption that a framework approach necessarily excludes the idea of progression through the days. E.g., he claims that day 4 cannot parallel day 1 since day 4 has the sun placed in the "firmament" which is created in day 2; likewise, the fish of day 5 are called fish of the "sea" which is prepared on day 3. (In fact, it is simply the gathered waters of day 2 in order for land to appear.) But the framework view has never denied the progression of creation and hence would naturally expect the ancient author to take account of what happened in the intervening days when he parallels the days. I am at a loss to understand why Grudem seems to think that our author lacks the sophistication to integrate both progression and parallel.

Entirely in keeping with Genesis 1:2, we have two sets of three days: the first concerning giving form to or structuring what was formless and the second concerning filling the newly created but empty forms. Furthermore, in both sets there is a progression from heaven to earth, with the preparation of the land and the formation of humanity respectively as the climactic moment. This progression is further highlighted by the nature of Yahweh's creative acts. Days 1 and 4 have a single act, days 2 and 5 one creative act of two parts, and finally days 3 and 6 consist of two creative acts. It seems to me that unless we have a previous agenda this kind of detailed and highly stylized literary patterning strongly cautions against taking this account too concretely. This is not to say it is not true, only that its truth claims may not be of the kind we associate with "literal" reading.

So much for formal indications. What about the content? The first thing we note is the twenty-four hour period—or, to be more precise, a working period of twelve hours from morning to evening (the day ending with evening and the following announcement of morning indicating the beginning of a new day). While it is true that "day" (yom) can elsewhere mean a longer period (e.g., Ps 90:4), it seems to me that the use of evening/morning terminology and Yahweh's rest on the seventh day (in the light of the Sabbath commandment, Exod 20:11; more on this below) makes it all but undeniable that twenty-four hour periods are in view. We also note that there is no mention of any ending of the seventh day. This is probably because the narrative has arrived at Yahweh's rest in his completed creation, and there is no need to go further.

More to the point perhaps is the question: why did the various creative acts of the six days take the same amount of time? One would have thought that creating the sun, moon, and stars with all their mind-numbing extent throughout our vast universe would require considerably more time than creating birds and fish. And why would separating the waters above and below take as long as creating all of the land-dwelling creatures? Even the notion of a firmament in which the heavenly bodies are placed is hardly in keeping with what we now understand. And why exactly twelve hours and not two or forty-seven and a quarter? Why should it take God any time to do anything? Why should he work only in daylight hours? Surely he does not need to rest at night, and the idea that it was too dark for him to see is ludicrous. And what about the flightless land birds and the amphibians which seem not to fit any of the categories? Then we notice that Genesis 2:4-7 suggests that the creation of plants was delayed until apparently the creation of humanity to work the fields. But in Genesis 1 plants are created several days beforehand. It is hard to understand how three days without tillage could be such a problem. None of this is intended to be taking cheap shots. It is, however, intended to suggest something about the genre, and thus about the kind of truth communicated in Genesis 1. When we ask questions and get answers like these, our customary response is to recognize that whatever the truth claims of the account might be, it is not what we normally call "literal" history. Strangely, some readers of Genesis at this point suddenly decide to ignore the genre contract between writer and reader which they customarily and everywhere else observe. One cannot help but wonder if there is some other agenda at work.

Based at this point solely on the text itself and applying the same standards we use everywhere else for assessing genre, that is, to consider form and content, it appears that Genesis 1 is not intended to be read "literally," at least in the popular usage where it usually means "concretely" or strictly and without the possibility of metaphor, hyperbole, or symbol.[5] This does not mean Genesis 1 is not true. It does, however, mean that its truth claims are of a different nature.

Genesis 1 in Its Ancient Near Eastern Environment

How then are we to approach our reading of Genesis 1? As in the reading of any document, it helps to have some familiarity with comparable materials, in this case other ancient creation stories. What we are after, in dealing with the ancients' view of origins, is some idea of the kinds of questions they asked and how they answered them. Again, this is not to assume that Genesis 1 is identical to, or of the same genre as, these other stories or has borrowed from them. We are simply interested in trying to understand what issues a second-millennium B.C. culture might have been interested in. I am, however, assuming that they were not trying to do modern science nor attempting to show that Darwin was wrong—hardly likely since neither was around at the time. It is impossible here to carry out a thorough comparison of ancient creation stories, but a cursory overview will be helpful in giving us a feel for the

---

[5] Technically speaking, "literally" in its original medieval derivation means reading a document in keeping with the literary genre, in the sense the author intended. On this meaning, the reading proposed here would be the literal sense.

kinds of concerns that the first audience of Genesis 1 might have brought to the text.[6]

(1) *Sumerian* — We have very little from the Sumerians of the third millennium B.C. They have no epic origins poem, and instead all we have are some brief indications in introductions legitimating their social order. One story describes a very early division between heaven and earth where Enlil, god of the air, separates An and Ki (heaven and earth). Another begins with Nammu, a watery goddess, who then becomes mother of heaven and earth and all the gods. As increasing order emerges from an amorphous whole, and humans, who had previously been animals, become a special kind of creature.

(2) *"Babylonian"* — Although often regarded as "Babylonian," the *Atrahasis* and *Enuma Elish* myths are probably of more complex origins. Not only had Babylonian culture inherited materials from the Sumerians, but it was also influenced by a mid-third-millennium incursion of Semites and a late-third-millennium takeover by the Amorites. Although most of our sources derive from the Assyrian or Neo-Babylonian period, the traditions themselves are probably more ancient.

The *Atrahasis* myth, whose earlier form is found in the Sumerian account of *Enki and Ninmakh*, was probably the standard Babylonian version of the creation of humanity. At first the gods and humans were not differentiated. The weaker gods, the *Igigi*, performed irrigation and drainage, but growing tired, they threatened rebellion. Humans were then created, by mixing clay with the blood of a god, to take over these tasks.

Our earliest records of the *Enuma Elish* have been dated from the 1300s, although they too are probably derived from earlier sources. More recently this account has been regarded as a late and sectarian story concerned with the localized elevation of Babylon and her god Marduk

---

[6] Rather than fill this chapter with footnotes, which would be inappropriate in a volume of this kind, the following works provide easiest access to most of the data included here: Alexander Heidel, *The Babylonian Genesis: The Story of Creation*, 2d. ed. (Chicago: University of Chicago Press, 1951); W.G. Lambert, "The Babylonian Background of Genesis," *JTS* 16 (1965): 287-300; Helmer Ringgren, *Religions in the Ancient Near East*, trans. John Sturdy (Philadelphia: Westminster, 1973); James K. Hoffmeier, "Some Thoughts on Genesis 1 & 2 and Egyptian Cosmology," *JANES* 15 (1983): 39-49; James P. Allen, *Genesis in Egypt: The Philosophy of Ancient Egyptian Creation Accounts* (New Haven: Yale Egyptological Seminar, 1988); John D. Currid, *Ancient Egypt and the Old Testament* (Grand Rapids: Baker, 1997). I am especially indebted here to Hoffmeier and Currid.

as both rose to prominence around 1500 B.C. In any case, Tiamat, the seawater, and her husband, Apsu, the fresh groundwaters, are the first to rise from primeval chaos, and their intermingling engenders other generations of gods. Apsu, seeking rest in his maturity, becomes agitated at the increasing activity and noise of the younger deities and plots their extermination. He is thwarted, however, by Ea, the god of the heavens, who casts a sleeping spell upon him, murders him, and builds his palace upon Apsu's water-corpse. Ea and his wife, Damkina, have their first son, the precocious Marduk, who is twice as strong, wise, and glorious as any other god.

In time, the younger deities seek to avenge Apsu's murder, and Kingu, new consort of Tiamat, is chosen as their leader. The other gods, terrified, choose Marduk, son of the usurper Ea. As battle is joined, Kingu is cowed by Marduk's magnificent appearance, but Tiamat with an accompanying host of serpent monsters is undeterred. However, with the help of the mighty north wind that distends Tiamat's watery body, Marduk shoots an arrow down her gullet. He celebrates his victory by dividing her watery carcass in two, creating heaven and earth, then the stars, plants, and other living things. After the battle, Kingu and his host are reduced to servitude but soon complain that this role is not fit for deities. Kingu is slain and his blood mixed with earth to create humans who are now to perform forced labour for the gods. They are particularly to provide for Marduk in his Temple at Babylon, which is then established. There is no mention of humans being made in the image of the deities, although the reference to the Lamga gods may imply some sense of humans reflecting divine statuary.

It should be noted, however, that this story is not primarily an explanation of creation, but is rather an aetiology to elevate Marduk, the chief god of the Babylonian pantheon, showing how he attained his supremacy in cosmological terms and to explain why Babylon (with its Temple) is the chief city. Some fifty names celebrate Marduk as the sustainer of life on earth and in heaven. His glorification undergirds and legitimates both divine and human institutions of governance, namely, the Temple and the kingship, which are the *sine qua non* of great Babylon's existence.[7]

(3) *Egyptian* – Surprisingly, although Israel had just spent 400 years in Egypt, relatively little attention has been given to Egyptian creation accounts which one might otherwise expect to provide the dominant

---

[7] R. J. Clifford, "Cosmogonies in the Ugaritic Texts and in the Bible," *Or* 53 (1984): 185.

background against which Genesis 1 was heard or read. And considering that Genesis is traditionally described as one of the books of Moses, from a literary standpoint it seems right to read it in the light of Israel's exodus. At the outset, it should be noted that there is no unitary or common Egyptian creation story but rather a range of variations depending on which deity is in view. Egyptians apparently accepted a variety of myths and rejected none with the result that the often meagre data derives from a range of diverse texts. Nevertheless, some characteristic themes emerge.

Unlike the Mesopotamians who believed in a number of creator gods, the Egyptians held only one deity responsible for their universe—referred to as "heaven and earth"—whether in the New Kingdom or in Memphite theology. The act of creation is described in various ways. In the Pyramid texts (c. 2350-2176 B.C.) there is a sudden emergence of a primordial mound(s) or hillock(s) (which the Pyramids symbolized) out of the watery void of Nun, upon which Atum materialized in an act of self-creation. These became the sites—the Holy Places of creation—upon which Temples were built. Atum then creates the lesser gods, all of whom are personifications of various elements of the natural world. In the Memphite texts (Old Kingdom, c. 2500-2200 B.C.) which polemicize against Atum theology, Ptah not only creates all, he is also the primeval waters that begat Atum.

In the little known stela of Ptah and Sekhmet we find the idea of creation through lordly speech where Ptah's tongue commands what his mind thinks—"One says in his mind (heart) 'Look, may they come into being'"—no preexistent material is used (cf. Ps 33:6). This idea of creation by decree is also found in a Coffin Text, where life is created "according to the word of Nun in Nu..." and Atum creates animal life through his command. One notes that Genesis 1 is thoroughly, even characteristically, permeated by the idea of Yahweh speaking creation into being.

Creation emerges from the deep, the darkness, the formlessness and emptiness, and the wind. The Coffin texts mention the Hermopolitan Ogdoad (also known as the Octead, see below) who are eight primordial beings—four pairs of cosmic forces and their consorts with the four males being toads and the four females snakes—who inhabited the primeval slime from which creation proceeds. There is some debate over their identification. On one view, Nun is a formless deep, Keku is darkness, Amun is a breath, and Hehu (the least clear) is some kind of illimitable chaos. On another reading, these eight consist of

Nun and Naunet, representing primordial matter and space, Kuk and
Kauket, the idea of the illimitable and the boundless, Huh and Hauhet,
for darkness and obscurity, and Amon and Amaunet, representing the
hidden and concealed. In Memphite theology these arise from Ptah, and
out of them emerges the sun. Interestingly, the biblical record begins
with Elohim and then speaks of a formlessness and emptiness, a deep, a
darkness, and a hovering wind (Gen 1:1-2).

    In terms of the order of creation, the god Re first creates light out of
darkness, and only after this the sun-god. This resembles Genesis 1
where Elohim creates light before the creation of the sun. Separation is
also a key idea with Ptah separating earth and sky and Atum separating
Geb (earth-god) from Nut (sky-goddess). In the Hermopolitan story the
primordial hill becomes the firmament which divides the upper and
lower waters. Given that the biblical idea of the "firmament" has
connotations of beaten metal, it is interesting that another Egyptian
tradition describes the resurrected king as taking possession of the sky
and then splitting or separating its metal.[8]

    In the Hymn to Khnum, we are told that the god "made plants in
the field, he dotted shores with flowers; he made fruit trees bear their
fruit," and this apparently precedes the creation of human beings. A
similar sequence is found in the Great Hymn to Amon, who puts the
stars in his path, and creates fish to live in the rivers and birds to live in
the sky, while Atum forms the Nile and calls it "the lord of fish and rich
in birds." One notes here the similar sequence of Genesis 1, beginning
with the sun, moon, stars, and then birds and fish, with the latter
together in the one set and even in the same order (Gen 1:20-21). The
fashioning of the animals and humanity is also linked in the Egyptian
accounts, as it is in day six in Genesis 1:24-26.

    Unlike the Babylonian traditions, the Egyptians grant a special role
to humans. According to the Great Hymn to Atum, the god "created
mankind and distinguished their nature and made their life." We also
find the making of man from clay with either Khnum being seen as a
potter molding humanity on his wheel (Great Hymn to Khnum) or Ptah
molding humanity with his hands. In the Instruction of Amenemope,
"Man is clay and straw, and God is his potter" and in a few texts there is
even the idea that humanity is made in the image of the god, as per the
Instruction of King Merikare: "They are his [Re] own images proceeding
from his flesh." The Egyptian word used here (snnw) is often written

_____

[8] Hoffmeier, "Some Thoughts," 43-45.

with a determinative in the shape of a statue. This is similar to Genesis 1's notion of humanity being made from the dust of the earth in Elohim's image (*tselem*), a word which initially meant a piece cut from an object and which would be entirely appropriate for a piece of clay cut for a sculpture.

As far as I can ascertain there is no notion in Mesopotamian stories of humanity being imparted breath by the gods. But in the Instruction of King Merikare—"[A]nd he (Re) made the air to give life to their (men) nostrils"—the impartation of life occurs through the breath of the creator-deity. On the other hand, the reason for the creation of humanity is unclear, though it seems a possibility that it was to carry out the creator-god's purposes.

Finally, the idea of the deity as craftsman is implied by the use of words that describe the metal worker who hammers and casts, or the master potter who molds, which would fit with the concept of a hammered firmament and with humans being fashioned from the earth.

Comparisons between Genesis 1 and Ancient Near Eastern Creation Myths

Some significant contours should be evident.[9] For the ancients the very order and coherence of the natural world implied some kind of personal agency. There is not a hint of the idea that the ordered world emerged from chaos by purely natural means. My point here is that no one wrote these texts to argue for the existence of the gods. That much was simply assumed. On this basis, Genesis 1 is unlikely to offer much succour for those who want to argue against Darwin. It was never designed to do so. More probably it was designed to answer the question: *which* god/s ordered and filled the heavens and the earth?

Whereas for moderns the process of creation is thoroughly materialistic, with the earth emerging merely as part of a larger solar system, and life, if discussed at all, being considered in only the most primitive form, for the ancients the primary concern is with the earth as the setting for the appearance of a fully formed human community and culture. In terms of the starting points, the motifs of water/watery deep, wind/storm, and formlessness are common, and, in the Egyptian Coffin Texts, one also finds the primeval darkness. Thus most stories, including in part Genesis 1, begin with either an amorphous mass or primeval

---

[9] For much of the following, see Clifford, "Cosmogonies," 185.

chaos, out of which through increasing differentitation heaven and earth are separated and ultimately a particularly social order emerges. Genesis 1 is unusual in that although it begins with the same basic elements it is more universal and seems uninterested in legitimating a specifically Israelite social order, though in the larger context of the Torah one might be expected to understand as much. In contrast to modern origins stories which utterly reject any psychologizing of what is seen as a purely "objective" materialist account, ancient stories—with the exception of Gensis—simply assumed a continuity between personified "nature" and the appearance of humanity.

Though absent from Egyptian or Sumerian accounts,[10] the idea of warfare is prominent in the "Babylonian" stories, and particularly in the defeat of the chaos-storm-monster (cf. the allusions in Job 26:12; Ps 89:10; Isa. 51:9). In such stories cosmogony was essentially a conflict of wills from which one party emerged victorious (so Ea/Apsu; Marduk/Tiamat; cf. Baal and Yam/Mot[11]). Babylonian stories also involved the use of magic on the part of the deities. In Egypt, however, there is only one creator god who creates and this by fiat through divine speech. But even so, their stories are still theogonic, that is, concerned with the emergence of the gods as personifications of aspects of nature. Apart from the single creator and creation by speech alone, none of these features is found in Genesis 1.

Humanity's purpose, while unclear in the Egyptian sources, in the Babylonian materials is to labour for Babylon's gods who then rest after they create humanity to do their work. The notion of humans bearing the deity's image is found only in Egypt and Genesis 1. In the latter, humans act as Elohim's vice-regents superintending his creation. Apart from Genesis 1 there appears to be no concern with duration or a literary framework wherein time is broken into a series of consecutive days. Only in the Baal palace-building story—and again there is debate over whether this is a creation narrative (fn. 11)—is there mention of a seven-day program to build Baal's palace-temple (cf. seven years for Solomon's temple; 1 Kgs 6:37-38).

---

[10] H.G. Güterbock, *JCS* 6 (1952): 29, 52-4; where a "saw" (uncertain word, based on etymology) is used.
[11] I have not included this story since there is some debate as to whether it is a creation story though I tend to agree with those who see it as such; cf. Loren R. Fisher, "Creation at Ugarit and in the Old Testament," *VT* 15 (1965): 313-24; and Clifford, "Cosmogonies."

Before considering this temple connection further, it is worth recalling Israel's exodus experience. They had just seen Yahweh, the god of the Fathers, uncreate Egypt by overturning the rule of Pharaoh, son of Amon-re, with the ten plagues that effectively dissolved the boundaries that gave the land of Egypt its order and form. And then at the Reed Sea (Exod 14:19-31) they had witnessed Yahweh cause light to shine in the darkness and a divine wind to drive back the deep of the *Yam Suph* (a sea that the Egyptians also regarded as the being at the edge of the world and the abode of Apophis the chaos serpent)[12] and so to reveal dry land.

Not only so, but Pharaoh's crown carried a Urea, an enraged female cobra, which functioned both as a symbol and the actual repository of Egypt's power.[13] Pharaoh's "father," the sun-god Re, after traveling through the heavens, would descend into the watery underworld of the dead, the sea of reeds. Escorted by two fire-breathing cobras he would do battle with Apophis the chaos serpent and emerge victorious each morning to bring life to Egypt. Like father like son, Pharaoh was to bring order and justice to Egypt by restraining the chaos of lawlessness.[14] One can understand why Pharaoh, as Amon-Re's son, thought he too could send his armies into the watery deep of the *Yam Suph* and emerge victorious. But as with Moses' first sign—the transformation of his judicial staff and symbol of his authority into a serpent that swallows those of Pharaoh's magicians—so too with the last, when Pharaoh's Urea-led armies are engulfed by the unrestrained sea, and that at Yahweh's command. It is hardly surprising, then, that the sight of their dead bodies on the shore of the *Yam Suph* (cf. the Sea of Reeds and Pool of the Dead[15]) had a considerable impact on Israel (Exod 15).[16] It is, therefore, probably not by accident that one can hear echoes of light in the darkness, the wind over the deep, and the appearance of dry

---

[12] J.R. Towers, "The Red Sea," *JNES* 18 (1959) 150-53; Walter Wifall, "The Sea of Reds as Sheol," *ZAW* 92 (1980): 325-32; and Bernard F. Batto, "Red Sea or Reed Sea?" *BAR* 10 (1984): 57-63.

[13] On the cobra and serpent in Egypt see Currid, *Ancient Egypt*, pp. 142-55.

[14] Wifall, "Sea of Reds," 325-32.

[15] Wifall, "Sea of Reds," 325-32.

[16] I wonder too if this might explain the choice of the serpent motif in the Garden of Eden. Are we to see in Eden a polemic against Pharaoh's anti-garden, that is, Egypt, replete with its own river of life (the Nile) and cosmic mountains (the Pyramids; cf. Ezek 28:13-14) wherein death instead of life prevails? Is the entry of the serpent a not-so-subtle declaration that it is the Pharaoh-like craftiness (Gen 3:1; cf. Exod 1:10) and god-like autonomy which has overtaken humanity that is the cause of humanity's present distress and alienation from the garden life that God intended?

land in Genesis 1: they had seen Yahweh do this when he delivered them at the *Yam Suph*.

This considerable similarity with the Egyptian accounts raises a very interesting question. It is sometimes suggested that the other ancient creation stories are distorted echoes of the original creation story, namely Genesis 1. This is always a possibility. But then one is left with a strange fact. How does one explain that it happens to be Egyptian stories, the place where Israel has just spent 400 years and which stories antedate considerably Israel's stay in Egypt, whose scattered details on the whole bear a greater resemblence to Genesis 1 than those, for example, of Mesopotamia? Might not a better explanation be the exact opposite? Namely, that it was the details of the varied Egyptian accounts that have influenced the language of Israel's creation story precisely to make it all the more effective against the gods of Egypt? Might it not be that Genesis 1 was written with a particular concern to declare that it was Israel's God, Yahweh, and not Ptah, Atum, or any other of Egypt's failed deities, who was alone responsible for the good and perfect order of creation?

It might also be that the clear literary art and architectonic patterning of Genesis 1 is a deliberate artistic device intended to underline the good order and patterning of Yahweh's creational activity. If so, what do we do with the order of the parallel three days? It seems to me that they are designed to reflect the same emergence of increasing order—form and fullness—we have seen elsewhere in the ancient world and particularly Egypt, but now at Yahweh's command. But why "three" days? I suggest it comes from the ancients' perception of the basic structures of their reality. The fundamental given of human existence is the experience of night and day, no matter whether one is above or below, or on sea or land. The next level of complexity is above and below, and then finally, on the below, the division between land and sea. These three days together delineate the fundamental structure of the ancient world as the ancients experienced it. But the structure was not created to remain void or empty, and so on the second set of three days Yahweh fills each of the realms with, as it were, their rulers (cf. Gen 1:16) up through finally the appearance of the image-bearer (Gen 1:26-27; see below).[17]

To return to the temple motif noted earlier, a key feature in a number of the stories is that the gods, having defeated the chaos

---

[17] Meredith Kline, *Kingdom Prologue* (South Hamilton, Mass.: privately published by Gordon-Conwell Theological Seminary, 1993), p. 25.

monster, construct their palace-temples. (In Hebrew "palace" and "temple" are represented by the same word, which in certain circumstances is synonymous with "house"—e.g., house of Yahweh—the idea going back to the Sumerians, where the word for temple is "big house"). As Arvid Kapelrud has argued, when one has defeated one's foes, be one human or divine, and has established one's realm, one builds a palace or temple.[18]

Creation as God's Palace-Temple

I want to pick up for a moment on the palace-temple image. If we ask how ancient peoples might have conceptualized their world, the answer seems to be as a palace-temple, such that creation becomes an act of palace-temple building. Egyptian sources contain hints of this, with several traditions mentioning some poles that lift the heaven over the earth and which are oriented toward the cardinal points. This might also explain the Egyptian practice of building Temples at various sites associated with the Holy Place/s of creation.[19] At the same time, the Egyptian cultic complex of the exodus period was a model of cosmic origins, with its lake of reeds and stately temple.[20]

In the "Babylonian" *Enuma Elish*, the outcome of Ea's victory over the watery god Apsu is not creation but the building of a palace-temple on the body of his foe.[21] Likewise, after Marduk's defeat of Tiamat he divides her corpse and stretches out one half like a roof to form the heavens, apparently forming the earth from the remainder, though the text breaks off at this point.[22] Similarly in the Canaanite story of Baal's victory over Yam, after Baal gains dominion, a house (temple) is constructed for him (as already noted opinions are divided over whether this is an account of creation but my interest here is the form of conceptualization). Baal's temple is a microcosm, and temple-building corresponds to creation such that creation, kingship, and temple-

---

[18] Arvid Kapelrud, "Temple Building, a Task for Gods and Kings," *Or* 32 (1966): 56-62.

[19] See James K. Hoffmeier, *'Sacred' in the Vocabulary of Ancient Egypt*, OBO 59 (Freiburg: Universitäts Verlag, Vandenhoeck und Ruprecht, 1985), pp. 171-77.

[20] E.A.E. Reymond, *The Mythological Origin of the Egyptian Temple* (Manchester: University Press, 1969).

[21] Tablet I.72.

[22] Tablet IV.129-32; cf. R. Labat, "Les origines et la formation de la terre dans le poeme babylonien de la creation," *SBOr* 3 (1959): 205-15.

building all belong together.[23] Interestingly Baal's temple is created in seven days and Yahweh's Jerusalem Temple, itself a microcosm, in seven years (1 Kgs 6:37-38).[24]

This metaphor is hardly surprising if one reflects for a moment on the realities of the ancient world. If the biggest threat to a settled agricultural existence was chaos, usually through war, lawlessness, or flood, then who was it that established order and security? Naturally, it was the great king who defeated the enemy, who promulgated and upheld the law (his word), and who supervised and orchestrated the building of dykes, etc., to restrain the devastating floods. Having established his realm he would then build his palace. If kings do this on a micro scale, then surely the gods do it at a cosmic one. In fact, it is in recognition of this connection that victorious kings, having entered into their rest, built temples for their deities.[25]

But is there any evidence of this notion in the Bible? The data is overwhelming. In Psalm 104:2-3 we are told that Yahweh "wraps himself in light as with a garment; he stretches out the heavens like a tent and lays the beams of his upper chambers on their waters." Isaiah 24:18 declares that "the windows of heaven are opened, and the foundations of the land tremble." One notes especially Job 38:4ff:

> Where were you when I laid the earth's foundation? ....
> Who marked off its dimensions?
> Surely you know!

---

[23] Fisher, "Creation," 313-24, strongly suggests a conceptual link between creation, kingship and temple building. Clifford agrees that the Baal texts are cosmologies because they focus on the final well being of humanity ("Cosmogonies"). See also J.C.L. Gibson, "The Theology of the Ugaritic Baal Cycle," *Or* 53 (1984): 203-19, who thinks that on the one hand the cosmological material of the first two tablets (Baal's defeat of Yam) have been shaped toward a seasonal reading, whereas in Baal's defeat of Mot (5 and 6) the seasonal has been shaped toward the cosmological. If so, then this suggests that the Baal story has already begun to take on cosmological overtones.

[24] On Yahweh's temple as a microcosm, see e.g., John D. Levenson, *The Theology of the Program of Restoration of Ezekiel 40-48*, Harvard Semitic Monographs 10 (Missoula: Scholars, 1976); Susan Niditch, "Ezekiel 40-48 in a Visionary Context," *CBQ* 48 (1986): 208-48; Margaret Barker, *The Gate of Heaven: The History and Symbolism of the Temple in Jerusalem* (London: SPCK, 1991); Ben F. Meyer, "The Temple at the Navel of the Earth," in *Christus Faber: The Master-Builder and the House of God.* (Allison Park: Pickwick, 1992), pp. 217-79; and John F. Kutsko, *Between Heaven and Earth: Divine Presence and Absence in the Book of Ezekiel*, BibJudStud 7 (Winona Lake: Eisenbrauns, 2000).

[25] Kapelrud, "Temple Building," 56-62.

Who stretched a measuring line across it?
On what were its footings set,
or who laid its cornerstone ....
Who shut up the sea behind doors ....
When I fixed limits for it and set its doors and bars in place ....
Have you entered the storehouses of the snow
Or seen the storehouses of the hail?

In fact, the Hebrew Bible is awash with architectural imagery when describing creation. It speaks of the foundations of the earth (Ps 18:15; 82:5; 102:25; 104:5; Prov 8:29; Isa 51:13,16; 2 Sam 22:8,16; Zech 12:1; cf. 2 Sam 22:8), the pillars of the earth and of the heavens (1 Sam 2:8; Job 9:6; Ps 75:3; Job 26:11), the heavens' windows (Gen 7:11; 8:2; Isa 24:18; Mal 3:10; 2 Kgs 7:2; Ps 104:2), the stretching out of the heavens like a canopy/tent (Isa 40:12,22; 42:5; 44:24; 45:12; 48:13; 51:13; Jer 10:12; 31:37; 32:17; 51:15; Amos 9:6; Zech 12:1; Job 9:8; Ps 102:25), and storehouses (Deut 28:12; Jer 10:13; 50:25; 51:16; cf. Ps 33:7; 135:7; Job 38:22).

But what kind of building is this? As Isaiah 66:1 makes clear, "Heaven is my throne, and the earth is my footstool. Where is the house you will build for me? Where will my resting place be?" Where does one find a throne and a footstool if not in a palace, and what is the palace of Yahweh if not a temple?[26] And note too the image of resting in his house (= Temple) in the light of Yahweh's resting in his completed abode on the seventh day of Genesis 1. In this sense, the whole of creation is seen as Yahweh's palace-temple, and hence the reason for his Jerusalem temple itself being a microcosm, a mini universe: it serves to remind Israel that the whole world is Yahweh's.[27] Granted, Genesis 1 does not explicitly describe Yahweh as actually rolling up his sleeves and "building" — why should it when a truly Lordly Yahweh would merely have to give the word? But given the rather widespread Ancient Near Eastern notion linking creation, defeat-of-chaos, and temple-building, and the thorough-going architectural imagery which characterizes the biblical conceptualizing of creation, it would be very odd if Genesis 1 were not to be understood along the lines of cosmic palace-temple building. As the Great King, Elohim naturally creates realms for the lesser rulers (cf. Gen 1:16) as he forms his palace-temple out of the deep

---

[26] See Kline, *Kingdom*, pp. 17-18.
[27] Cf. Crispin Fletcher-Louis, "The Temple Cosmology of P and Theological Anthropology in the Wisdom of Jesus ben Sira," in *Of Scribes and Sages: Studies in Early Jewish Interpretation and Transmission of Scripture*: SSEJC 8, ed. C.A. Evans (Sheffield: Academic, 2002); Josephus, *War*, 5.5.4 (5.212-14).

and gives order to and fills it. And as the Great King, having ordered his realm, he now rules over all in "Sabbath" rest (see Exod 20), sitting in the great pavilion of his cosmos-palace-temple (cf. Ps 93).

This might also explain some elements of John's Revelation where he describes the New Jerusalem as coming down out of the heavens to earth (Rev 21). One striking feature is the absence of any Temple (Rev 21:22). The odd cube shape of the city might explain this. The only other biblical objects in a similar setting that are cube-shaped are the Holy of Holies in the Tabernacle (10 cubits, probably) and Solomon's temple (20 cubits; 1 Kgs 6:20; 2 Chr 3:8; cf. the Holy Place in Ezekiel's temple, 500 cubits square, Ezek 42:16-20; 45:2). If so, then this suggests that the reason there is no temple in the New Jerusalem is because the city itself has become, not just the Temple, but the very Holy of Holies (cf. also Ezek 45:2-3). But what about the surprising size of the city: 12,000 stadia (approximately 1,500 miles) along each axis? The significance of these dimensions might lie in the observation that the size of the city corresponds to that of the then-known Greek world, while the height emphasizes the co-mingling of heaven and earth.[28] In other words, the climax of the new creation is not the abandonment of the earth, but instead the coming of Yahweh himself to the earth to dwell among us. Here, then, is the climax of Genesis 1's seven-fold affirmation of the goodness of creation with its progression in both sets of days from heaven to earth. The final goal is not the destruction of creation, but rather the unification of heaven and earth such that the renewed earth itself now becomes Yahweh's very throne room.

Further support for this palace-temple conceptualization is found in the final act of creation: the forming of humanity, male and female, in the image of Elohim. Long the subject of debate, the image of God language makes a great deal of sense within the palace-temple context. After all, what is the last thing placed inside the deity's house, if not his image? So here in Genesis 1 on the last creative day, Yahweh fashions his own image and places it in his palace-temple. At the same time, as Shelley's poem *Ozymandias* so evocatively describes, ancient kings frequently placed images of themselves throughout their realms as signs of their power and sovereign authority. It is highly likely that in the biblical account humanity serves the same function. Thus, both Israel (Exod 4:22) and her king (Ps 2:8) are called to be God's son in the sense of

---

[28] See G.K. Beale, *The Book of Revelation*, NIGTC (Grand Rapids: Eerdmans, 1999), pp. 1073-74.

being faithful bearers of his image, that is, to reflect his character and to act as his vice-regents as they live in his palace-temple.

From this perspective, Genesis 1 is a "poetic" account in which Yahweh, Israel's god, is alone proclaimed the builder of creation, his palace-temple. It is he and no other who by the fiat of his kingly command provided the fundamental structures of ancient human experience and who filled these sub-realms with their rulers, over all of which he has placed humanity, his image-bearer, as his vice-regent.

Conclusions

What might we conclude about the truth claims and significance of Genesis 1? Given its genre—a highly stylized form and unrealistic content—I would suggest that it is not to be taken "literally" in the popular modern Western sense as a blow-by-blow, chronologically accurate, account of creation. No one in the ancient world, apart from the isolated account of the time taken to build Baal's palace, seems particularly concerned with these kinds of questions. Our chronos-fixated age measures things in nanoseconds and smaller—but not theirs. Rather, the pattern of days probably derives from the ancients' understanding of the structure of their world—day/night, above/below, and land/sea—this being conceptualized in terms of the deity's construction of his palace-temple as he gives it form and fills it. The fundamental issue is that it is Yahweh, Israel's God, a God who cares for slaves, non-entities, and even non-Israelites (cf. the mixed multitude who are also delivered from Pharaoh's genocidal proclivities; Exod 12:38), who brought order to the world, not the failed deities of oppressive Egypt nor, to a lesser degree, those of Canaan or Mesopotamia. And in doing so, it uses the language and imagery to which that world, and particularly Egypt, was accustomed. This is hardly suprising.

On this reading the twenty-four hour periods, or more accurately dawn-to-dusk days, probably reflect the notion of the customary daily periods of work. Yahweh is the builder, and each day he speaks and thus by divine fiat builds or fills a discrete part of his realm. Consequently, the injunction to keep Sabbath is less intent on imitating six literal twenty-four-hour days of creation than it is a summons for Israel to live out her creation story—structured as it is in the nature of the case by six days with a seventh to rest—and so to declare herself to be Yahweh's "son," imitating him in continuing his creation work of bringing order with the ultimate goal of Sabbath rest.

So in what sense is this true? If this kind of metaphor, symbol, or antiquated way of seeing the world is all that is intended, how does it translate into our modern world? In what sense can this be meaningful for us? The answer is surprisingly modern. We recall that for the ancients the fundamental concern of their stories was the emergence of humanity, society, and culture. It was the same for Israel. Yahweh has designed this palace-temple, this pavilion, to be the habitation of his image-bearer, namely, humanity. This, it seems to me, is nothing other than the ancient version of the recently formulated Anthropic Principle, which in its various forms reflects the fact that the fundamental structures of this world, the observed values of its cosmological and physical quantities, appear to have been fine-tuned with human existence in view.[29] To observers both then and now there are strong hints that this creation was designed for us. And Genesis 1's answer, it seems to me, is not so much concerned with the "how" in the technical or mechanical sense as it is with the "who," namely, Yahweh. It is Israel's God who has created this world, and humanity will never truly know what it means to be human until we learn to reflect his image. There is truth here, but it is more like the pungent and memorable truth of Blake's "Tiger, Tiger" than the serried ranks of mathematically precise gene maps.

Two final observations. If this creation is Yahweh's palace-temple, then we had best take good care of it. Far too many of us treat our homes far better than we treat this creation. We would never tolerate toxic waste or unbridled pollution in our living rooms, and yet we seem happy to do so when it comes to God's palace-temple. While some have mistakenly read the apocalyptic language of purging fire as a *carte blanche* to do whatever they will to this present earth,[30] we might do well to remember the warning in Revelation 11:18: God will destroy those who destroy his earth. Given that it is his palace-temple, and that far from people going

---

[29] See e.g., John D. Barrow and Frank J. Tipler, *The Anthropic Cosmological Principle* (Oxford: Oxford University Press, 1988).

[30] A classic case is the older translation of 2 Pet 3:7-13, in which the earth was to be destroyed. But as more recent translations recognize, the better reading is "the earth and all that is done in it will be disclosed." The imagery of this chapter derives from Israel's experience at Sinai where the heavens were moved aside, and amid fire and thunder, Yahweh came face to face with his creation. The fire then concerns not destruction but purging, and just like with the flood the wicked will be swept away, while the purified earth will remain.

to heaven, heaven is coming here (at least if Revelation 21 is to be believed), God's anger against violators of the earth is perfectly understandable. It is his palace-temple they are defiling, whereas he is committed to renewing it.

Second, if humans are made in God's image, then the repercussions are serious indeed. In the ancient world, to deface the image of the king or deity was tantamount to high treason. If one did not want to live in his realm or under his kingship, that could be arranged, either by exile or death. If we take the Genesis 1 account seriously, namely, that every human being is made in God's image, then we need to know that any act of abuse against another human being is an act of high treason against the God whose image we bear and to whose kingship and sovereignty we therefore inherently bear witness. With this in mind, it is not hard to comprehend why Jews and Christians have historically put such a high value on human life, whether women, slaves, gladiators, newly born, or even unborn children.

It seems to me that this kind of reading of Genesis not only makes good sense of the text within its cultural horizons, but puts the emphasis back where it belongs. Perhaps it is time to stop warring, for example, over the length of the days and instead to recall what Genesis 1 is more likely about. This world is God's temple-palace and he has not abandoned it. If we are truly to bear his image, then neither should we. Not only so, but every human being is made in God's image. From this perspective, it makes a great deal of sense for Jesus as God's son among us not only to cleanse Israel's microcosmic temple, but also to restore our image — opening blind eyes, deaf ears, raising the dead, etc. Nor is it hard to see why he sums up the Law and the Prophets with the dual command to love God and neighbour. Little wonder Paul speaks of a new creation. With these truths firmly in mind and heart, it would be difficult for Christians not to change the world.

Chapter 8

Biophilia and the Gospel:

Loving Nature or Worshipping God?

John R. Wood

Recent Television news shows have run film of a pod of killer whales swimming within sight of Seattle. What remains so alive in us that we willingly interrupt our consumption of the ritualized stories of violence, economic intrigue, and political scandal to watch spellbound? Could it be that we have not lost our instinct for grace, that, at heart, we desire the salvation of being at home in a peaceable kingdom ruled by laws we cannot divine?

John Leax, **Approaching the Narrows.**[1]

W hat creature do you love? By the thread of that simple question hangs a tale that I think affects us all. The world seems to divide itself between those who love creatures of the earth and others who are seemingly indifferent or even occasionally hostile to what we call the creation, or nature. I sometimes ask people, "What creature do you love?" When posing this question in a Christian audience I can easily be misunderstood. "What are you, some kind of New Ager?" Perhaps that question also goes through some of the readers' minds. But

---

[1] John Leax, *Out Walking: Reflections on Our Place in the Natural World* (Grand Rapids: Baker, 2000), p. 140.

how is it that we have come to a place today where loving God's creation is taken as a sign of infidelity to the Creator?

The love of life in contemporary scientific terms has been called "biophilia."[2] It expresses the tendency to orient ourselves to living things, and to pay attention to movement in life-like systems. Even a casual observer can see this happening every day. We invariably orient ourselves to other people and often pay close attention to the domestic animals and even the plants that fill our lives. We spend time and money on preferred forms of nature, and we make emotional attachments to an astonishingly wide variety of creatures. The term "biophilia" was coined by Edward O. Wilson to explain what he regards as the "innately emotional affiliation of human beings to other living organisms."[3] The biophilia hypothesis incorporates this positive reaction to other species. But it also includes the negative response we may have to living things. Our fears, disgusts and phobias, it is said, also reveal how deeply we are psychologically entwined in living systems. "We need other species not only for the promise of material and physical sustenance but, just as important," Stephen Kellert says, "for the raw material they offer for our psychological and intellectual growth."[4] If Kellert and Wilson are right, then this biophilia tendency is profoundly part of what it means to be human. And as such it should be evident in the biblical descriptions of the human-nature relationship.

The technical term "biophilia" has an awkward sound to our ears. But such words can help us see a relationship that we might not otherwise recognize. The Scripture calls this concept simply our kinship of common creatureliness.[5] And it both recognizes and resolves the tension produced by our being placed in a network of biophysical relationships. The Lord God brings the animals to Adam "to see what he would name them" (Gen 2:19). Now if we only focus on the fact that "no suitable helper was found" we miss the first point of this story. Humans

---

[2] Edward O. Wilson, *Biophilia* (Cambridge: Harvard University Press, 1984), p.1.

[3] Stephen R. Kellert and Edward O. Wilson, ed., *The Biophilia Hypothesis* (Washington: Island, 1993), p. 31.

[4] See Kellert and Wilson, *Biophilia Hypothesis*, p. 457.

[5] Technically the human-nature relationship is said to be one of tension, and our *hypostasis* is a necessary polarity of transcendence and immanence. See Colin E. Gunton's Didsbury Lectures, *Christ and Creation* (Carlisle: Paternoster; Grand Rapids: Eerdmans, 1992), pp. 35-46. See also Richard A. Young, *Healing the Earth: A Theocentric Perspective on Environmental Problems and Their Solutions* (Nashville: Broadman & Holman, 1994), pp. 65-68.

are creatures, too. God brought the creatures to Adam out of an existing relationship. They are also the dust of the earth. This is what biology texts sometimes call in shorthand "SPONCH" (or "CHNOPS"). Each letter in the acronym is the symbol of a chemical element on the periodic chart. These six elements—sulphur, phosphorous, oxygen, nitrogen, carbon, and hydrogen—are the most common chemical building blocks of life. Together they comprise between 90 and 99% of the atoms in the molecules of the bodies of most living organisms on earth. Of course, this mnemonic device needs to be qualified because there are other common elements, too.[6] The device is nonetheless helpful in drawing our attention to the fact that both the Old Story (the biblical account) and the New Story (the scientific account) of creation are important.[7] The colourful term "dust" is so commonplace that we easily miss the punchline of the story. We, like all the other creatures are the SPONCH of the earth—a fact of which Adam is forcefully reminded later, in Genesis 3:19. So, our relatedness as creatures begins with our common chemical composition. The New Story then extends our insight from elemental building blocks to the incredibly complex macromolecules of DNA that carry the code of life. From Adam to elephants, David to dugongs,[8] and from Solomon to sabre-tooth tigers, we are the SPONCH of the earth. These building blocks, from the chemical elements to DNA molecules, make up the rose of Sharon and the cedar of Lebanon, and our Cornflakes and coffee, too. In short, they make up us.[9]

Biophilia, it is said, may provide "a framework for an inter-disciplinary research agenda on understanding the human relationship

---

[6] Helena Curtis and N. Sue Barnes, *Invitation to Biology*, 5th ed. (New York: Worth, 1989). There are actually many more than these six elements that are critical to life. Among the other vital components are sodium, potassium, calcium, iron, magnesium and other metals. The SPONCH elements, however, illustrate nicely our dependency on complex biogeochemical cycles that are mediated by living systems.

[7] Loren Wilkinson notes that "[m]uch recent religious thought on 'the environment' proceeds from the assumption that the 'Old Story' of Christian orthodoxy has been exhausted...." Hence the need for a New Story of the cosmos. But he concludes "that Trinitarian Christian orthodoxy provides us with a more adequate framework for the care of creation than any of the variations of monism now being prescribed" ("The New Story of Creation: A Trinitarian Perspective," *Crux* 30, no. 4 [1994]: 26–36).

[8] Dugongs and sea cows are close relatives of the Florida manatee.

[9] See Theodore Hiebert for a discussion of the theological basis and importance of these facts in "Rethinking Traditional Approaches to Nature in the Bible," in *Theology for Earth Community: A Field Guide*, ed. Dieter T. Hessel (Maryknoll, New York: Orbis, 1996), p. 28.

with nature."[10] But since this theory still needs rigorous scientific testing it is tempting to dismiss it out of hand as merely speculative. However, closely examining these challenging ideas may help us see nature with fresh eyes and help us gain new insights into Scripture. The starting point of biblical faith is that God creates everything. We are all creatures, and that places us in a web of horizontal and vertical relationships.[11] The message of modern biology—both the speculative biophilia hypothesis and the biochemical facts of life—is forcing us to look again at who we are as human beings. We are also being challenged by the impact our technologies have on the environment to reconsider our relationship with the creatures of the earth. The biophilia concept may help us see both nature and the gospel with fresh eyes.

God has chosen to sustain our lives through cosmic and planetary processes in a complex web of physical and biological relationships. This New Story of scientific discovery has been told through the media and in schools so often that even children learn its outline. We must first of all recognize that this is one way in which God sees us.[12] We are SPONCH-ly creatures of recycled star stuff, curiously poised between heaven and earth. And as David says in Psalm 8, remarkably, we are the objects of our Creator's interest. But there is a tendency among some individuals to over-play, and among others to down-play, the significance of this narrative. The problem seems to be twofold. We either view ourselves as only animals, although God gives this particular species dominion (e.g., Ps 8), or we claim we can use the world in any way we please, although God is in fact the master (e.g., Ps 24:1-2). Perhaps, as James Houston and others have pointed out, we need to see the heavenly humour in our cosmic situation and in our refusal to see ourselves as God does.[13]

Loving Nature

We like nature and are drawn to it in many ways. Our most common responses to creation are simple pleasure, aesthetic wonder, and even deep emotion. The natural world is a source for much of our recreation

---

[10] Peter H. Kahn, *The Human Relationship with Nature: Development and Culture* (Cambridge: MIT Press, 1999), pp. 25, 43.

[11] Gunton, *Christ and Creation*, p. 36.

[12] Loren Wilkinson notes that "when the New Story of creation is centered on the cross, and the self-giving of the creator which it expresses, then we can understand how that New Story fits into the larger narrative of the Old Story ("The New Story of Creation," 36).

[13] James M. Houston, *I Believe in the Creator* (Grand Rapids: Eerdmans, 1980), p. 222.

and leisure time activities. A recent survey has shown that each year over two-thirds of Canadians visit natural areas for a variety of activities.[14] We like nature so much that we construct expensive facilities (zoos, aquariums, and museums), and it turns out that more people visit them than attend professional sporting events.

But it isn't just wild nature to which we love being near; gardening, lawn care and other horticultural activities are also very popular. We bring everything from pet rocks to parakeets and from fish to fungi into our homes. The billion-dollar pet industry has blossomed into a multi-national enterprise, complete with big box chain stores. The array of pet related products and services rivals that available for humans. Today we can arrange for our animals to have a veterinarian surgeon, a psychologist, vacation care, and cleaning specialists, or even a mortician.[15]

We have found that pets are important to our well-being. Companion animals of various kinds are a growing part of health care, especially with an ageing population. Other pets become working animals, like the so-called "dogs with jobs." Our affinity for pets can run deep, and we grieve for the broken relationship when a pet animal is lost. We may debate the relative merit of the companionship of pets for humans; we must admit, however, that the feelings we have for them are real. As more than one person has said, "Dogs are little people in fur coats." Whether this is a good attitude to take or a moral misjudgement on our part is widely debated.[16] Yet even the Scripture acknowledges the

---

[14] Federal-Provincial-Territorial Task Force on the Importance of Nature to Canadians, *The Importance of Nature to Canadians: Survey Highlights* (Minister of Public Works and Government Services Canada, 1999).

[15] This growth provides an opportunity for specialized Christian witness and evangelism. In the last two decades a number of Christian professionals in the animal care field have joined together in associations, such as the Christian Veterinary Mission, to use their gifts in professional veterinary medicine and in this way share the love of Christ around the world.

[16] The debate often begins by someone asking a question actually intended to end it: "Will there be pets in heaven?" For a positive case for transforming our response to animals see Richard A. Young, *Is God a Vegetarian? Christianity, Vegetarianism, and Animal Rights* (Chicago: Open Court, 1999); or Stephen H. Webb, *On God and Dogs: A Christian Theology of Compassion for Animals* (New York: Oxford, 1998). For a more restricted view of their place based on the work of St. Thomas Aquinas in *Summa Theologiae*, see Joseph Kirwan, "Greens and Animals," in *The Cross and the Rain Forest: A Critique of Radical Green Spirituality*, ed. Robert Whelan, Joseph Kirwan and Paul Haffner (Grand Rapids: Acton Institute; Eerdmans, 1996), ch. 3. Some animal rights

value of pets. The story that the prophet Nathan used when rebuking King David only works because the lamb is the poor man's pet, a "member of the family" (2 Sam 2). David is outraged, and he reacts emotionally because he recognizes that the lamb is an object of genuine care and concern.

But there is also a dark side to our interest in animals. Animals in our care are not only at risk of neglect, but also of direct abuse. Our treatment of animals, both domestic and wild, has historically been contested ground.[17] British and North American Christians vigorously advocated humane standards in the early nineteenth century.[18] The harm we inflict does not always occur deliberately. Pets purchased on a whim, especially around the holidays, are often released outdoors or humanely destroyed. The introduction of unwanted native and exotic species is a concern to conservation biologists because they can become serious, billion dollar pests.[19] So our love affair with the natural world can sometimes go sour, with lasting consequences. But negative interactions and even the anxiety and fear engendered by nature are also part of biophilia as it is broadly defined. We have, it is claimed, for good and for ill, an innate affinity with nature.

God Loves Nature Too

It may seem surprising to suggest that God is in love with this world, but these are the very words used in Psalm 145:17. He has an immense affinity with both the living and non-living things of the earth.[20] His care for creation is evident when it says that he is good to the animals (Ps 145:9), preserving them (Ps 36:6), and providing for them (Ps 104:10-14; Matt 6:26). [21] Scripture is filled with metaphors and descriptions of a lovingly crafted creation. The story of God's love in the Song of Songs is

---

activists see a sinister face in domesticaton, e.g., Paul Shepherd, "On Animal Friends," in Kellert and Wilson, *Biophilia*, pp. 284-88.

[17] Andrew C. Isenberg, *The Destruction of the Bison: An Environmental History, 1750 - 1920* (Cambridge: Cambridge University Press, 2000), pp. 143-46.

[18] Andrew Linzey, *Animal Gospel* (Louisville: Westminster John Knox Press, 1998), pp. 11-17.

[19] George W. Cox, *Alien Species in North America and Hawaii: Impacts on Natural Ecosystems* (Washington: Island, 1999).

[20] The meaning of the terms "world" and "worldly," "earth" and "earthly" have been problematic for Christians and the source of dualistic and Gnostic readings of Scripture, says Young, *Healing the Earth*, pp. 244-49.

[21] For a longer treatment of God's love of nature, especially animals, see Young, *Is God a Vegetarian?* pp. 83-86.

moulded from rich earthy language. In this book the pages drip with environmental metaphors for love.[22]   The whole of creation history, according to Robert Farrar Capon can be pictured as a love story. The Trinity is "creating the world out of pure fun," he says. And Christ (the Word) in this epic boy-meets-girl drama is "romancing creation into being and becoming incarnate to bring it home."[23]   God delights in his craftsmanship, especially in humble humanity (Prov 8:30). Looking at creation through the eyes of love changes everything.

In Genesis 9:8-12 God declares, "I now establish my covenant with you and with your descendants after you and with *every living creature* that was with you ...." Reading these words today as a biologist, I find their implications intellectually staggering. God is love, and the process of creating (and sustaining) the cosmos is an act of love.[24] One of the clearest expressions of this love of the creation, biblical commentators point out, is in the book of Job. The speech to Job, beginning in chapter 38 and continuing to chapter 41, is the longest narration by God recorded in Scripture. The answer to Job's deepest questions is not given in terms of the wonder of humanity, but instead God directs Job's attention to the marvel of the created order. Although modern science might partially answer some of the ecological questions raised here, the cosmos remains a place of deep mystery. His love for it and us still does not yield to easy formulas.

If we notice God's loving attitude toward all that he has made, our attitude changes. We can more easily see the reciprocal praise of God by his creatures. The new insights in ecological science can also help us in reading Scripture in this relational way.[25] The very earth is urged to sing out, we read in Psalm 148. All of the created order gives voice, and—of special interest to entomologists—so do the "*small creatures*" (Ps 148:10). The ecological spectrum here is majestic in its sweeping breadth. When

---

[22] Janice and Donald Kirk drew my attention to the environmental connection of this love language in *Cherish the Earth: The Environment and Scripture* (Scottdale: Herald, 1993), p. 12.

[23] Robert Farrar Capon, *The Romance of the Word: One Man's Love Affair with Theology* (Grand Rapids: Eerdmans, 1995), p. 237.

[24] R. Scott Rodin, *Stewards in the Kingdom: A Theology of Life in All Its Fullness* (Downers Grove: InterVarsity, 2000), p. 69.

[25] Brian J. Walsh, Marianne B. Karsh and N. Ansell, "Trees, Forestry, and the Responsiveness of Creation," in *This Sacred Earth: Religion, Nature, Environment*, ed. Roger S. Gottlieb (New York: Routledge, 1996), pp. 423-35. This paper closely relates to my thesis. They ask, "Can we listen to trees, and through new paradigms in forestry and tree biology facilitate such a listening?" p. 423.

the psalmist wrote "small creatures" he was probably thinking of some tiny birds or mammals. But the Hebrews were keen observers of insects, too; so I like to imagine that he had insects and perhaps other invertebrates in mind. We might pause to meditate for a moment on the fact that all of these little creatures are busy in their ecological communities, oblivious to us, but doing exactly as their maker bids them. And we should carefully consider, too, that God is in love with this bio-diverse creation.

Nature, the Gospel, and Worship

Yet, for all our interaction with nature, and our knowledge that God loves it, we seldom see it as a serious part of our Christian experience of worshipping God. True, if you check the index in a hymnal there are songs that feature nature or creation.[26] And these songs contain rich theological insights into the multi-faceted relationship between God, humans, and the rest of creation.[27] But the majority of worship choruses, both contemporary and classic, that are sung by evangelicals are focused single-mindedly on Christ, God as Father, the Holy Spirit and us. "The things of earth," we sing, "will grow strangely dim, in the light of His glory and grace."[28] Choruses are often love songs to Jesus. It is true that in the arms of a passionate lover all else does fade away, and rightly so. But we do not live forever in embrace, or always in the mountain top experience.[29] There is more than one way to fully comprehend a lover's attributes. And one of the greatest ways to experience God is within the creation itself. But we often close the doors in our worship of God to all but the human-built dimensions of creation. The rest of the created order is mostly absent from our regular worship.

There are, however, some important ways in which nature does enter into our religious experience. We have a set lexicon of Bible stories in the Sunday school curriculum that feature nature themes. They are important starting points for learning about our relation to both Creator

---

[26] The "God in Creation" section of a typical Protestant hymnal contains about twenty songs out of the standard 450-500 hymns.

[27] S. Paul Schilling, "God and Nature in Hymnody," *The Hymn* 42, no. 1 (1991): 24 - 28. He also notes that the newer mainline and ecumenical hymns recognize ambiguity in our position in creation.

[28] Helen Howarth Lemmel, "Turn Your Eyes upon Jesus" (Grand Rapids: Singspiration; Zondervan, 1922).

[29] This commonly used Christian analogy is remarkable in that for most people it has little to do with the actual experience of mountains.

and creation. These stories are helpful because the moral points they make are widely and readily understood. However, since we adults already know both the plot and the moral it becomes difficult to hear the message of these stories in our changing cultural context. If we see them mainly as children's stories, the force of these narratives can be lost on us. The message of Noah and the Ark is an example. Over the years Cal DeWitt has worked to help us hear anew the message of Noah and the Ark. He claims, but not without contention, that it speaks directly to the endangered species question of our day.[30]

But perhaps our most common experience of worship in a natural setting occurs in summer camps. Here we actively seek out scenic natural settings for worshipping God. Missionaries have taken this tradition around the globe, and para-church organizations specialize in it.[31] Our affinity for nature is used as a venue for intensive evangelism. It is not an accident that the most successful camps are found in wondrous scenic locations in the mountains, the forests or overlooking the lakes or oceans. We love nature, and in retreating to it, as we say, we mimic, though imperfectly, the wilderness experience of the prophets and desert saints. When we draw away into nature we are drawing closer to God.[32] Recently a number of thoughtful writers have urged us to direct our attention toward more fully recovering this experience of God's grace in the setting of nature. The essays of John Leax come to mind, as well as book-length treatments by Lionel Basney, Janice and Donald Kirk and Scott Hoezee.[33]

---

[30] Calvin B. DeWitt, "The Price of Gopher Wood," in *The Best Preaching On Earth: Sermons on Caring for Creation*, ed. Stan L. LeQuire (Valley Forge: Judson, 1996), pp. 181-84; or his *Caring for Creation: Responsible Stewardship of God's Handiwork* (Grand Rapids: Baker, 1998), pp. 21-23, 52-55; for Thomas Sieger Derr's caution on the Noah story, see pp. 82-83.

[31] Christian Camping International and Young Life are but two of many examples.

[32] Susan Power Bratton has written extensively on the concept of wilderness and Christian formation. See her *Christianity, Wilderness, and Wildlife: The Original Desert Solitaire* (Scranton: University of Scranton Press, 1993).

[33] Lionel Basney, *An Earth-Careful Way of Life: Christian Stewardship and the Environmental Crisis* (Downers Grove: InterVarsity, 1994); Scott Hoezee, *Remember Creation: God's World of Wonder and Delight* (Grand Rapids: Eerdmans, 1998); Kirk, *Cherish the Earth*; Leax, *Out Walking*. Also see the many articles in *Creation Care* published by the Evangelical Environmental Network.

Loving Nature *or* Worshipping God

If we have the capacity both for responding lovingly to nature and for worshipping God, then we should be restless without these attributes in our lives. But isn't there a danger of confusing loving nature with our love of God, and of worshipping it instead of him? Yes, this is certainly possible. And there are a number of good reasons why evangelical Christians have been cautious about the relationship between nature and faith. We have the clear biblical warning not to worship created things (Exod 20:4-6; Deut 4: 15-19). And because it is easy for humans to get mixed up, this warning is repeated throughout Scripture (Isa 40:19ff; 44:9ff.; Rom 1:18-23). But the simple option of loving nature *or* worshipping God implied by the title of this chapter turns out to be a false dilemma. Here Francis Schaeffer's powerful insight into our relationship with creation can help us gain some clarity. "If I love the Lover," he comments, "I love what the Lover has made." He goes on to suggest, "Perhaps this is the reason why so many Christians feel an unreality in their Christian lives. If I don't love what the Lover has made—in the area of man, in the area of nature—and really love it because He made it, do I really love the Lover at all?"[34] So it may be that we are actually too cautious here and, as Susan Bratton notes, our "fear of idolatry may now inhibit any spiritual exercise in nature."[35]

Over the last decade there has been a rich flow of biblical scholarship and pastoral counsel on this subject. John Stott puts it this way: "It is not only possible to love and enjoy the rich diversity of the natural world," he says, "it is required of us."[36] The works of the Lord, he is saying, are the subject of our stewardly study. The enormous variety in the universe becomes the subject of our worship, but it is explicitly not the object we are worshipping. We need to remember, Stott counsels, that the deeds of the Lord are the reasons for which we give praise to the Creator. And Alister McGrath adds significantly that "[t]here is no place in Christianity for the worship of nature ... God alone is to be worshiped. Yet we must respect and care for nature as the work

---

[34] Francis Schaeffer, *Pollution and the Death of Man: The Christian View of Ecology* (Wheaton: Tyndale, 1970), pp. 91-92.
[35] Susan Bratton, "Teaching Environmental Ethics from a Theological Perspective," *REd* 85 (1990): 28.
[36] John R.W. Stott, "The Works of the Lord," in *Best Preaching*, ed. LeQuire, pp. 78-83.

of the same God who loves and redeems us."[37] But today we seem to be trapped in a fear of cultural contamination that won't let us express our rightful appreciation of creation.

Do We Have a Theological Blind Spot?

The Hebrews often mixed up the distinction between worship of God and worship of nature. And so can we. That is why the warnings in Scripture are so clear. But whenever Israel asks itself the question, "why should we worship God?" repeatedly it answers by asserting that we worship God because he is both our Saviour *and* the Maker of heaven and earth. The biblical writers deliberately and self-consciously link the themes of salvation and creation.[38] Recently evangelical theologians have begun to emphasize this fact.[39] They note that redemption is never separated from the sustaining action of God in creation. But throughout most of the twentieth century, North American Protestants have not noticed this connection. And so, Jonathan Wilson claims, "we have failed to maintain a proper dialectic of creation and redemption."[40] What he means is that what we know (and believe) about God's work in nature needs to interact with what we believe about the gospel. The saving grace of Christ, who redeems me, is also made available to the rest of creation (e.g., Col 1:15-16, 19 - 20; Rom 8:19). "This does not demean the work of Christ, but rather amplifies it."[41] If this is true, why do we so seldom think of our attitude about the environment as a matter of faith?

It seems, according to John Jefferson Davis, that we have developed a theological blind spot. His survey of systematic theology textbooks shows that in discussing the doctrine of creation theologians

[37] Alister E. McGrath, "Recovering the 'Creation': A Response to Hugh Montefiore," *Trans* 16 (1999): 80. Also see Ron Sider, "Tending the Garden without Worshiping It," in *Best Preaching*, ed. LeQuire, pp. 30-40.

[38] The following are a few examples: Ps 33; 96:11-13; 115; Isa 44:24-26; Jer 12; 14:15-17; Acts 17:27; 1 Cor 4:1-2; 1 Cor 16: 25-36.

[39] For a summary of the literature on the cosmic nature of Christ's redemption see John Jefferson Davis, "Ecological 'Blind Spots' in the Structure and Content of Recent Evangelical Systematic Theologies," *JETS* 43 (2000): 275, n. 11.

[40] Jonathan R. Wilson, "Evangelicals and the Environment: A Theological Concern," *CSR*, 28 (1998): 298-307.

[41] Fred Van Dyke, David C. Mahan, Joseph K. Sheldon and Raymond H. Brand, *Redeeming Creation: The Biblical Basis for Environmental Stewardship* (Downers Grove: InterVarsity, 1996), pp. 86-87. See also Ronald Manahan, "Christ as the Second Adam," in *The Environment and the Christian: What Does the New Testament Say about the Environment?* ed. Calvin B. DeWitt (Grand Rapids: Baker, 1991), ch. 2.

focus more on evolution than on the environment.[42] It is not surprising, then, that pastors find little reason to mention caring for creation when they preach these central biblical texts. When we have thought about the creation at all, it has been the creation-past that has loomed largest for us. The contemporary-creation in which we live has faded from theological view. Even the popular appeal of Francis Schaeffer a generation ago, as Davis notes, or that of Tony Campolo today, is not enough to change our minds.[43]

Losing the Opportunity for the Evangel

There is in our generation a greater danger than nature worship. Unless we rethink our Christian relationship to nature the testimony of the evangelical church is in danger of failing to speak effectively to this generation.[44] To the extent that we ignore the natural world or treat it as mere matter or simply a stage for the human drama we diminish our capacity to speak to our culture. I have little fear of most people mistaking the creatures for the Creator. The bogeyman of "New Age" is largely that, an empty argument.[45] Few evangelicals are in danger of falling into that trap. Rather, our problem is that we are missing an opportunity to speak faithfully and redemptively to some of the most pressing issues of our day.

Evangelism, Michael Northcott points out, is the underlying motivation for the Evangelical Declaration on the Care of Creation.[46] The great irony, according to William Dyrness, is that "announcing the good news of the New Covenant has been sometimes seen as a retreat from

---

[42] Davis, "Ecological 'Blind Spots,'" 273-86, and Hoezee, *Remember Creation*, pp. 1-4.

[43] Schaeffer, *Pollution*; Tony Campolo, *How to Rescue the Earth without Worshiping Nature* (Nashville: Nelson, 1992).

[44] See Wilson, "Evangelicals and the Environment," 307; Ron Sider, "Biblical Foundations for Creation Care," in *The Care of Creation: Focusing Concern and Action*, ed. R. J. Berry (Leicester: Inter-Varsity, 2000), p. 44; and Young, *Healing the Earth*, pp. 24-25.

[45] For a detailed review of this point see Loren Wilkinson, "New Age, New Consciousness, and the New Creation," in *Tending the Garden: Essays on the Gospel and the Earth*, ed. W. Grandberg-Michaelson, (Grand Rapids: Eerdmans, 1987), p. 7; and more recently Young, *Healing the Earth*, pp. 25, 265-67.

[46] Michael S. Northcott, "The Spirit of Environmentalism," in *Care of Creation*, ed. Berry, p. 167.

the problems posed by the environment."[47] We need to learn better ways to exegete not only Scripture, but also our culture, especially with respect to its deep yearning for a meaningful connection to earth. Nature provides a powerful incentive to hear the gospel. Paul understood this, and he used it evangelistically a number of times in various settings.[48] The testimony of creation leaves all of humanity without excuse for rejecting God's grace in Christ Jesus. This yearning, that Kellert and Wilson call biophilia, is nothing less than a manifestation of our common God-given creatureliness. And it confirms the reciprocal relation of biophilia and the gospel. "Our environmental responsibilities not only *include* evangelism," as William Dyrness says, "they *begin* there."[49]

Rethinking Our Relation to Creation

While the general public is strongly drawn to nature, conservative Christians as a whole, although somewhat supportive of environmental concerns, remain cautious. A number of surveys have shown that there is an inverse relationship between regular church attendance and interest in the natural world.[50] To be sure, this observation is full of ambiguity. The easy formulation of "faith-in-God equals disregard for the environment" does not hold. In my experience many evangelicals care very deeply about the environmental problems facing us. But they may not express this in ways that a secular pollster or environmentalist would easily recognize. The suggestion by historian Lynn White that "[e]specially in its western form, Christianity is the most anthropocentric religion the world has seen," has been vigorously debated for over thirty years.[51] It is only recently that we have begun to move beyond this impasse to a more fruitful understanding of the role of the Church in

---

[47] William A. Dyrness, "Environmental Ethics and the Covenant of Hosea 2," in *SOTT*, ed. Robert L. Hubbard, Robert K. Johnston, and Robert P. Meye (Dallas: Word, 1992), pp. 263-78.

[48] Paul used the argument from nature on several occasions, including at Lystra (Acts 14:8-18), Athens (Acts 17:24-28), and in a different context in Corinth (1 Cor 10:26), and in Rom 10:18.

[49] Dyrness, "Environmental Ethics," p. 274.

[50] Robert Booth Fowler, *The Greening of Protestant Thought* (Chapel Hill: University of North Carolina Press, 1995), pp. 24-26.

[51] Joseph K. Sheldon summarizes much of the literature on the Church's reaction in *Rediscovery of Creation: A Bibliographical Study of the Church's Response to the Environmental Crisis*, ATLA Bibliography Series, no. 29 (Metuchen: Scarecrow, 1992).

environmental concerns.[52] But that does not free us from our hesitancy to witness regarding God's love for creation. It is unfortunate that the voice of creation has been muted in proclaiming the gospel. But as R.J. Berry notes, "[T]here has not been — nor is there — any general agreement about Christian commitment on priorities or actions about creation care."[53] This will likely continue until we repair the unfortunate separation of both books of God's revelation (Ps 19).

One way to unhinge from this situation, I am suggesting, is to begin rethinking our relationship to the creation. We can do this by asking ourselves, "What creature do I love?" The discomfort we feel with this question is perhaps a measure of the distance that has grown between us and the rest of creation.[54] Let's begin by returning to Adam's story. Perhaps it will tell us something more about how we should relate to nature. The first thing that Adam did in seeking out a suitable helper was to establish his nomenclatural relationship with the creatures. On a biological field trip students often begin their investigations with, "What is this called?" So, biologists are quick to point out that a basic human task is biological nomenclature. We take the time to name the things we value.[55] Today, the naming of new species is buried in the specialist domain we call Systematics. Scientists in this area have yet to complete the job. We do not know, for instance, within an order of magnitude, how many species of life inhabit the earth.[56] This diverse organismal array is the basis for a considerable portion of human wealth.[57] These creatures not only provide raw materials for our economy, but also

[52] See Hiebert, "Rethinking," p. 25; Young, *Healing the Earth*, p. 10. Fowler reviews the evangelical disagreement in "Dissent and Protestant Fundamentalism," in *Greening of Protestant Thought*, pp. 45-57.

[53] R. J. Berry, in *Care of Creation*, ed. Berry, p. 15.

[54] Walsh et al. have said, "To the degree that we are unable to countenance this language, however, we also find ourselves alienated from much of the biblical tradition" ("Trees, Forestry," p. 425).

[55] Peter De Vos, Calvin De Witt, Eugene Dykema, Vernon Ehlers and Loren Wilkinson, ed., *Earthkeeping in the Nineties: Stewardship of Creation* (Grand Rapids: Eerdmans, 1991), p. 288; Young, *Healing the Earth*, p. 168.

[56] Robert M. May, "How many species inhabit the earth?" *SA* (1992): 42-48. This gap in our knowledge limits our capacity to be effective stewards of the earth. For instance, because we have not fully studied many species we can only approximate the number and rate at which they are lost to extinction. See also Michael L. McKinney, "High Rates of Extinction and Threat in Poorly Studied Taxa," *ConBio* 13 (1999): 1273-81.

[57] According to Edward O. Wilson, "[e]very country can be said to have three forms of wealth: material, cultural and biological,", *SA* 261(1989): 108-117.

maintain vital natural ecosystem services that we can replace only at great cost, and in most instances not at all. The array of nature's services includes cleaning air and water, flood control, temperature regulation, pollinating crops and much more.[58] So, our first task may be going on a field trip and getting to know nature well enough so that we can ask the biophilia question.

Ugh! It's a Bug

But the creatures of earth have worth beyond their utilitarian value as natural resources for food, clothing and shelter. The French anthropologist, Claude Levi-Strauss, has suggested that animals, and by extension all living things, are "good to think with."[59] And Peter Steinhart claims, "Animals are far more fundamental to our thinking than we supposed. They are not just a part of the fabric of thought: they are a part of the loom."[60] We wrap up some of our most important mental images in creaturely analogies and metaphors. When Adam was naming the creatures he didn't say, "Oh, here comes a pork chop, and there is a hamburger; or is that a hot dog?" The plants of the Garden of Eden were not "fibre," or "paper stock," or "board feet" or any other unit of production. These were first of all fellow members of creation, not gastronomic delights or mere natural resources. To the extent that our culture forgets this lesson it will be impoverished spiritually, and eventually physically as well.[61]

Today, however, we seldom see ourselves in a relational way to creation—and especially not to the "small creatures."[62] I often bring live insects into the classroom. One of the most common responses is, "Ugh! Is it going to sting me or hurt me?" And for others it is, "Oh, it is so gross!" This happens frequently enough that it might seem that we innately dislike these creatures. It appears that we do have a partly genetic predisposition to biophobia or a fear of threatening animals.[63] But our disgust reaction to insects is not innate; it is a learned behaviour.

---

[58] Gretchen C. Daily, ed., *Nature's Services: Societal Dependence on Natural Ecosystems* (Washington: Island, 1997), pp. 3-6.

[59] Claude Levi-Strauss, *The Savage Mind* (Chicago: University of Chicago Press, 1966).

[60] Peter Steinhart, "Dreaming Elands," in *The Norton Book of Nature Writing*, ed. Robert Finch and John Elder (New York: Norton, 1989), p. 812.

[61] De Vos et al., "Valuing Creation," in *Earthkeeping*, pp. 237-54, 282.

[62] De Vos, et al., "Valuing Creation," in *Earthkeeping*, p. 285.

[63] Roger S. Ulrich, *Biophilia, Biophobia, and Natural Landscapes*, in Kellert and Wilson, *Biophilia Hypothesis*, pp. 85-86.

Although psychologists may tell us that our reactions are not rational, a complex mixture of experience and prejudice still sweeps over us.[64] We are happier, we say, to be left in our ignorance. And this says more about our attitude both toward the natural world and the Creator than we might think. Insects are merely a cipher for a wider class of responses to nature. Our negative reaction to them indicates that we are ill at ease with much of the natural world.[65]

The reason we are disgusted and fearful of insects isn't puzzling to most people! There is a legitimate concern over insects that bite, sting or make us ill. So it is simply enough to know that they might hurt us. Entomologists have tried to reassure us that insects are not all harmful, but with little success. Our reactions, they say, are entirely out of proportion to the degree of risk we face. But does it make any difference whether we dislike these creatures? Or, for that matter, whether we dislike any particular creatures? For some time now, a wide range of scientists, philosophers and theologians have been trying to tell us that it does matter. Our attitude toward nature, or the creatures of earth, is important.[66]

This debate over the place of insects in creation lies near the heart of the modern environmental dilemma. It was, after all, Rachel Carson's book, *Silent Spring*, that triggered a public response to the negative aspects of our "war on insects."[67] It seems to me that it takes a brave person to tell the Creator that insects are ugly, or a mistake. They may be foreign, but nevertheless they have a place in God's economy. And God seems to value creatures differently than we do. "[C]oncern for even the weakest and apparently most useless creatures," Tom Finger says, "is clearly rooted in the concern and suffering of Jesus for even the least of creatures."[68] Cal De Witt makes a similar point when he says, "God finds

---

[64] For more on these fears, see the review by John R. Wood and Heather Looy, "My Ant Is Coming to Dinner: Culture, Disgust, and Dietary Challenges," *ProtJI* 17 (2000): 52-56.

[65] Stephen R. Kellert has conducted extensive investigations of our attitudes toward invertebrates and other organisms. He lists nine basic values, indicating the complexity of our relationship to nature (*The Diversity of Life: Biological Diversity and Human Society* [Washington: Island, 1996], pp. 10-26).

[66] See Rodin, *Stewards*, pp. 101-03.

[67] Robert Gottlieb, *Forcing the Spring: The Transformation of the American Environmental Movement* (Washington: Island, 1993), pp. 81-86.

[68] Tom Finger, "An Anabaptist/Mennonite Theology of Creation," in *Creation and the Environment: An Anabaptist Perspective on a Sustainable World*, ed. Calvin Redekop (Baltimore: Johns Hopkins University Press, 2000), p. 167.

it necessary in the presence of Job to praise the unlovely, uncuddled, and the little-cared-for kinds." So perhaps "[t]hrough the appreciative eyes of God we may see what to human eyes may seem ugly."[69]

The Death of an Owl

So far, I have focused on insects. But the problems we face are much larger than mere insects. They include the dying of large parts of creation, something that we assume is a necessary part of our modern economy. Not long ago, as I walked along a roadside, I saw an owl lying in the grass. [70] The feathers were silky soft to my touch and the body still pliable. This northern hawk owl had been struck and killed only a few hours before. These low-flying birds hunt during the dawn and dusk hours along the wetlands and forest edges so common in Canada. A medium- to small-sized owl, it was beautiful to look at, especially close-up. The yellow eyes, with huge jet-black pupils, were starting to collapse. But the plumage, from the barring on the breast to the chestnut mottled sides and back, was still breathtakingly beautiful. Here was one of God's good gifts to us. I wanted somehow to try and hold the beauty a little longer, and to reanimate it, but that was no longer possible.

So, what should I do with the dead owl now? Pick it up and carry it back to the lab to prepare a study skin? Or leave it to be reclaimed by a host of scavengers who patrol this area? But to leave it would only create a greater hazard, inviting small mammals to be struck, in turn, as they sought to feed on the carcass. And what happens to the countless other animals that are struck on highways every day? What do you do when your automobile hits an animal? Stop? Keep going? Or perhaps even make a joke about buying a book of road-kill recipes? The small dilemma that the death of one creature presents to us is symptomatic of a larger problem we face today.[71]

The daily slaughter on the highways of commerce is a normal aspect of our lives. We cannot escape the fact that not only do we eat organisms, but also many of our other actions are tied in with the death of some creature. The controversy over animal rights is one of a number of signals telling us that something must change in our relationship with

---

[69] DeWitt, *Caring for Creation*, p. 50.

[70] An earlier version of this story appeared in my monthly column, "Creation Waits," written for the *ChCour*, 13 December, 1999.

[71] In this chapter I do not address the environmental implications of natural evil or theodicy. On these vital questions see Rodin (*Stewards*) or Young (*Healing the Earth*).

the earth. Artists, poets and musicians are often at the forefront of those who are protesting against our view of animals as mere commodities.[72] We are shocked when a display in the name of art is filled with rabbit carcasses, or when, as recently happened, a Danish museum exhibits live goldfish swimming in food blenders that are plugged in, ready to be turned on by the viewers. These artists are using shock to break through the habitual mental barriers that constrain us. We should be dismayed, and so we are, at this treatment of creatures.

The youth culture, weaned on "dolphin-safe" tuna campaigns, has begun expressing a vegetarian preference. [73] Animal rights activists like PETA (People for the Ethical Treatment of Animals), the anti-whaling campaign of Green Peace, and the anti-sealing efforts by the Sea Shepherd Society have gained strong international followings. But not everyone sees these issues the same way.[74] The protests against medical research on dogs, cats, and primates has continued on and off since the beginnings of the anti-vivisection movement. Now the debate over transgenic crops and other genetically modified organisms (GMOs) is sharply in focus. The veggan food and animal rights protesters are demonstrating at a growing range of recreational activities including the circus, rodeo, sport fishing, and hunting (most recently fox hunts in Britain). We are, it seems, in the midst of a great cultural rethinking of our relationship with animals. The animal rights movement is, however, only a sub-text of a much larger adjustment that we are making through the broad scope of the environmental movement.

He's Got the Whole World in His Hands — Or Does He?

I have said that our attitude toward nature has not kept pace with our understanding of nature and its needs. And a number of things have happened to make this so. First, our view of our position in the natural world has been dramatically altered in the last forty years. Consider two illustrations of the earth, each with a pair of hands holding the globe. The

---

[72] Loren Wilkinson has drawn attention to the tension that results from ignoring elements of either the new or the old story in our search for truth in science, in art, or in environmental debate ("The Truth of Creation in the Present Age," *Crux* 34, no. 2 [1998]: 3-17).

[73] For a recent summary of these developments in the context of Christian concern for creation, see Young, *Is God A Vegetarian?* pp. 33-37.

[74] Rev. George Kallapa, a Makah native and member of a whaling family on the Olympic Peninsula of Washington State says that the real issue is racism (personal communication). See my article, "A Whale of a Way to Die," *ChCour*, 28 June 1999, 3.

first illustration is from the cover of *Maclean's* magazine (16 December, 1991). In a special report, entitled "The Fate of the Earth," a pair of hands holds a luminous globe. The subtitle reads, "World Leaders Will Negotiate the Planet's Future." For the second illustration, imagine that you are sitting in church in the early 1950s. The same picture of a globe and hands is in front of you. What do you see in these two pictures, and to whom do the hands in each picture belong? In the 1950s they are obviously the hands of God. Gospel tracks with such pictures were common in that era—just as the familiar chorus asserts, "He's got the whole world in his hands." But only a half-century later we have made a dramatic shift in perspective. The images from the Apollo lunar program are only the most visible evidence of this change in our thinking. They signify how dramatically our technological abilities have increased. This shift means that the mental models for our relationship with the earth that served us well only a generation ago, will need renewal.[75]

Second, from an ecological perspective, humans are a keystone species *par excellence*. We exceed all other creatures in reshaping ecosystems on earth. The term "human-dominated ecosystems" once applied only to pastures, farm fields or cities, but now it can be used almost everywhere on earth, even in "pristine" environments.[76] Ecologically, a keystone species is one that organizes or significantly alters the structure of the community in which it lives. A dominant species, on the other hand, may influence its community simply by its great size (technically, its "biomass") or large numbers. But our biological influence is greater than either our proportional biomass or population size, and so we function as a keystone species. The myth of an ecologically pristine wilderness world, free of human influence, has been challenged on a number of fronts.[77] While the impact of our management may have seemed mostly local in the past, it was not. But now we are more than a biological force on a global scale. Recent studies have shown that the power of humans to alter the planet has grown to the point where we now rival geologic processes on earth. Human

---

[75] Hiebert notes that "land is the very realm of redemption" for Israel ("Rethinking," p. 29). It seems to me that since the Enlightenment the mind has become our realm of redemption. See also De Vos, et al., *Earthkeeping*, p. 172.

[76] Peter M. Vitousek, Harold A. Mooney, Jane Lubchenco, and Jerry M. Melillo, "Human Domination of Earth's Ecosystems," *Sc* 277 (1997): 494-99.

[77] See William Cronon, "The Trouble with Wilderness; or, Getting Back to the Wrong Nature," in *Uncommon Ground: Toward Reinventing Nature*, William Cronon, ed. (New York: Norton, 1995), p. 83.

excavations move more earth and rock than either rivers or glaciers do on the planet.[78] It is tempting to ask if we have been thoughtful of the implications of this power. Our recent history suggests that we are engaged only lightly in thinking about our place as either a biological or creational agent of planetary change.[79]

Third, when a human-built project is contemplated it has often been assumed, until quite recently, that the creatures would move or die. How they would adjust or where they would go has not been our particular concern, unless perhaps we were a biological specialist. This assumption that nature will simply move out of the way for us has been proven false.[80] Endangered species legislation, pioneered in the United States thirty years ago, is the most visible evidence of our efforts to alleviate this problem. There has been sharp disagreement among evangelicals about the wisdom of this law. Whether one agrees or disagrees, it is clear that we are facing a challenge with respect to how we act in nature.

All of these insights are changing our understanding of the stewardly role we play on earth. From a biblical perspective the human management of creation has been mandated from the beginning. Christian environmentalists are recognizing that our care for the earth is a deeply religious issue.[81]

Is Creation Mindless or Mindful?

Throughout this chapter, I have been using the terms "nature" and "creation" synonymously. Nature, as an independent entity, separate from humans, is largely a Greek concept. It has been adopted widely and used effectively during the rise of modern science. The word "nature" communicates an abstraction that is thought to be free of metaphysical accoutrements. But this notion has worked mischievously to relegate humans to intruder status as a "non-normal" part of nature. The Hebrew mind did not recognize this division between nature and humans. The

---

[78] See the report of Roger Hooke's work in Yvonne Baskin, *The Work of Nature: How the Diversity of Life Sustains Us* (Washington: Island, 1997), p. 155.

[79] See Fred Van Dyke's challenge to evangelical environmentalists on this point in "Bridging the Gap: Christian Environmental Stewardship and Public Environmental Policy," *TJ* NS 18 (1997): 139-72.

[80] See Vitousek et al., "Human Domination," or almost any issue of *Conservation Biology, Ecological Applications* or numerous other scientific journals.

[81] See Rodin, *Stewards*; Van Dyke et al., *Redeeming Creation*; and De Vos et al., *Earthkeeping*.

hand of God, the Hebrews believed, created everything in what we call "nature." Although we can recognize the enormous value for research of an abstraction such as "nature," the term under-specifies our relationship to the natural world. It puts all of the emphasis on the material and impoverishes the spiritual and normative aspects of the created order.[82]

I deliberately use both "nature" and "creation," because as a scientist and as a Christian I move freely back and forth between these two senses of earth. Together, these words, as they are commonly understood today, capture something of the dual qualities of reality. I agree with my colleagues that creation is the richer, more accurate term.[83] And I would add that I use it often in my teaching. But in the context of the science-faith debate today, both terms are used in a sectarian fashion. We will not resolve these differences until we develop a richer view of our relationship to the natural world. Perhaps we cannot come to any common agreement on their content. And so for the moment I simply acknowledge the awkwardness of using both terms.

How we view the natural world is vitally important. It is now widely recognized that nature, as we call it, is a modern mental construction. One of the challenges of environmentalism is to give voice to a voiceless nature. This is important because "[b]y constructing nature as deaf and dumb, we have made ourselves deaf and dumb in relation to that nature."[84] But can mindless matter have a relationship? It has rightly been observed that simply "[w]anting to listen, however, does not mean that we can listen."[85] If these creatures have no agency, no ability to respond independently from us, then the notion of giving voice to nature is a nice sentiment, but little else.

Here I think that Moses can help us see this question in a new light. At the end of his life he is reviewing with the children of Israel all that God has taught him. In Deuteronomy 30 he puts before the people a blessing and a curse in hope and in warning. The interesting thing is the identity of the witnesses he calls to this covenant. It would seem reasonable that he might call on the many enemies that surround Israel and who will presumably harass them if they fail to keep their end of

---

[82] For more details on this important distinction, see Van Dyke et al., *Redeeming Creation*, p. 15; De Vos et al., *Earthkeeping in the Nineties*, pp. 347-48, and Steve Bouma-Prediger, *The Greening of Theology: The Ecological Models of Rosemary Radford Ruether, Joseph Sittler, and Jürgen Moltmann* (Atlanta: Scholars, 1995), pp. 274-76.

[83] Van Dyke et al., *Redeeming Creation*, pp. 39-40.

[84] Walsh et al., "Trees, Forestry," p. 425.

[85] Walsh et al., "Trees, Forestry," p. 425.

this bargain. But instead he calls upon heaven and earth as witnesses against the people. This may simply be hyperbole, but the affirmation of Psalm 19 suggests that it is not.[86] In this psalm we see that even without words these creatures speak the testimony of God. And yet there is, as Loren Wilkinson notes, "a curious incompleteness about that news." "The truth of creation," as he puts it, "is incomplete without the truth of Scripture." If we can read past the words of Moses without noticing that the rest of creation participates in this covenant making agreement we risk missing a substantial message from our Creator. It will pay us richly if theologians and natural scientists would together carefully consider what a relational reading of Scripture might tell us.

Calling for a New View of Creation

I began this chapter by emphasizing that humans are chemically and biologically one with the creatures. This scientific insight quickly leads in some environmental writing to a levelling of all differences among species. A bio-egalitarianism or a philosophical monism is the result.[87] From this perspective humans are simply one species among many that are competing for their respective rights. The Gaia hypothesis proposed by James Lovelock suggests that the biophysical world is one interacting system. This is a testable scientific hypothesis. But when it is extended to a metaphysical framework for the meaning of life, it is no longer science.[88] Dorion Sagan and Lynn Margulis make this extension in the context of biophilia, claiming that humans have no discernible purpose beyond their evolutionary destiny. In these authors' view, "it is better to think of ourselves as all just a part of Gaia and not even, in any way, the most important part."[89] The gospel stands in sharp contrast to these conclusions. Christian thinking, from the Apostles' Creed to contemporary Christian scholarship, asserts by faith that humans are more than their constituent parts. And in this way we are manifestly different from the rest of creation. Although this difference is located in facts that may be easy to state (we are made in the image of God), it is

---

[86] See Wilkinson, "Truth of Creation," 11-12.
[87] See James Nash, *Loving Nature: Ecological Integrity and Christian Responsibility* (Nashville: Abingdon, 1991), p. 181 and De Vos, et al., *Earthkeeping*, pp. 184-85.
[88] There are many cogent critiques of this type of reductionism. For a recent one that addresses the Gaia hypothesis explicitly, see Malcolm A. Jeeves and R.J. Berry, *Science, Life and Christian Belief: A Survey and Assessment* (Leicester: Inter-Varsity, 1998), p. 228.
[89] Dorion Sagan and Lynn Margulis, "God, Gaia, and Biophilia," in Kellert and Wilson, *The Biophilia Hypothesis*, p. 351.

wonderfully mysterious, and it can only be apprehended by faith (Ps 8:4; Col 1:23, 27). A generation ago, Donald MacKay called the tendency of taking scientific explanations as exhaustive "nothing-buttery."[90] From science we will discover that we have a necessary relationship with the earth, but in itself this is not a sufficient or satisfactory answer to the question who we are. Our place in the creation is defined not only by our physical and biological linkage, but also by our responsibilities reflected in the New Covenant in Christ.[91] Yes, we are insightful SPONCH, but we are also more than that because we are the children of God.

Steve Bouma-Prediger, a philosophical theologian at Hope College, has said that Christians need to take seriously the creation's responses. The natural world is not essentially an autonomous and unresponsive entity called "nature." Our perspective should shift to seeing the material world as graceful, grace-filled and responsible.[92] All creation is a place of grace. Does what we now see in creation give us hope for renewal in the future? As John Leax asks, "Could it be that we have not lost our instinct ... that we desire the salvation of being at home in a peaceable kingdom ruled by laws we cannot divine?"[93] James Houston thought so when he said that just as "creation is not merely an objective world, whose phenomena we abstract to study, but the dynamic interaction of relationships, so the new creation is the fullness of relationship."[94] It is our calling "to restore creation's goodness by loving it and caring for it."[95]

But is there, as the biophilia hypothesis maintains, an innate tendency in human beings toward other living things? I think that there is, but it is only in part a biological tendency. What scientists call biophilia has more than a biological basis in genetics. It is also a reflection of the image of God in every one of us. The remarkable thing about the gospel, as James Nash says, is that the incarnation "justifies 'biophilia,'" and because God values the whole creation "Christians are called to

---

[90] Donald M. MacKay, *The Clockwork Image* (Downers Grove: InterVarsity, 1974). See also his discussion of determinism in *Science and the Quest for Meaning* (Grand Rapids: Eerdmans, 1982).

[91] Dyrness, "Environmental Ethics," 265.

[92] Bouma-Prediger, *Greening of Theology*, p. 281.

[93] Leax, *Out Walking*, p.140.

[94] Houston, *I Believe*, p. 249.

[95] Rodin, *Stewards*, p. 91.

practice biophilia."[96] This is, Francis Schaeffer believed, a central feature of "the Christian view of nature." And so he was able to say to the buttercup, "Fellow creature, fellow *creature*, I won't walk on you. We are both creatures together."[97] Here we have a clear theological statement of biophilia. In it our biblical relationship to other creatures is operationalized. So once again I ask, knowing that we stand redeemed by the love of Christ, "What creature do you love?"

---

[96] On the incarnation, James Nash says, "The Incarnation confers dignity not only on humankind, but on everything and everyone, past and present, with which humankind is united in interdependence" (*Loving Nature*, pp. 109, 137).
[97] Schaeffer, *Pollution*, p. 93.

Chapter 9

The Jabs of Justice:

Towards a Christian Understanding of Punishment[1]

Christopher D. Marshall

Punishment is a universal feature of human social life. It plays a significant role in both private settings, such as in family life, and in public settings, such as in the civil and criminal justice systems, which is my interest in this chapter. Punishment may be defined as *"the deliberate infliction of an unpleasant or painful experience on a person, such as the deprivation of something greatly valued, like freedom or money or even life itself, as the sequel to a perceived offence and corresponding in some way to the action that evoked it."*[2] Interestingly, criminal offending could equally be defined as "the deliberate infliction of an unpleasant or painful experience on a person, such as the deprivation of something greatly valued, like freedom or money or even life itself." Both crime and punishment, in other words, entail the calculated imposition of pain on a

---

[1] For an extended treatment of this question, see chapter 3 of my book *Beyond Retribution: A New Testament Vision for Justice, Crime, and Punishment* (Grand Rapids: Eerdmans, 2001). I am grateful to the publishers for permission to contribute an abbreviation of that chapter to the present volume.

[2] For expanded definitions of punishment, see Walter Moberly, *The Ethics of Punishment* (London: Faber and Faber, 1968), pp. 35-36; Barbara A. Hudson, *Understanding Justice: An Introduction to Ideas, Perspectives and Controversies in Modern Penal Theory* (Buckingham: Open University Press, 1996), pp. 1-3; Nils Christie, "Crime, Pain and Death", *NPCJ* 1 (1984): 1-4.

third party. Yet one is legal, the other illegal. One is regarded as wrong, the other as right. One is considered a social blight, the other as a social necessity.

This paradoxical situation underscores a very important fact about punishment: its legitimacy needs to be established; it is not self-evident. The practice of punishment requires particular ethical justification. This has long been recognized by moral and social philosophers. There has been an enduring debate, stemming back into Greek antiquity, over both the *purpose of punishment* (Why do we punish? What are our goals in administering punishment?) and its *moral justification* (What entitles us to punish? How much should we punish? If it is wrong to inflict pain, and two wrongs do not make a right, what justifies adding the pain of punishment to the pain already caused by the offence?) From this discussion, several different theories or explanations of punishment have emerged. Each theory has held sway at certain periods in Western legal thinking, and each continues to have an influence on current penal practice. Each explanation has both strengths and weaknesses, and each can claim some biblical warrant, which is not surprising given the bewildering diversity of biblical teaching on the theme of punishment.

In this chapter, I want to offer a Christian critique of some of the dominant theories of punishment that have shaped the Western criminal justice system. I will briefly summarize both the strengths and weaknesses of each theory, then propose a way of thinking about punishment that seeks to be consistent with the redemptive nature of God's justice as revealed to us in the Christian Scriptures. My argument is that the premeditated pain delivery that is punishment is morally and theologically defensible only if it serves a restorative rather than a "payback" intention. Only if punishment is qualified by a redemptive concern for all those affected by the criminal action can it be adequately justified from a Christian perspective.

The Rehabilitation Theory

One of the three most common ways of justifying punishment in the modern era has been to appeal to its capacity for generating change in the recipient. The pain of punishment is considered acceptable because it serves to rehabilitate the offender. It might even be thought of as a system of social hygiene that "cures" wrongdoers of their unfortunate propensity to offend.

That an important, though subordinate, aim of punishment is the reform of the offender was a relatively novel idea when it was mooted by the eighteenth-century philosopher Jeremy Bentham (1748-1832). The existing system of punishment was largely arbitrary and often brutal, with a much greater emphasis on hurting the body than reforming the mind or character of the offender. But as the idea of rehabilitation steadily took hold, it contributed considerably to mitigating the severity of criminal law. In the space of forty years, the number of capital offences in England fell from several hundred to just four. The function of imprisonment also changed from being primarily a means of holding people awaiting trial or of inducing payment of fines, to becoming a mode of punishment in its own right, as a more humane alternative to death or exile. "The age of sobriety in punishment had begun," Foucault observes, even if the intention was "not to punish less but to punish better" — better because now the mind or soul of the criminal was being targeted, not just the body, and it was being done so away from the public gaze behind prison walls.[3] Prisons were built throughout Western Europe and America with the intention not merely of incarcerating offenders but also of reforming them through a mixture of work, discipline and penance. In twentieth-century penal theory and practice, there has been unprecedented concern for the rehabilitation of criminals and their reintegration in society.

The most obvious strength of the rehabilitative approach is the way it recognizes that an offender does not stop being a member of the community whilst under correction. The offender's interests are part of society's interests, and it is in everyone's interests that lawbreakers are rid of their anti-social behaviour. From a Christian perspective, rehabilitation is consistent with the strong biblical emphasis on repentance and forgiveness. "Whether in the judgment of Israel in the Old Testament or the discipline of church members in the New," observes Robert McQuilkin, "God's primary purpose in punishment has always been the restoration of the sinner. 'Do I take pleasure in the death of the wicked? says the Sovereign LORD. Rather, am I not pleased when they turn from their ways and live?" (Ezek 18:23).[4]

---

[3] Michel Foucault, *Discipline and Punish: The Birth of the Prison* (New York: Vintage, 1979), pp. 14, 82. See also David Cayley, *The Expanding Prison: The Crisis in Crime and Punishment and the Search for Alternatives* (Toronto: Anansi, 1998), pp. 89-164; Hudson, *Understanding Justice*, pp. 26-31.

[4] Robert McQuilkin, *An Introduction to Biblical Ethics* (Wheaton: Tyndale, 1989), p. 357.

However, criticism has been levelled at the rehabilitation theory of punishment on both theoretical and pragmatic grounds.[5] Philosophically, critics have warned of the dangers of regarding punishment as a kind of treatment, since that presumes that crime is a type of disease or abnormality to be cured rather than the expression of moral choices for which the offender stands accountable. This in turn rests on a deterministic view of human nature which diminishes the moral autonomy of the offender and locates the cause of crime in some inherited psychological predisposition, or in social factors such as poverty, unemployment or family upbringing. Such denial of personal liability can lead to two opposite kinds of injustice—laxity and tyranny. In the former case, criminal behaviour is too easily excused and the criminal exempted from taking responsibility for his or her actions. In the latter case, because the object of the "treatment" is to render the criminal unlikely to reoffend, there is the potential for punishment to be extended for an unjustly long period of time until social conformity is secured. There is also little to prevent abusive or inhumane techniques being used to achieve success. Our track record in treating the criminally insane is a salutary warning in this respect.

More significantly, it is questionable whether punishment itself has any inherent power to rehabilitate someone. As George Bernard Shaw once observed, "If you are to punish a man retributively you must injure him. If you are to reform him you must improve him. And men are not improved by injuries."[6] The pain or prospect or routine of punishment may succeed in producing external behavioural changes. But behaviour based on fear or habituation is not the same as a genuine transformation of one's moral character and volitional disposition. Permanent organic change requires the criminal's personal co-operation and commitment, and these are not readily elicited by deliberately hurting him.

There is also a major pragmatic objection to the reformative theory: it appears not to work! Despite the introduction of rehabilitation programs, recidivism rates remain high. New Zealand is typical in this respect: around 30% of current female prisoners and 60% of current male

---

[5] A classic critique is that of C. S. Lewis, "The Humanitarian Theory of Punishment," in *Essays on the Death Penalty*, ed. T. Robert Ingram (Houston: St Thomas, 1963), pp. 1-12. Less impressive, in the same volume, is E.L.H. Taylor, "Medicine or Morals as the Basis of Justice and Law," pp. 81-102.

[6] George Bernard Shaw, *The Crime of Imprisonment* (New York: Citadel, 1961), p. 26.

prisoners have already served previous prison sentences.[7] It has even been said that the only thing that rehabilitates criminals is old age! Although this is unduly pessimistic, what Karen Kissane calls Western society's "creeping sense of helplessness about its ability to rehabilitate those who commit crime" is arguably *the* major reason for the declining influence of the reformative theory of punishment.[8] Many criminologists now insist that rehabilitationism has had its day, and by the 1980s, many western jurisdictions had effectively given up reformist goals in favour of alternative aims in punishment.

The Deterrence Theory

According to the deterrence theory, punishment is designed to discourage future wrongdoing, whether by the offender (so-called "specific deterrence") or by others tempted to follow his or her example ("general deterrence"). Punishment is deemed the most appropriate way of instilling in the offender, and reinforcing in the wider community, respect for the legal and moral code that has been violated. The pain of punishment is justified on the utilitarian ground that it averts the even greater pain that would ensue if future offending were not deterred.

Now there can be little doubt that the likelihood of apprehension and punishment does have some deterrence value. Avoiding foreseeable and unproductive pain is a common human trait. Deterrence works best with certain premeditated crimes, particularly those aimed at material gain, such as fraud, and with certain sections of the population, especially those who would generally be law-abiding citizens. Insofar as deterrence is achieved, exemplary punishment serves to protect innocent victims from further crime. Scripture is filled with admonitions for the protection of the innocent, and the Bible seems to recognize a deterrent dimension to punishment. The outcome of the death penalty for rebellion in ancient Israel was that "all the people will hear and be afraid, and will not act contemptuously again" (Deut 17:12-13; cf. 13:11; 21:21; Rom 13:3-5). A similar rationale underlies instructions relating to church discipline in 1 Timothy. "Those who sin are to be rebuked publicly, so that the others may take warning" (5:20; RSV; cf. Acts 5:11).

However, it needs to be recognized that punishment by itself is usually not an adequate deterrent for serious crime or for crimes of

---

[7] Cited in Helen Bowen and Jim Consedine, ed., *Restorative Justice: Contemporary Themes and Practice* (Lyttleton: Ploughshares, 1999), p. 84.
[8] Karen Kissane, "Punish and Be Damned," *TM*, 28 June, 1993, 29.

desperation. Punishment will do little to deter offending in social contexts of economic despair, political hopelessness or systemic violence. Deterrence reasoning also assumes a high level of rational control and freedom of choice on the part of potential offenders. It presumes that criminal activity is the outcome of carefully made calculations of self-interest. Sometimes this is the case. Yet many serious offences, such as murder and assault, are crimes of impulse committed in the heat of the moment, with no thought to personal consequences or likely penalties. Those who commit them often live chaotic lives, unable to measure present decisions and actions in light of their longer term consequences. And even in premeditated crimes, as long as the culprit thinks there is a sporting chance of getting away with it, the allotted punishment will have little deterrent value.

The deterrence approach also encounters a range of empirical quandaries. How do we know just how severe penalties have to be in order to make people decide against crime? Individuals are different: what might deter one person will not necessarily deter another. And how can we be sure that potential offenders will learn about the penalties engaged to deter them? The theory requires that intending offenders will know about the sentences which the courts hand down for particular crimes and have these uppermost in their minds at the moment they are tempted to offend. But not all criminals read newspapers or court reports, much less criminal legislation. Again, how can we verify deterrence effects? It is very difficult to determine *real* crime rates, since statistical fluctuations may reflect reporting or detection rates rather than actual offending rates. If the real offending rate is hard to know, how much harder is it to know whether the rate has been affected by particular penalties or their absence. Even if real reductions in particular crimes could be pinpointed after the use of deterrent penalties, such reduction may be due to growing public disapproval of particular behaviours, like drunk driving, rather than to the specific fear of punishment.

But there are two more substantial criticisms of the deterrent theory of punishment. The first is that it depersonalizes the offender. It is not interested in criminals (or victims) as individual human persons, but only in securing compliance with the law in society at large. There is a real danger that the individual rights of the offender will be sacrificed for the sake of the higher good of crime prevention. There is also nothing in the deterrence theory that supplies normative criteria for limiting the extent of the punishment. The severity of the penalty is determined by the message the courts want to send to the community, not by the gravity of the offence or the circumstances of the offender. And if the prescribed medicine fails to effect a communal cure, the strength of the individual dose must be increased, which might result in penalties out of all proportion to personal culpability.

The other main criticism is that deterrence reasoning circumvents the moral basis of punishment. The reason for punishing is purely utilitarian. It is not the moral guilt of the offender that is primary, but whether a particular behaviour is thought to represent a danger to society. This may result in covert scapegoating, in that an individual offender is made to suffer not only the consequences of her or his own misdeeds, past and potential, but also the full weight of communal anxiety about specific behaviours. But to bypass issues of moral guilt, just deserts and the potential of atonement in explaining punishment is to rob moral life of all meaning, and to provide inadequate safeguards against unjust treatment of individual offenders.

The Retributivist Theory

Social thinkers who recognize such weaknesses as these in utilitarian theories of punishment often insist that retributivism is the only satisfying alternative. There are several different versions of retributivism as a penal philosophy, and consequently there is considerable conceptual confusion in the literature. But for my purposes here, four key elements in the retributivist theory of punishment may be identified.[9]

The first is the notion of *guilt*. Criminals are regarded as morally responsible agents who, by voluntarily breaking the law, incur personal legal guilt which must be dealt with. From this flows the concept of *desert*. Punishment is meted out solely because it is morally deserved, and because it would be unjust *not* to punish offences against the transcendent moral order. No other justification is necessary. Proponents of retributivism frequently use metaphors for punishment such as "restoring the balance," "neutralizing the poison," "repaying the debt to

---

[9] Howard Zehr identifies five key elements of retributivism: (1) crime is understood essentially as lawbreaking; (2) when a law is broken, justice involves establishing guilt, (3) so that just deserts can be meted out (4) by inflicting pain (5) through a conflict in which rules and intentions are placed above outcomes, (*Changing Lenses: A New Focus for Crime and Justice* [Scottdale: Herald, 1990], pp. 63–82).

society," "wiping the slate clean," "cancelling out the crime."
Punishment is considered to achieve something that is morally, even
cosmically, important. It is an act of homage to the moral order. The third
key concept is *equivalence* or, as is more commonly expressed today,
proportionality. In order to be just, the punishment inflicted should be
proportionate to the harm done, in the words of the Mikado, a
punishment that "fits the crime." The fourth concept is *reprobation* or
denunciation or *public censure*. Punishment serves as the fundamental
means by which society communicates its abhorrence for certain deeds
and sets the boundaries of acceptable behaviour.

After an interlude in which utilitarian approaches to punishment
dominated the penal scene, retributive justice has, in the past three
decades, made a strong comeback, both in popular sentiment and in
penal philosophy. This is, at least in part, because of the inherent
strengths of the retributivist theory. For example, in contrast to
deterrence thinking, retributivism focuses on the criminal as an
individual, not simply on the betterment of wider society. It rightly
recognizes that wrongdoing entails personal choice and moral
responsibility. It takes seriously the entitlement of the criminal to be
treated as a rational human being, a dignified moral agent who is
accountable for his or her actions. Retributivism rightly insists that
punishment is only justified if it is just, it is only just if it is deserved, and
it is only deserved if the crime is the result of free will. It follows from
this that punishment must be limited to the guilty party alone. Notions
of collective or vicarious punishment are excluded in retributivism. All
citizens can therefore be assured that whether or not they are punished
depends entirely on their own actions and choices. This means that the
protection of the innocent is anchored more normatively in retributivism
than in utilitarianism. The guilty are also afforded greater protection,
since the retributive concepts of just deserts and proportionate
punishment, if applied carefully, ought to eliminate vindictiveness,
cruelty, and race-, class-, and gender-bias in punishment.

These are real strengths, which are of fundamental importance to
any adequate theory of punishment. Notwithstanding these strengths
however, retributivism is still open to serious criticism on philosophical,
moral, biblical and theological grounds. I want to review these criticisms
in some detail, for two reasons: first, because retributive justice is often
championed by Christians as being the theory most consistent with a
Christian approach to issues of crime and punishment; and secondly,

because restorative justice, which I regard as more authentically Christian, often sets itself expressly in contrast to the reigning paradigm of retributive justice.

(1) To begin with, retributivism is *philosophically inadequate* as a justification for punishment.[10] It is not enough to say that crime should be punished because of its inherent wrongness, or that lawbreakers deserve punishment simply because of their moral wrongdoing. For not *all* moral transgression is deemed by society to be criminal, and the state does not invariably mete out punishment (or reward) whenever it is deserved. To say that punishment is merited is not to say that it is necessary, or that there is an inescapable moral obligation to deliver it. It is only particular misdemeanours, in particular historical periods, that are deemed worthy of legal punishment, and the decision as to which acts should be penalized usually includes culturally specific utilitarian considerations.

Retributivism's core principle of proportionate punishment runs into at least three interrelated problems. It depends, in the first place, on the ability to rank crimes in terms of their seriousness. But not only do judgments about seriousness vary over time (as changing attitudes to child abuse, sexual harassment or drunk driving indicate), but there are so many variables involved that it is impossible to come up with a satisfactory scale of gravity. It may be possible to secure general agreement about the most and least serious offences, but problems arise in ranking offences between these poles. Is shoplifting more or less serious than minor tax evasion? Is cruelty to an animal more or less serious than burglary or arson? Some just desert theorists have attempted to devise ways of measuring the seriousness of crimes in terms of their impact on the living standards of the victim. But the emotional or psychological impact of a crime often bears little relation to the material or physical loss suffered.

A second difficulty relates to determining what constitutes a commensurate punishment for a specific crime. Hypothetically it is feasible to graduate penalties from least severe to most severe. But how are the levels of punitive severity to be objectively correlated with degrees of seriousness in offending? What are the anchoring points on the scale? On what grounds can it be decided whether 15 or 20 or 50 years in jail, or some different penalty, is proportionate to the loss of a

---

[10] See, for example, David Dolinko, "Some Thoughts about Retributivism," *Eth* 101 (1991): 537-59.

victim's life? And how would such a scale work in practice, since the same penalty will have a different severity for different parties? A $10,000 fine may be deemed a proportionate penalty for a particular crime, but it will have a more severe impact on a poor person than on a wealthy one. It is impossible to measure pain in standard doses. What hurts one person moderately may hurt another very severely.

The third problem concerns the measuring of guilt. In practice the severity of penalties is determined not only by the nature of the crime but also by the degree of moral culpability of the criminal. Not just the criminal act but the intentions behind the act (*mens rea*), and the circumstances in which the act occurred, are considered relevant to deciding on the appropriate punishment. Rightly so. Yet no human court can ascertain true moral character. Moral guilt is not coterminous with legal guilt. Moral culpability cannot be quantified objectively. It varies from person to person and depends on innumerable intricate circumstances. Nor, from a moral (or theological) point of view, are guilt and innocence mutually exclusive categories. As Volf observes, "From a distance, the world may appear neatly divided into guilty perpetrators and innocent victims. The closer we get, however, the more the line between the guilty and the innocent blurs and we see an intractable maze of small and large hatreds, dishonesties, manipulations, and brutalities, each reinforcing the other."[11]

What these observations amount to is a recognition that while moral blameworthiness may be an *essential* ingredient in the justification of punishment, it is rarely a *sufficient* reason. Retributivism is better able to tell us when *not* to punish (i.e., when the person is innocent of legal wrongdoing) than to tell us when *to* punish, since it is neither expedient nor necessary to punish every moral infringement. Consequently, just as utilitarian theories of punishment must take the moral dimension of punishment into account to be adequate, so retributivist theories must take utilitarian considerations into reckoning to operate effectively. As a social institution, punishment occupies the borderland between morality and social expediency. It cannot be understood without reference to morality, as retributivism insists, but it cannot be governed solely by moral considerations, as utilitarians are quick to point out.

---

[11]Miroslav Volf, *Exclusion and Embrace: A Theological Exploration of Identity, Otherness, and Reconciliation* (Nashville: Abingdon, 1996), p. 81; so too L. Gregory Jones, *Embodying Forgiveness: A Theological Analysis* (Grand Rapids: Eerdmans, 1995), pp. 116-17.

(2) Retributive practice is also dogged with its own *moral problems.* Retributivism appeals to the darker, more fearful side of human nature, and tends to sanction society's most punitive reflexes. For all their theoretical weaknesses, historically it has been utilitarian rather than retributive theories of punishment that have contributed most to moderating the severity of criminal law. The massive institutions of punishment which characterize the present criminal justice system are sustained largely to service the popular demand for retribution, with a corresponding lack of imagination being shown in the development of alternative mechanisms for dealing with crime.

Again, the concepts of "just deserts" and of "the punishment fitting the crime" are open to question on moral grounds. As general principles they have some value in guiding the administration of justice. But while it makes moral sense to repay good deeds with further good, it is quite another matter to requite evil deeds with further evil. Malevolence is a vice, and to insist that evildoers be repaid in kind is surely to make a virtue out of a vice. It also runs directly counter to perhaps the most distinctive emphasis in the moral teachings of the New Testament—the obligation to love one's enemies and to overcome evil with good (e.g., Rom 12:9-21).

Retributivism also tends towards an exaggerated moral individualism. It treats crime primarily as an offence against the law by an autonomous individual rather than as an injury to the community, by a member of the community who has been fundamentally shaped, for good or for ill, by that community. (After all, what is it that turns innocent babies into adult criminal monsters?) The retributivist emphasis on personal responsibility is valuable and important: individuals do *choose* to commit crimes. But choices are constrained by environmental circumstances, and it is naive, if not dishonest, to speak of crime solely in terms of personal free will. Under certain social conditions people will turn to crime who in other social climates would remain law-abiding. Poverty, unemployment, racial inequality, social prejudice, and drug and alcohol abuse all have a role in fostering crime. It is crucial therefore to inquire into the societal causes of, and collective responsibility for, crime rather than being content to divide individuals into categories of guilty and innocent, and calculating commensurate punishments for the guilty.

It is also important to recognize that the law which criminals break is not a neutral transcription of absolute morality. It is an irrefutable fact, Barbara Hudson insists, that the law is predominantly reflective of the standpoint of the powerful, property owning, white male, and that the justice system bears down more heavily on the poor and disadvantaged than on the rich and the powerful.[12] (One recent study in New Zealand shows how the government puts far more money and resources into cracking down on welfare benefit fraud than on combatting white collar crime, even though the cost of white collar crime and corporate fraud is up to ten times higher than the cost of all other crime combined.)[13] Hudson also points to a significant link between business cycles and punishment:

> Whether or not times of depression really do lead to increased crime is debatable, but what is not debatable is that in times of recession the vocabulary of justice becomes harsher. Blame is attached to individuals, and social responsibility for crime is denied; lack of investment in areas of high unemployment is blamed on crime rates rather than on the flight of capital; the unemployed are said to be happy to depend on welfare payments, to have a different (pro-crime) set of values from those of the rest of society. Theories of justice in such times inevitably emphasize punishment rather than help or treatment, and the economic down-turn has indeed seen the demise of rehabilitative orthodoxy and the rise of deterrence, retribution and incapacitative strategies.[14]

Retributivism thus faces the problem of explaining how there can be "just deserts" for individuals in the context of an unjust society, and a society where the justice system most benefits those with vested interests in maintaining the status quo. As Howard Zehr notes, by separating criminal justice from wider questions of social justice, retributivism attempts "to create justice by leaving out many of the relevant variables."[15]

This almost exclusive focus on the individual offender also highlights a further weakness in retributivism: its neglect of the victim. Justice is held to be satisfied by the vindication of the law and punishment of the lawbreaker. There is no need to refer to the real victim at all, and even more so when the system redefines the victim as the impersonal State, not the human being actually injured by the crime. But crime nearly always involves the rupturing of relationships. Not only is

---

[12] Hudson, *Understanding Justice*, pp. 149-50.
[13] The study is by Michael Thornton of Victoria University of Wellington, reported in the campus newspaper *Salient* 61, no. 12 (1998).
[14] Hudson, *Understanding Justice*, pp. 109-10.
[15] Zehr, *Changing Lenses*, pp. 72-73.

the proper relationship between victim and offender distorted by the crime, but the emotional, material, and physical hurt experienced by the victim radiates out through his or her relational world. When conceived as the fracturing of relationship between victim and offender, and their respective relational networks, punitive retribution is clearly an inadequate response, since it does little or nothing to bring about relational recovery.

(3) It is questionable, thirdly, whether retribution is as foundational to *biblical conceptions of law and justice* as sometimes claimed. This is extremely complex territory to traverse, since the biblical data is so vast and interpreters operate with different definitions of retribution. But some initial comments may be ventured.

Certainly it is not difficult to find evidence of retributivist language and concepts in the Bible. The four central concepts of guilt, desert, equivalence and censure are widely attested in Scripture. The notion of guilt and atonement underlies certain parts of the Old Testament sacrificial system and is foundational to many of the procedures of Pentateuchal law. The concept of desert is expressed in the frequent assertion in Scripture that God's judgment is just because it is impartial and strictly according to deeds,[16] as well as in the principle that "The soul who sins is the one who will die" (Ezek 18:4; RSV).[17] The idea of proportionate recompense is captured in the *lex talionis*,[18] "an eye for an eye, a tooth for a tooth." And the notion of reprobation or censure is perhaps echoed in the oft-repeated refrain in Deuteronomy, "so you shall purge the evil from your midst"[19] and in instances where punishment is inflicted for revelatory purposes, so that others might know God's character and power.[20] Retribution is most clearly in view when God's wrath destroys the objects of judgment, thus ruling out any hope of their reformation or restoration,[21] and in texts where God is said

---

[16] For example, Ps 9:8,11; 37:9,33; 58:12; 62:12; Job 34:11; Prov 10:16; 24:12; Eccl 12:14; Isa 3:10-11; 59:18; Jer 17:10; 25:14; 32:19; Lam 3:64; Hos 4:9; Matt 12:37; 16:27; 23:35; Rom 2:1-16; 14:7-12; 1 Cor 3:1-17; 4:1-5; 5:1-5; 6:9-11; 9:24-27; 11:27-34; 2 Cor 5:9-10; Gal 5:19-21; 6:7-10; Col 3:25; Eph 6:8; 1 Tim 5:24-25; 2 Tim 4:14; Heb 2:2; 1 Pet 2:14; Rev 22:12.

[17] Cf. Exod 20:5 (note the qualification "of those who reject me"); Deut 24:16; 2 Kgs 14:6; Ezek 18:1-32.

[18] Exod 21:24; Lev 24:19-22; Deut 19:21; cf. Matt 5:38-48; Luke 6:27-45. See also Exod 4:23; Jer 14:13-16; Mic 2:1-5; Ps 18:26; Prov 3:34; Isa 59:18; Jer 34:17; Joel 3:4-8.

[19] Deut 13:5; 17:7, 12; 19:19; 21:21; 22:21,22,24; 24:7; Jdg 20:13.

[20] Exod 7:17; 10:2, cf. Ps 9:16; Ezek 6:11-13; 7:4,9,27; 38:22-23.

[21] For example, Deut 7:4; 9:8,19,25; Num 16:21; Ezek 22:31; 43:8.

to inflict punishment by the agency of natural phenomena—such as plagues (Exod 7-11), disease (Num 11:33; 2 Sam 24:15), drought (Jer 14:1-7), famine (Ezek 5:12,16), earthquake (Isa 29:6; Amos 8:8), and lightening (Num 11:1)—since such punishments cannot be seen as the inevitable result of wrong human choices.

Clearly, then, there is a theme of retribution in the Bible. But this is *not* to say that the Bible advocates a fully-fledged, coherent theory of retributive justice, and certainly not in the classical Western sense. Indeed, biblical law and justice operate according to certain values, convictions and assumptions that are largely foreign to the model of retributive justice in the Western tradition. Klauss Koch argues, for example, that assertions in the Old Testament about Yahweh's punitive intervention in human affairs need to be understood in light of the basic worldview conviction that deeds carry their own inherent outcome. There are forces at work within the actions themselves that carry the doer along in their wake, bringing either blessing or bane, depending on whether the deeds are good or bad. It is not that Yahweh assesses deeds according to some higher norm and allocates proportionate rewards or punishments accordingly. Rather actions and their consequences are intrinsically linked, so that there is a "sin-disaster" connection on the one hand, and a "righteousness-blessing" connection on the other. "Misfortune pursues sinners, but prosperity is the reward of the righteous" (Prov. 13:21; RSV). This connection is the basis on which the problem of theodicy arises. That the wicked prosper while the good suffer is a paradox precisely because deeds and consequences are supposed to be related.

This is not understood, Koch is careful to explain, as some kind of impersonal cause-effect mechanism that operates independently of God. Yahweh is pictured as intimately involved in the process. God sets the "deed-consequence" construct in motion and consents to its operation. God sometimes hurries it along and ensures that it works, that the results of actions are directed back on those who performed them. But this is intended not simply to bring retributive punishment on the wicked but is "motivated by the long-range purpose of restoring Israel to the status of being blessed." Furthermore, in acting this way, God is not keeping some metaphysical order of justice finely-tuned; he is preserving the covenant. Every action, whether good or wicked, spreads out to affect, or infect, others within the covenant community. God proves true to his covenant commitments by purging evil from the land, and thereby protecting his covenant people. And he does so through establishing and sustaining the deed-consequence construct, and symbolically dramatizing it in judicial procedures and penalties.[22]

Koch's approach has been subject to considerable criticism and it does not, as he claims, entirely dispose of the theme of retribution in the OT.[23] But his study is an important warning against over-emphasizing the extent and unity of the theme, conceptualizing it wholly in forensic terms, and treating it in isolation from the wider conceptual framework in which deeds carry inherent consequences and where God's vengeance is activated primarily by his commitment to the covenant.

In this covenantal setting, criminal offending was viewed by Israel, not as an unbalancing of the moral or cosmic order demanding retribution, but as a breaching of covenant relationships. The basic concern in administering justice was to restore the relational integrity of the community. "In contradistinction to Roman and Western justice," J. T. Renner observes, "the fundamental purpose of a trial in the Old Testament was to settle disputes so that the community might thrive and prosper. Indeed, all punishments were designed to help communal living..."[24] In this setting, Forrester explains, "justice is not 'due process' or 'giving each his due.' It is about the restoration of relationships."[25] While it is true that certain religious offences and crimes against human life carried the death penalty, the execution of those guilty of such crimes was not simple tit-for-tat judicial retribution. It was a kind of cultic atonement or ceremonial expiation of evil which, if left unchecked, threatened the actual survival of the community. In non-capital offences, the emphasis in biblical jurisprudence falls on restitution rather than retribution (Lev 17-27; Num 5-8). As John Hayes explains: "The basic principle operative in Israelite laws dealing with injured parties was restitution. That is, the concern of Israelite law was for restoration of the

---

[22] Klauss Koch, "Is There A Doctrine of Retribution in the Old Testament?" in *Theodicy in the Old Testament*, ed. James L. Crenshaw (Philadelphia: Fortress; London: SPCK, 1983), pp. 57-87 (quote from p. 68).

[23] For critiques of Koch, see Y. Hoffman, "The Creativity of Theodicy," in *Justice and Righteousness: Biblical Themes and Their Influence*, ed. H.G. Reventlow and Y. Hoffman (Sheffield: Sheffield Academic Press, 1992), pp. 117-130; H.G.L. Peels, *The Vengeance of God: The Meaning of the Root NQM and the Function of the NQM-Texts in the Context of Divine Revelation in the Old Testament* (Leiden: Brill, 1995), esp. pp. 302-05.

[24] J.T. Erich Renner and Victor C. Pfitzner, "Justice and Human Rights: Some Biblical Perspectives," *LTJ* 24, no. 1 (1990): 5.

[25] Duncan B. Forrester, "Political Justice and Christian Theology," *SCE* 3/1 (1990): 13.

victim to the status prior to the wrong rather than punishment of the offender."[26]

Specific acts of restitution are prescribed in Mosaic law, based broadly on equivalence of value (Exod 21:26-36). A retributive element might be seen in the way some offences demanded double restitution or more, according to the seriousness of the offence and the attitude of the offender (Exod 22:4,7). But where fourfold, fivefold, even sevenfold reparation is required (Exod 22:1,4,9; Prov 6:30-31), the intention was not merely to hurt the offender but to bring both restitution and compensation to the victim, as well as to "mark" the gravity of the situation. If the thief could not pay, he might be taken as a slave by the injured party until he had worked off the debt (Exod 22:3). Slavery was not as ghastly in the ancient orient as in modern times; in fact Hebrew slavery was arguably a more humane institution than its modern equivalent of imprisonment.

It is one thing, then, to identify certain *retributivist dynamics* in biblical law and narrative; it is quite another to read out of the text a wholly *retributivist theory* of punishment that can be transferred directly into the secular criminal justice system today. The retributivist features that exist need to be understood and evaluated in light of several things, such as the Hebrew understanding of the intrinsic connection between deeds and their consequences, the use of rhetorical flourish for emphasis, the cultic and covenantal character of Israelite society, the restorative goal of covenantal justice, and the role of non-retributivist features, such as undeserved mercy and forgiveness, in the operation of divine justice.

(4) There are, finally, *theological reasons* to question the assumption that God's order operates according to the principle of retributive justice. Space permits only one brief comment. In his penetrating critique of penal theologies of the atonement, Thomas Talbot argues that the retributivist theory of justice is fundamentally flawed because punishment as punishment can never satisfy the demands of justice to the full. Justice is only fully satisfied when the harm caused by wrongdoing is undone, when the damage is repaired, when the bad consequences of wrongful actions are cancelled out. Punishment does none of these things. Inasmuch as sin is anything that separates us from God and from each other, Talbot writes, "perfect justice requires reconciliation and restoration. It requires, first, that sinners repent of their

---

[26] John H. Hayes, "Atonement in the Book of Leviticus," *Int* 52 (1998): 11 (author's emphasis).

sin and turn away from everything that would separate them from others; it requires, second, that God forgive repentant sinners and that they forgive each other; and it requires, third, that God overcome, perhaps with their own co-operation, any harm that sinners do either to others or to themselves."[27] Paul Fiddes makes the same point: "What justice demands is not payment but repentance; it is finally 'satisfied' not by any penalty in itself but by the change of heart to which the penalty is intended to lead."[28] In short, God's justice cannot be vindicated ultimately by retribution, but only by reconciling forgiveness and healing, for only thus are things made right.

To sum up: the ideas of reform, deterrence and retribution have been the dominant categories used in the long-running debate over the rationale for punishment. Other categories, such as, most recently, human rights theory,[29] have also been used, and various combinations proposed. The current Western justice system is itself a hybrid of many different, and to some degree conflicting, theories of punishment. Yet, as Howard Zehr argues, the Western penal system remains largely committed to retribution. A fundamentally retributive model has been subjected to a number of utilitarian adjustments to make it work better or appear more humane. But none of these adjustments have remedied the basic dysfunctionality of the undergirding retributive model. What is needed, Zehr argues, is a new paradigm of *restorative justice*, committed not merely to administering punishment, but to making right what has gone wrong through crime, and employing appropriate institutional mechanisms for doing so.

I am convinced that this is the way ahead. But I have observed that advocates of restorative justice are often reluctant to speak of punishment at all, or to justify it on theoretical grounds, for fear of reinforcing the punitive instincts they are seeking to supplant. And yet, as retributivism reminds us, the link between justice and punishment is too important to be ignored, and the theme of punishment is too

---

[27] Thomas Talbot, "Punishment, Forgiveness and Divine Justice," *RS* 29 (1993): 151-68 (quote from 163).

[28] Paul Fiddes, *Past Event and Present Salvation: The Christian Idea of Atonement* (London: Darton Longman Todd; Louisville: Westminster John Knox, 1989), p. 104.

[29] For a summary with references, see Hudson, *Understanding Justice*, 67-74. On the biblical grounding of human rights principles, see my extended essay, "'Made a Little Lower Than the Angels': Human Rights in the Biblical Tradition," in *Human Rights and the Common Good: Christian Perspectives*, ed. Bill Atkin and Katrine Evans (Wellington: Victoria University Press, 1999), pp. 14-76.

entrenched in Scripture to be disregarded or minimized by Christians. The real question to be asked is whether "the 'P' word" has a positive role to play in the attainment of restorative justice.

Restorative Punishment?

I wish to suggest that it does, that there is such a thing as "restorative punishment," that the idea of restorative punishment is both a meaningful concept and a necessary one. To explore this further, I propose that we should, on the one hand, broaden the concept of punishment to include the suffering involved in working for restoration, and, on the other hand, understand the role of external punitive sanctions in essentially symbolic terms.

Punishment as the Pain of Taking Responsibility

It is now widely conceded that a significant weakness in the conventional criminal justice system is that it takes too little account of the needs of victims in dispensing justice. Technically the victim of crime is the impersonal State, and the responsibility of the courts is to enforce State law. In criminal law, the category of punishment is usually distinguished from that of restitution. If the offender is ordered to pay compensation to the actual victim, it is typically in addition to some other punishment which is imposed for the act of law-breaking itself and which is intended to satisfy the demands of justice. But not only is justice truly satisfied when the harm done to the *real* victim is addressed, there is no reason why a serious and concrete contribution to doing so should not be regarded as an essential ingredient of the punishment itself. It might be argued that restoring what has been unfairly taken in the first place is not really a punishment; it is simply returning things to their original condition. But we ought not to underestimate the shame and pain entailed for offenders in confronting the personal consequences of their actions, accepting responsibility for them, seeking reconciliation with those whom they have harmed, and working to restore, so far as is realistic, the damage caused. The suffering entailed will be intense, sufficiently intense to qualify as a kind of punishment.

Of course, the extent to which genuine restoration can be achieved in the wake of crime will vary from case to case. Never will it be easy or pain-free, for offenders or for victims. But it will be suffering in the service of restoration, not simply as a way of "getting even" with the culprit. It will be a form of punishment that stands in creative *opposition* to the wrongs done, that seeks to arrest its influence and undermine its sway, not the kind of punishment that stands in *continuity* with wrongdoing and extends it further through inflicting commensurate suffering on the offender. Naturally, in cases where an offender refuses to enter the process of reparation, or remains a serious danger to the safety of others, alternative punishments may be justified. But even here the goal of the exercise should be to facilitate a situation where the offender finally awakens to his or her responsibility for putting right what has gone wrong, and is prepared to do so.

Punishment, by definition, entails the deliberate imposition of pain on an offender as the sequel to an offence. Arguably the most exquisite pain and the most profound shame associated with criminal offending comes, not from incurring secondary penalties, but from facing up to one's responsibility for violating another human being and striving to remedy its consequences.[30] Such pain and shame is an inherent punishment, one imposed by the offence itself and by the offender's deliberate acceptance of responsibility for it. It is a restorative punishment, a punishment that promises healing. Can the same be said for the imposition of external, secondary sanctions?

Punishment as Symbol and Invitation

Some 30 years ago, Sir Walter Moberly identified two basic, perhaps universal, human drives which motivate the practice of punishment: the drive to see wrongdoers get their just deserts, the feeling that punishment "serves them right" for doing wrong, and the drive for annulment, the deep craving to see the wrong that has been committed undone or cancelled out.[31] The singular attraction of retributivism is the way it speaks directly to these two drives. Its great weakness, however, is that it sees punishment, in and of itself, as the way of achieving both goals when in fact it achieves neither. The reason for this, Moberly suggests, is that the true consequences of wrongdoing, and the means by which those consequences are undone, belong to the moral and spiritual

---

[30] The seminal work on the role of shame in criminal punishment is John Braithwaite, *Crime, Shame and Reintegration* (Cambridge: Cambridge University Press, 1989).
[31] Walter Moberly, *The Ethics of Punishment* (Connecticut: Archon, 1968), 210-225; see also Elizabeth Moberly, *Suffering, Innocent and Guilty* (London: SPCK, 1978), pp. 61-101.

realm, whereas legal punishment belongs to the material and social realm. Punishment is external and physical, something that is "added" to the crime. In that sense punishment is neither the automatic result of wrongdoing, nor does it possess the power to cancel out the effects of wrongdoing. Yet it derives its significance from its relation to both these ideas.

This distinction between the moral and the material realms is crucial to grasp, especially when working from a Christian perspective. Crime is an evil of the first realm; it is primarily a moral offence that carries its own inevitable repercussions. For the offender, the result of crime is a process of moral and spiritual deterioration in his or her own person. This moral degradation, this bondage to sin, is the true retribution for crime. The most terrible punishment for criminal wrongdoing is not what the courts do *to* them, but what they do to ourselves, what they become. The New Testament is full of this idea. It is what Paul means when he says that "the wages of sin is death" (Rom 6:23). Death is not "added" to sin as a secondary penalty; it is the inherent outworking of sin within our personality. For society too, the true damage of crime is its impact on the moral fabric of the community, while for the victim the most injurious aspect of an offence is usually emotional and spiritual more than physical and material.

Given the moral impact of criminal offending, society is duty bound to react against crime, lest it spread like a disease. It is in this connection that punishment has an important role to play—but not principally as a means of retribution (or deterrence for that matter). As already noted, legal punishment is not the true retribution for wrongdoing. (The true retribution is moral and personal corruption.) Nor is it the true undoing of wrong. (The real battle between good and evil takes place in a region deeper than any external punishment can reach.) But punishment has a role in reflecting the battle between good and evil, and may even influence its course. How does it do this? By symbolizing or dramatizing what is going on in the invisible moral and spiritual sphere, and thereby inviting the kind of response which will defeat the evil unleashed by the offender and promote redemption. Let me expand on each side of this relationship.

(1) On the one hand, punishment *symbolizes* the corrupting impact of the offence on the wrongdoer's own person. The emotional pain or material loss inflicted by the punishment are a garish but powerful picture of the spiritual injury the offender has inflicted, both on himself

and on others. The external indignity of legal punishment is an enacted parable of the invisible spiritual and moral indignity which the criminal has visited on himself and others.

Consider this analogy. In the biological realm, physical pain serves as the body's danger signal that serious injury may occur. Sensate suffering externalizes the internal organic damage that has begun to occur. Similarly in the social realm, punitive pain symbolically externalizes the moral evil unleashed by the criminal act. It is intended to awaken criminals to the danger they are in of doing permanent damage to themselves, as well as to the personal and emotional damage they have already done to others. The pain of punishment is not itself the real retribution for the wrongful act. It is a dramatic foreshadowing of such retribution (which is personal ruin) that is intended to arrest, not effect, the experience of retribution. This leads to the other symbolic dimension of punishment.

(2) As well as signifying the inner, moral consequences of wrongdoing, thus satisfying the underlying drive to see the offender held accountable for his or her actions and receive in some sense their just deserts, punishment also signifies the *reversal or cancellation* of wrongdoing, thus satisfying the underlying drive to see things put right.

Once again, annulment is a fundamentally moral and voluntary matter. It requires repentance and reparation from the offender. No external punishment can, of itself, cancel out a crime (as retributivism claims). Only repentance and forgiveness can do that. Punishment is no more than a vivid gesture that symbolizes the need for the crime to be cancelled out, and invites the criminal to face the reality of the hurt he or she has caused and to strive to make amends. The goal is not some abstract cancellation of wrong in virtue of having suffered sufficient pain under punishment. The true undoing of crime is the reformation of the offender, the healing of the victim and the repair of relationships. Punishment is but an invitation (albeit forcibly imposed) for this process to commence and run its course. It is a restorative punishment insofar as it invites restoration to wholeness.

Conclusions

The question I have tried to pursue here is how the legitimacy of punishment may be established within a Christian concept of redemptive or restorative justice. I have tried to outline a theory of "restorative punishment" that both honours the moral seriousness of retributivism and the social goals of utilitarianism. To administer punishment in the absence of guilt would be a monstrous injustice — this is the irreducible truth of retributivism. To punish solely because of guilt would be impossible, for we are all sinners and decisions must be made about which wrongs to punish. That punishment must serve some end beyond itself is the crucial insight of utilitarianism. Restorative justice unites both. It places emphasis on the moral and spiritual obligation that comes with crime to respond in ways that endeavour to put right what has gone wrong, to bring healing to the relationships ruptured by crime. It is more interested in reconceptualizing "justice" than in justifying punishment. But issues of prosecution and punishment cannot be side-lined in any adequate theory of justice.

Among the criticisms levelled at restorative justice is that it underestimates the social and moral function that the ceremonies of criminal law and infliction of penalties play in relieving the feelings of victims and the community and in clarifying its values. It is also ill-equipped to deal adequately with those who refuse to admit guilt or who represent an ongoing threat to the safety of the community.[32] Whatever the merit of these criticisms, they underline the need for restorative justice to articulate a theory of punishment that matches its agenda.

Such a theory would understand punishment, not as retribution, but as an instrument for accessing the moral and spiritual realm. It does so by dramatizing or mirroring, albeit imperfectly, the moral, personal and relational pain caused by criminal offending, thereby inviting transformation of the offender and restoration for the victim. From this it follows that the mode of punishment should be what is most conducive to achieving this goal. Since punishment is but a symbol of, and an invitation to, penitence and restoration, it will not achieve automatically the realities it seeks to portray, since any real change in the moral sphere demands the exercise of the offender's free choice. The potency of the appeal issued by the punishment depends almost entirely on what form punishment takes. As an ingredient in restorative justice, restorative punishment is partly a matter of restitution or compensation for the victim, which brings with it a sense of vindication; it is partly a matter of resolving grievances between victim and offender, and their wider

---

[32] Cayley offers a sympathetic review of some of the problems and pitfalls associated with restorative and other alternative modes of handling criminal offending in *The Expanding Prison*, pp. 358-65.

relational networks; and it is partly a matter of promoting restoration or healing within the offender's own character and conduct. Measured against these criteria, many of the punishments employed in the current penal system, such as long periods of incarceration, are far from restorative. They are inherently destructive; they make matters worse.

Some criminal justice specialists now speak of the "tragic quality" of punishment: it is simultaneously necessary, yet destined to a degree of futility. But both the tragedy and futility of punishment would be eased by developing modes of punishment that focus on the goal of restoration rather than simply on more effective pain-delivery. The notion of restorative punishment coheres well with Christian themes of repentance, forgiveness, reconciliation and redemption. The message of the gospel is that God does not requite evil with further evil, but with a counter-action that seeks to reclaim the sinner and heal the damage done. That fact alone, upon which the universe itself turns, is reason enough to justify the questions I have asked here, even if my attempt to answer them is inadequate or unconvincing.

Index

www.ingramcontent.com/pod-product-compliance
Lightning Source LLC
Chambersburg PA
CBHW031249090426
42742CB00007B/380